GETTING YOUR
Shift
TOGETHER

Making Sense of Organizational Culture and Change

Introducing **Cultural Due Diligence**™

D1052443

by P.J. Bouchard and Lizz Pellet

Published by CCI Press
Phoenix, AZ

Getting Your Shift Together:
Making Sense of Organizational Culture and Change

Copyright © 2000 by P.J. Bouchard and Lizz Pellet

Published 2000 by CCI Press

Printed in the United States of America

Produced by Five Star Publications, Inc., Chandler, Arizona

Linda F. Radke, president • www.BookProducer.com

Requests for permissions should be addressed to:

CCI Press

41455 N. Ironwood Bluff

Cave Creek, AZ 85331

Phone: (480) 595-9874 • Fax: (480) 595-9874

e-mail: change4u@aol.com

Library of Congress Cataloging-in-Publication Data

Bouchard, P. J.

Getting your shift together: making sense of organizational culture and change: introducing cultural due diligence / P. J. Bouchard, Lizz Pellet. — 1st ed.

p. cm.

Includes bibliographical references.

ISBN: 0-9673248-0-7

1. Organizational change. 2. Corporate reorganization 3. Consolidation and merger of corporations. I. Pellet, Lizz. II. Title

HD58.8.B68 2000   658.16

QBI00-316

Editor: Salvatore Caputo
Contributing editor: Sally Starbuck Stamp
Book design and typesetting: Kim Scott

Dedications

To our families, without whom we would not be who we are or where we are today.

To the many, many leaders out there who believe in their employees and who continue to demonstrate a sincere commitment to understanding their organizational culture and creating a rewarding and encouraging place for employees to be.

To the Human Resource and Organizational Development professionals, who are willing to step over the edge and do whatever it takes to guide leaders through this cultural journey.

To Cody and Jake, who provided us with real diversions when we needed them most.

Table of Contents

Acknowledgments

As the famous Chinese saying goes, a book is like a garden that you carry in your pocket; this book like so many others has a plethora of gardeners.

A project of this magnitude could not have become a reality without the commitment, support, and ongoing encouragement of many people.

We would like to thank all of you who were involved in this exciting and, at times, very frustrating project. Thanks to all who listened to our ideas, challenged our assumptions and concepts, and offered ongoing encouragement at every juncture of this journey. Your input helped us to stay grounded in reality and congruent with ourselves. Sharing your personal stories and insight allowed us to tackle a nebulous topic like organizational culture and translate it into plain English.

Pauline Lyttle, thank you for planting the seed and spending hours of your time sharing your views about Cultural Due Diligence™. Your drive and belief in this concept took us down the path to developing the CDD™ Model and process.

To Sally Starbuck Stamp. Thank you for everything. Without your ongoing support *Getting Your Shift Together* would still be a figment of our imaginations. Thanks for keeping us focused, even though at times we know that was not an easy feat. Your willingness to do anything and everything to make this book a success is not only recognized, but also very much appreciated. Thanks for hanging in there, believing in us, and providing us with positive reinforcement when we needed it most. Thank you for your kindness. Sally, you have earned the dubious title of "Saint Sally Stamp."

No book project can be a true success without input from those whom the authors respect and trust, so thanks to Patti Saathoff, Barbara Novicki, Dr. Don Novicki, Matt McElrath, Ruth Ann Clark, Andy Riddell, Brenda Halpain, and Dr. Russ Jennings, for taking the time out of your busy schedules to not only read, but also to critique the manuscript. Your feedback was absolutely invaluable and because of you we have created a much better product.

A process such as Cultural Due Diligence™ starts out as a concept until theory and practical approaches are applied to it. Thank you, Dr. Lloyd C. Williams for your input in this regard.

Tony Gebarowski, thank you for taking the CDD™ model from computer speak to a readable format.

We are very grateful to Sal Caputo, our editor. Sal, you are the kind of editor every writer dreams about: passionate, insightful, always helpful, and yes, very direct—telling us we were all wet and then handing us a dry towel. And let's not forget that wonderful sense of humor. You did make us laugh. Thank you for that.

Linda Radke, thank you for your warmth, your directness, your professionalism and your charm, there is no one quite like you. We are extremely lucky to have you as a publishing consultant.

Kim Scott, our graphics guru, thanks for bringing our book to life and keeping us in the margins.

Doing a book project often brings you to a place you hadn't planned on visiting. For us, that place was the spirit and the critical role that spirit plays in all we do. Thank you Christian Amoroso, MD and Dr. Barry Berns for sharing your views and personal experiences. A special thanks to you, Barry, for sharing your personal story with our readership.

Another wonderful human being we encountered during this journey is Andy Riddell. Andy you are the consummate professional and a truly evolved CEO. We are extremely proud to have you as a contributor of *Getting Your Shift Together*. Thank you for your true commitment to organizational culture. It is CEOs like yourself who will make the business community a better place. Thanks for sharing.

In addition, we would like to thank the many professionals we interviewed. Without your stories and personal experiences *Getting Your Shift Together* would have been left with a huge void. In particular, we would like to thank: Jerry Hurwitz; Ben Gill; Andy Riddell; Steve Ruggles; Greg Daher; George Burkeholder, M.D.; Rebecca Leaper; Patti Saathoff; David Saathoff; Carol Mangold; Bill Mangold, M.D.; Betti Ward; Milt Bayer; David Starbuck, M.D.; Joe Dionisio; Sal Caputo, Jim Petrillo, Michael Lutin, and TEC group 840.

About the Authors

If you'll pardon us for saying it, authors **Lizz Pellet** and **P.J. Bouchard** really know their shift!

Lizz Pellet, for instance, brings more than 15 years of experience in human resources, cultural integration, training and development, and Total Quality Management to the table in her role as CEO of EMERGE. Lizz has held key management and leadership positions in a broad spectrum of industries. Before getting her shift together to form EMERGE, she held quality-management and human-resources positions with international manufacturing firms, major health-care organizations, and various service industries. Along the way, she has been a director for a major hotel chain, internal management consultant for a major acute-care hospital, and quality director for a major international manufacturing firm.

Lizz has served as key facilitator at strategic planning and "visioning" sessions with major manufacturing and health-care firms. She was a key player in a number of turnarounds, including one high-tech firm that was in Chapter 11. Lizz has managed the cultural-assessment and cultural-integration processes for high-tech firms going through mergers. She has also successfully led internal mergers and reengineering projects.

Lizz is co-author of *Getting Your Shift Together: Making Sense of Organizational Culture and Change—Introducing Cultural Due Diligence*™. She earned a Bachelor of Science in business from Lesley College, Cambridge, and a Fellowship in Change Management from Johns Hopkins University, Baltimore. She is certified in Myers-Briggs Type Indicator (MBTI). Lizz serves on the board of NAWBO—National Association of Women Business Owners.

P.J. Bouchard has seen plenty of shift, as well. For her part, **P.J.**, president of EMERGE, specializes in cultural assessment, cultural transformation and cultural integration. P.J. has more than 15 years of human-resources and organizational-development experience, earned in a variety of professional leadership positions, such as Director of Organizational Development, Director of Human Resources and Director of Training and Development for major, international manufacturing firms and health-care organizations. She also has held executive management roles in higher education and various service industries.

The co-author of *Getting Your Shift Together* is dedicated to helping companies successfully learn to manage change by creating the right culture. The hallmark of her success has been her ability to create healthy cultures that create solid bottom-line results.

Intimately involved in many major acquisitions, P.J. has successfully led several integration teams through the transition process. She has worked with firms across the country to not only assess their current organizational culture, but also to help them develop a culture that has improved the return on investment. P.J. has managed a number of organizational redesigns and has successfully restructured three major organizations.

She has a Bachelor of Science degree in Organizational Behavior from Lesley College, Cambridge and a Master of Business Administration degree from Boston University, Boston. She is certified in Myers-Briggs Type Indicator (MBTI), and serves on the board of St. Mary's Food Bank in Phoenix.

*"In business news today, trading of Favorite Airlines stock was sus-
pended after it fell 39% yesterday, following news of their merger
with Allright Air. Analysts agree that it will be extremely difficult to
make this combination fly in light of the significant differences in
business philosophy."*

*"In other news, The Bank of the People announced that 35 offices
will be closed in the aftermath of their 34 billion dollar acquisition
of The Peoples' Savings and Loan. None of the people are pleased."*

*"And still in other news, layoffs reached the 10,000 mark at All
American Software as their Doors 2000 failed to meet expected
sales projections for the third consecutive quarter. More doors are
expected to close as a result."*

Dear Reader

Business life used to be compared to a game of chess; a slow-paced, cerebral game of strategy aimed at outwitting your opponent. That was yesterday. Today's business life is more like a video game. Your success depends not only on how fast you are but on how well you know the terrain and how easily you maneuver through it. With so much change happening, let's talk about creating profitable work environments, one culture at a time.

Gone are the days when you could guarantee that your place of work, your business, or your carefully laid plans would be the same as they were when you left them the day before. The ever-increasing speed of doing business in today's economy makes it seem as if you're constantly rafting over white-water rapids. To survive, you and your organization must be smarter, faster, more resilient and innovative. Forget about the next year of your strategic plan, you've got to get through the next week.

With this understanding, we set out to develop a process to help you better understand the impact your "organizational culture" has on the financial success of your business and how to create an organizational culture that can SHIFT with rocket speed in today's business world. You must own up to the fact that SHIFT HAPPENS in every facet of your life—and you have to be able to "change a tire while the car is still moving" to stay in the race.

Through many years of real-life experience, we have had the distinct pleasure of learning the ropes through trial and error. We, too, have felt the pain that SHIFT brings. That's why many of our colleagues and friends encouraged us to share our experiences and the lessons we've learned with others.

Once we were convinced of the need to write a book offering a common-sense approach to organizational culture and change, we began a process that included an extensive review of the current literature. In addition to reading many, *many* books on a variety of subjects that included organizational development, change, mergers and acquisitions, culture, leadership, due diligence, and beyond, we examined and catalogued newspaper, journal, and Internet articles related to ongoing business-combination activities throughout the world. Then, in an effort to validate some of the conclusions that we were making, we conducted more than 100 interviews with business leaders from a wide range of organizations in various industries in the United States. To this, we added many of our own stories and those told to us by co-workers and associates. The end result is a research-based perspective, leavened with personal anecdotes and experiences, on an extremely relevant, contemporary issue.

We have tried to write a book that is not only fun and interesting to read but that is user-friendly as well. You can read the chapters sequentially or as stand-alone topics. Although we initially focused our book on organizational culture—what is it, how do you assess it, and how do you change it, we felt it would seem incongruous for us, as authors, to dive into the cultural assessment process without doing due diligence in preparing you, the reader.

To talk about any type of cultural assessment including our own Cultural Due Diligence™ (CDD™) process without talking about change would be like building a house without first pouring the foundation. A cultural-assessment process like CDD™ can create a major cultural shift in your organization and, therefore, is viewed as a *major business change strategy.* In order to enjoy as much success as possible with this process, you must first explore how you personally handle change. You must also examine what your track record with organizational change has been, and you should understand what mechanisms must be put into place before embarking on the path of any type of cultural assessment and beyond. That's why, after our initial "Call to Action," we focus on the nature of change in "The Change Game."

From "The Change Game," we move on to "Can We Talk—CEO to CEO?" It's about the role of the CEO in any type of change strategy. You will hear firsthand from Andy Riddell, a CEO who has had almost thirty years of turn-around experience. He will share with you the good, the bad, and the ugly. He also offers some wonderful insights and how-to tips on moving forward which you will find in the appendix.

Next is "The Culture Vulture," a discussion of this ever-elusive thing we call organizational culture. We have tried to provide you with

1. a pragmatic approach to the assessment and creation of any organizational culture,

2. a new way of thinking about culture,

3. a clearer understanding of what it is, and

4. the critical role it plays in overall organizational success and longevity.

Does organizational culture really make a difference in gaining market share, reducing employee turnover, hiring the right people the first time, and beating the competition without being gobbled up like a Thanksgiving Day turkey?

We unequivocally believe it does!

"Culture and Leadership" emphasizes the pivotal role of leaders in organizational culture and change and our need to be true to our core values in order to make organizational change succeed.

A discussion on "Due Diligence" then prepares you for our chapter on "The Cultural-Assessment Process." This chapter introduces Cultural Due Diligence™, a structured process for measuring and assessing your organizational culture. We use our process as an example to illustrate what any cultural assessment must encompass. A cultural assessment like CDD™ will give you a clear picture of what your organizational culture is, where the incongruencies lie, and how you must intervene to align your organizational culture to make it smarter, faster, more resilient and innovative, *and more profitable.* All of which makes you more competitive.

The subsequent chapter, "Moving Forward," is for those who decide to conduct a cultural assessment in the hopes of creating a cultural shift in their organizations.

The Afterword, "Spirit and Leadership," the closing piece by physician, lecturer, and author Barry Berns, M.D., is meant as a gift to you. After all this SHIFT, his personal journey of the spirit offers a real perspective on not sweating the small stuff. As we like to say, SHIFT HAPPENS.

When you have completed this book, you should have a good understanding of how Cultural Due Diligence™ and similar processes can improve your chances of success in any organizational change strategy or in this MAD (mergers, acquisitions and divestitures) world. At that point, you should know how CDD™, or any cultural assessment, might work in your organization. The rest we leave up to you. Here is where your personal commitment and ACTION truly begins. It is time to "SHIFT or get off the..." Well, you know the rest.

Call to Action

"If we listened to our intellect, we'd never have a love affair. We'd never have a friendship. We'd never go into business, because we'd be cynical. Well, that's nonsense. You've got to jump off cliffs all the time and build your wings on the way down."

—Ray Bradbury

This book is for leaders[*] who possess the courage, resilience, and fortitude to step over the edge, admit vulnerability, and take risks to try something innovative. Those who take our suggestions seriously will reap higher levels of success.

---

[*]For the purposes of this book, "leader" is a generic term used to describe anyone who is in a leadership position as defined by a particular organization. As authors and business owners, we include ourselves in this category.

It is not a book about wishful thinking or organizational fantasies.

It is a hard-core dose of REALITY.

Getting Your Shift Together takes you where many business books dare not go. You will be required to examine your role as a leader and determine how you can help create healthier and more effective work environments. We will work with you to take the mystery out of creating cultural consciousness and provide you with a better understanding of how organizational culture really does affect your bottom line.

This book is about collaboration. It is not just about what we, the authors, think and believe, it is about collective reality. We reached out to people in all industries and at all levels and asked them to share their stories. The overwhelmingly positive response and enthusiasm both surprised and pleased us. It also allowed us to include many more perspectives, which make this a truly collaborative book.

This book has been written with many stakeholders and leaders in mind—boards, shareholders, CEOs, CFOs, presidents, vice presidents, directors, managers, attorneys, investment bankers, venture capitalists, human resource professionals, organizational development professionals, practitioners, consultants, and students—the list is quite long.

Our original focus in writing this book was in support of business combinations—mergers, acquisitions, alliances, and joint ventures. As we got deeper and deeper into our research it became very apparent to us that a cultural assessment like Cultural Due Diligence™ is a "must do" for any business or individual going through any type of organizational shift. The shift can be:

- Implementing any type of business combination—merger, acquisition, joint venture,
- Adopting a new information-technology system,
- Embracing self-directed work teams,
- Introducing a 360-degree feedback system,

- Moving to open-book management,

- Shifting to a new way of conducting business; i.e. E-commerce.

All of these new business strategies are *change in disguise.* Therefore, we have expanded the application and use of a cultural assessment like CDD™ to include any and all business change strategies.

This book is written for anyone who is interested in effecting long-term, systemic organizational change successfully. A quick fix here and a little tweak there won't do. It will take hard core changes in your *thinking* and in your *actions.* And it's about your own personal commitment to change. It is about standing in front of the mirror naked—as scary as that is! Not just a quick glance, either—a long, hard look!

Think about this for a moment. Thousands of business books have been written on how you can improve your organization and become a more effective leader. We often talk about organizations in terms of things or shapes. How would you describe your organization? Fill in the blank: My organization is: _____ (flat, top-heavy, vertical, matrixed, silos, bottom-up, top down, pyramid, all kinds of things). We go so far as to refer to our organizations and their people as mammals or animals. "The 100th Monkey Theory," "Herding Cats," "Dancing with Elephants," "Swimming with Sharks," and being "A Peacock in a Land of Penguins." Oh, and, let us not forget "Dogbert's Top Secret Management Handbook," and "Dinosaur Brains." There's even a "Light Bulbs for Leaders," and an "Idiot's Guide to Managing People." The list goes on and on.

Writers have gone to great lengths to grab your attention. Has it done any good? Have you learned anything new and different about sustaining change? If so, why do some of us still fall for the flavor of the month (change strategies that are replaced as soon as a new brand is released)? Are we in the ice cream business? Even one who literally is into the flavor of the month, told us that there are no quick fixes for organizational leaders. "Nobody needs to reinvent the wheel," explained Milt Bayer, CEO of Kenwood Farms Ice Cream Company.

"The wheel is there." (1) He went on to tell us about how his business strategy focuses on maintaining effective past practices while responding to the changing marketplace. His flavor of the month is really the flavor of leadership style that he has developed over a lifetime in the food-products industry. That's the real scoop!

Another interviewee, who manages the training and development department for a health-care provider, agreed that we need to stop looking for a silver bullet that doesn't exist. "People are looking for a quick fix," she told us, but "the fix is investment in your people." (2) A quick fix is just like the TV commercial that promises a better body with awesome abs in two weeks or less—if it sounds too good to be true, it usually is. Long-term sustained change, of your body or your organization, requires more time and effort than many of us are willing to commit.

Creating a cultural shift as discussed in this book requires a commitment, a pioneering spirit and lots of courage. And the commitment to change must include a commitment to a lifetime of learning. That's the real bottom line.

Some leaders have fooled themselves into thinking that once they have achieved their goals—personally and professionally—then, in their mind they have arrived and can sail through the rest of their lives without much thought to continuing their formal and informal education. They have added a few letters to their name—OK, in some cases lots of letters: MBA, Ph.D., MD, CPCM, RN, MA, CPA and, of course, M.O.U.S.E.—and congratulations may be in order, but these are just milestones along the road. Too many of us forget that and allow the learning process to take a back seat on the rest of our journey.

You must be the self-appointed designated driver, remembering that you have a long way to go. And you must keep your wits about you when everyone else is intoxicated by these milestones—whether it's the honorary degree, faculty appointment or hefty bonus. You must keep your vision focused, consider the environment around you, and remember that each stop in your travels signals another opportunity to choose a new path. Stop going through life with blinders on. Don't get so caught up in getting there. The journey is where all the learning that life has to offer really happens.

Let's throw the damn map away—take the detours, try a new direction. Keep exploring and keep learning!

Some people have compared knowledge and skills to consumer products, suggesting they have a shelf life and expiration date. How many of us can expect to move forward in our careers if our skills are not updated regularly? Can anyone still say they don't see a need for computer literacy in their job and believe it? Would you promote the individual who never sees the need to meet the continuing education requirements? The shelf life of your education is limited. Just like bread, your career can get moldy and stale.

This can happen to your organization, as well. In a classic case of complacency, Howard Johnson Jr., who took over the huge highway hospitality chain after his father retired, allowed his competitors to capture much of his Middle America market share because he was unwilling to keep pace with changes. In a 1975 interview first published in *Forbes* magazine, as cited by Collins and Porras in *Built to Last*, Johnson admitted: "We are a reacting company. We don't try to anticipate the future. In this business, you can't look too far ahead, maybe two years." (3) How many orange roofs do you see along the turnpike these days? Unless we're mistaken, Golden Arches and others have replaced them. The shelf life of HoJo's definitely expired.

Getting Your Shift Together is also about a shift in thinking. You must continue to ask questions that help you get at the root cause of whatever ails your organization and you. You can no longer be satisfied with treating the symptoms. You need to examine:

- What is causing you to have chronic organizational migraines?
- Why is your business experiencing chronic failure rates?
- Why is morale down the tubes?
- Why do you keep losing precious intellectual capital and your best employees?

- Why is the cost of business rising and not shrinking?
- Why as a leader do you feel so damn isolated?

You can no longer rely on your accomplishments and your perceived infinite wisdom. You must go on a fact-finding mission. You must know what to examine and how to examine it in order to gather important concrete facts. You must know what questions to ask and whom to involve.

You need to start thinking and acting with your heart and not just with your head. That's the key! Like most leaders, we are sure that you are an expert tactician, but you must become an expert "touch-tician." As a leader, if you "talk the talk," you must "walk the walk" first. Your *actions* must speak LOUDER than your words. Employees demand this of a leader. This is where you begin to build a solid foundation for trust and respect with the work force. Remember: Genuine enthusiasm is caught, not taught.

Stop and think about a situation where you "talked the talk" but still didn't feel that you were in step. What was missing? Many leaders often go through the motions of walking without really thinking about it. They are persuaded to take action by external forces and then, like robots, play out their programmed response, the way it's always been done. Falling into the *current trend trap* will not help you improve your ability to "walk the walk," either. You must consciously think about and commit to an action so that you believe in it. Only such a deep commitment will make you feel in step.

For example, think about the trend toward self-directed work teams. Everybody's moving that way, and everything you read about it convinces you that you should, too. However, if you do not believe in or value employee involvement, then such a change initiative is doomed to fail. Why? Because you are doing it for the wrong reasons— because everyone else is doing it, and not because you're committed to the principles of the change. Remember what your mother always told you: "If Mary jumped off the bridge, would you jump too?" A leap of faith to embrace a business strategy that seems to be working for everyone else may cause you to jump ship when it fails.

You must also learn the difference between knowledge and knowing. You can have knowledge about growing up in an impoverished neighborhood—but unless you have received mail there, you don't know (can't feel) what it's like. Now, we are not saying that you must reach that level of knowing about all things; that would be an unrealistic expectation. But another way of knowing is to experience life through others. You can accomplish this by listening to their stories with your heart and not with your head. The ability to feel is a trigger far more powerful than our ability to think. Yes, there's that "F" word.

You should let feeling influence how you think, rather than let thinking influence how you feel. "Feeling is the language of the soul," according to author Neale Donald Walsch. "If you want to know what's true for you about something, look to how you're feeling about it. Feelings are sometimes difficult to discover—and often even more difficult to acknowledge. Yet hidden in your deepest feeling is your highest truth. The trick is to get to those feelings." (4)

Your inability to relate to those outside of your world has become a real handicap for you as a leader. You must allow yourself to listen and learn from others, especially those on the front line. Consider, for example, this story of a large hotel chain on the East Coast. The general manager became very concerned with the high turnover rate at one of the larger properties (over 75%) in the housekeeping department. His solution? Reprimand or fire the manager. In his estimation, she was incapable of running the department. However, he clearly wasn't listening to all available information. The turnover occurred largely because most of the employees lacked transportation to and from work. The hotel was located on a major highway with no local bus service. The majority of workers did not own cars and had to rely on others to get them to work. They readily admitted in exit interviews that they were forced to find other work that was more accessible. When this was brought to the general manager's attention, his reaction was, "Nice try, but everyone in this day and age owns a car." His inability to see the world through other lenses clouded his thinking and his ability to make good business decisions. Expanding the hotel shuttle service to include employee transport to and from a bus stop in the area might have allowed the organization to retain many of the workers who had been trained and were performing well. Instead, the high turnover rate grew even higher as other properties came to the area and offered additional work options for front-line employees. Within two years, this hotel went out of business, due in part to management's insensitivity to others and a resulting lack of creativity. The general manager refused to listen to and learn from those who had some of the answers: his employees. His view of the world was very myopic.

So now that we've built our case, we propose that you embark on this book-length journey. We will provide you with the road map. Your role is to first recognize that this journey cannot be traveled alone no matter what your position is; and, second, you must be willing to give up some level of control and allow us to truly be your guides. This will require another shift, in the way you perceive yourself and your approach to business.

We invite you to make a commitment to yourself *first* and *then* to your organization. Commit to an attempt to adopt new ways of thinking and acting in order to achieve great rates of success and excellence.

Organizational transformation must begin with you. It is about changing the current state of your organization and emerging as something totally new—with an unlimited shelf life. You must recognize the importance of understanding organizational culture, which will be critical in your efforts to stimulate learning and change within your organization. Your own behaviors are intricately intertwined with cultural creation and management. Therefore, you must begin to whisper the **SECRET**.

S = Sincere Commitment to Change

You'd better *walk the walk* when you *talk the talk*. To talk about something before you've shown your commitment through your **actions** is hypocritical.

E = Ego Toning

You really need to keep your ego in check. You must learn how to ask for help. Know when you need a coach, an advisor, or a guide to assist you in your journey. So find a friend who gets pleasure out of telling you that *you're all wet!*

C = Clarification of Purpose ... *yours and the organization's*

You cannot expect to lead the exploration team through the jungle without a clear destination and some idea of how to get there.

R = Reality Checks ... *every step of the way*

Remember, you must continually challenge what you see, think and feel, and ask the question: Is it imaginary or real?

E = Education

Here's that learning piece again. As a leader, you don't know it all. It is critical that you see yourself as a student of life and that you take the time to reflect on your track record, all of it—*the good, the bad, and the ugly*. You must learn from these experiences, and continue to grow and become more effective.

T = Tenacity

You really need to practice patience, something not a lot of us possess as leaders. You need to stop pulling the roots up to see if the plant is growing. There are more effective ways of tracking your progress.

In addition to asking you to embrace the SECRET, we ask that you not make this book required reading for your entire staff unless you are personally committed to lifting our recommendations off the page and

---

turning them into reality. Too often as leaders within an organization, we were given a copy of the *flavor of the month* book at a strategic planning session or annual retreat. Our leader would pass out the new publication and exclaim, "This is the best business book I have ever read, and I want all of you to read it and make this happen here at XYZ Company." You can just imagine how flat that sounded and how many of us sat there and said, "Here we go again." Please do not let this happen in your organization. It is much too painful for the management team and the entire organization.

Instead, let's work together. Let's breathe life into some of the more powerful human-resources and organizational-development models and theories that have been around for forty-plus years. Let's put them to work and make things happen. We like to call this *implementation mania,* and you must see yourselves as implementation instigators. Aren't you sick and tired of empty advice and hollow solutions? Breakthrough implementation is what you must demand and you should expect no less.

Stop talking about what you already know and get on with exploring what you don't know. Your organizational culture is crying out for your attention! Everyone has done a marvelous job of identifying the problems and challenges that you face as a leader. It's time to get off the soapbox and into the ring and get the contacts and energies flowing to create long-lasting results.

If you dare, please join us on this interesting, compelling, and yes, at times, frustrating journey. Our hope is that, as a leader, you will not only agree with, but also challenge our beliefs, convictions and assumptions; and that you will work your magic and turn our words into real-life success stories. Combine the knowledge gained from experiences yesterday with the best information available today and successfully meet the challenges of tomorrow. Become the contemporary tribal elder of your organization.

The Change Game

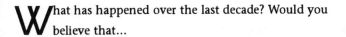

What has happened over the last decade? Would you believe that...

- More than half of all U.S. companies were restructured,
- Several hundred thousand companies were "downsized",
- More than 100,000 firms were acquired and merged,
- Nearly a million organizations sought bankruptcy protection in order to continue operating;
- More than 500,000 others outright failed.

SHIFT HAPPENS, and it's inevitable.

So why haven't more organizations mastered the change process yet? They have certainly had a lot of practice at it. Why do statistics show that

> **75%** of all attempted change initiatives (including mergers and acquisitions) fail within the first three years?—Failure is defined as the organization not meeting the strategic or financial goals in a defined time frame.

This figure includes business combinations as well as internal change initiatives. In light of this alarming failure rate, we felt compelled to explore the change process before we entered into a discussion about any type of cultural assessment and cultural shift process.

Change initiatives fail for many different reasons, but we have found through our own personal experiences and in-depth research that at the heart of many failed change initiatives sits a leader (or leaders) who lacks the true commitment and tenacity to make the necessary **personal** and **cultural** changes.

No one is really paying attention to organizational culture and the significant role it plays in supporting any internal or external change initiative. If you don't want to be part of that 75% failure rate, then you must start paying attention to the human and cultural side of your business.

Case in Point

Consider these real-life cases we experienced (cleverly disguised with fictional names):

- Supersmart, Inc. didn't want to be left behind as its competitors all got on the "360- degree feedback" bandwagon. So the company hired an external consultant to come in and teach the management team how to conduct 360-degree performance reviews. The organization's culture was averse to conflict, but conflict is a critical element in the 360-degree process. This issue was never addressed, and $500,000 in consultant fees later, the program was dropped, and top management came away from the experience with the stereotypical reaction that programs involving employees never work. Dollars lost in production totaled about $700,000. So this failed initiative cost this company a whopping $1.2 million.

- Bugs Are Us, a large international manufacturing firm, decided to create a team-based process for developing new products. The concept was very exciting for many employees, but very intimidating for most of the managers. The CEO decided to move forward and brought in a consultant at the price tag of $1 million. No one paid attention to the human factor involved in making these teams work. They simply introduced the new product-development process and said, "Poof! You will work as teams." Most of the teams outright failed. The organization's culture was not one that embraced or valued employee involvement and most managers didn't believe in the team approach, but no one thought about that when instituting this change. The process fell flat on its face, and after two years of total disruption to the organization and about $2.5 million in lost production time, the company's leaders decided that the team approach was not for them.

- Healthy You, a teaching hospital, was adding a new building to its campus. Plans for opening this new facility involved not only adding new staff, but also integrating a new software system for billing and accounting by the "go live" date. The organization made painstaking plans to integrate these changes. Consultants were hired to plan and design the training and education program so that all employees, long service as well as new, would be prepared for the new environment, equipment, and systems. All of the training was completed on time, "the switch was thrown," and the doors opened. However, management had failed to listen to its employees' concerns about the new software. The workers knew they could handle the software, as long as it worked, but they wondered what the backup system would be. Management's position was, "We don't care what you think. It has to be done, and it will be done this way, end of story." With no formal accounting or billing backup plan, the hospital lost more than a million dollars in billing in the first three months of operation, due to errors in coding and the inordinate amount of time it took to follow the paper trail when the new software program crashed, day after day. The external consultants had done their job and trained the employees, but the system did not work. The result was such a huge loss for the hospital that management had to go back to the budgeting committee and reallocated an additional $22 million to see the project through.

Although these organizations failed in their attempts to introduce new programs, these organizations did experience change. In fact, they are forever changed. We must remember that *even when change initiatives fail, things never go back to the way they were before.*

Many employees left these organizations during these chaotic and frustrating times, some were reassigned, and others stayed but became totally disillusioned with their organization. All three organizations lost significant human capital costing them millions of dollars.

To Change or Not to Change

In all these cases, trust levels plummeted, intellectual capital was lost, and both market share and financial performance were negatively affected. So, do failed initiatives cost organizations money? Absolutely. Are they disruptive to organizations? Absolutely. Therefore, it is imperative that before you embark on any change initiative, you take the time to understand all the underlying elements of your culture. Had these organizations taken the time to answer the following questions their outcomes would have been very different.

- Is our culture ready?
- Can our culture support the new change strategy?
- Do our values support moving in that direction?
- How successful have change strategies been in the past? Why have they failed? Why have they been successful?
- Do our stated values really reflect our day to day actions?

We are not saying that because of these alarming statistics you should stay away from change. In these times of constant SHIFT, *not changing* is not an option—*change is inevitable.* Therefore, you must take control of the change effort and lead change in a meaningful direction.

However, a word of caution is in order. Do not change for the sake of change. That's not a meaningful direction. Change for the sake of change is as bad as trying to avoid change. If you have real goals that you want to achieve and you need to change things to achieve them, it's your job to find the right tools to make those changes. You can't just expect to buy medicine off the shelf (the flavor-of-the-month route) and force-feed it to your organization. You want to become a doctor who'll make an accurate diagnosis and begin the appropriate program of care. Your patients will thank you.

When we talk about change efforts, we are referring to *sustainable change* or *meaningful change.* This type of a change must be consistent with your organizational culture. If your culture doesn't welcome change and is not equipped to deal with change, prepare to become another statistic in the tally of failed change initiatives.

If your culture doesn't support or value the change that you are contemplating and if you are not willing to look at your organizational culture and make the necessary changes, then do not proceed with the change. It is too costly and too painful, as reflected in our examples.

Tool Time

When new concepts or management tools are introduced, they are often viewed as the panacea—the answer to all our problems. The tool is **not** the answer. The tool merely eases the SHIFT from one point to the next. When you have a flat tire, you may have the tire iron and the pump you need to fix the flat, but if you don't know how to use these tools, the flat won't get fixed. You've got to work to fix the flat. You might have to do less work if you have a more sophisticated tool, but you still have to work, unless you call for roadside assistance. However, if you call roadside assistance, you will never learn how to use the tools and you will never be able to fix the flat yourself. With change being necessary every day, do you really want to be dependent on outsiders every time you make a change, or do you want to learn to do it yourself?

Another example of how tools are not the solution comes from a real change initiative. There was a client who knew that a particular process was broken. The organization had just gone through many months of training on process-improvement tools, presented by a leading consulting firm. As the newly trained individuals investigated the "broken" process, they decided to use flow charting as the diagnostic tool. To investigate the process, a team of seven people got together for two hours a week over an eight-week period. As they got into their work, they used *Pareto* analysis, flow charting, and fishbone diagrams to collect reams of data. As they reviewed all of the collected data, they found gaps, "rework loops," and determined how to fix the process. The next steps were to develop the "new and improved" process, write the policies, and implement the new plan. It was a thing of beauty. The major "oops" in this situation was that the team forgot to consult the end-user (or the subject-matter expert) as it developed the new process. When the team members brought the new process down to the line and explained the new way to do things, they were laughed out of the room. The end-users (for good reason) shot holes in almost every suggestion that was presented. It turned out that the group had wasted its

---

time, and the company's money—about $250,000 worth of meeting time and document preparation. The new procedures, when taken to the application stage, failed miserably, not for lack of good tools, but for lack of inclusion of the right people and a solid process.

In order to increase the odds for successful implementation, it is important to understand the context in which a cultural assessment tool, such as Cultural Due Diligence™, is used. Therefore, it's essential for us to review the key factors of change.

Change Agent: Master of the Change Process

(We realize that some of you are probably thinking, "If I hear or read one more thing about that damn *C* word, I'll scream!" Go ahead. Screaming is great for the lungs, the heart, and even the soul. Now that you've gotten that out of your system, let's proceed.)

Through all of our research and personal experience, we have determined that, in order to be successful at any change initiative (including a cultural shift), you, as a leader, must first understand how you personally deal with change. From that point, you must then move into the role of change agent and be personally committed to the change.

Change agents are no longer the "soft-skilled people" looking for a change in assignment; they are hard-charging professionals who understand the business side of doing business but can also relate to the intrinsic needs of people. As a change agent you must help employees understand the need for change, point out alternatives to existing problems, dramatize the importance and effect of these problems on the business, and help employees recognize their own capabilities to not only cope with the situation but to change it. Employees must see these behaviors in your daily actions. No change tool will make you more successful in your efforts unless you are willing to take the necessary steps. You must drive the change bus. In other words, conducting a cultural assessment isn't enough. You must be prepared to make the necessary changes that are identified during the assessment phase.

How Deep is Change?

Changing one's values, which is true cultural change, requires years of changing many things in an organization. It will require changes to your training programs, reward systems, and management behaviors. Yes, it even means painting over the names on the reserved parking spaces. It is a gut-wrenching and often agonizing experience. As one of our interview respondents told us, "Cultures just don't change that quickly; they might change on paper, but they don't change in reality for a long time." (1)

So why the worry about organizational change? Is it really something that affects you? For anyone who is aiming to make a difference in a business, change is on the agenda: Creating it, managing it, and mastering it is the only survival tool in today's business climate.

In addition to the direct effects of organizational shifts on individual employees, what impact does all of this have on you as a consumer? You can answer this question by asking yourself a few questions:

- How many different telephone bills do I get (long distance, local, cellular, pager)?
- Which gas station now honors my Mobil (Exxon, Shell, etc.) card?
- What is the name of my health plan this month and is my doctor still on it?
- How quickly did the last computer I bought go "out of date"?
- Why do I question why a package sent "second-day air" takes so long?
- Why is the concept of using real money, instead of a credit or debit card, such a foreign idea?

As a leader, you are faced with even more effects of change. *"Don't I know that,"* you exclaim. Just when things seem to be going pretty well, the SHIFT hits the fan! And it blows in every direction. For example:

- Mergers often lead to duplication of management staff and positions—and guess what? Two heads are not always considered better than one.

- Business combinations, downsizing, and restructuring often result in the loss of intellectual capital. "My GOOD people are all leaving," lamented a physician who had combined his successful practice with another group to improve community access to quality care and to survive in the managed-care marketplace. (2) The change obviously affected the GOOD people (employees) and their decision to leave, but it also affected their leader, the doctor, and ultimately the patients he was committed to serve.

- The consolidation of operations and streamlining efforts that often include plant closings or retooling modifications (and subsequent changes) are SHIFTs that affect the leaders left trying to do their jobs. They may even be faced with relocation and/or retooling their own skills.

Future Focused

By now we all agree that the business community has seen huge SHIFTs in operations. But what does the future hold? Surely, merger mania and rampant restructuring will slow down. What do the experts think?

BE PREPARED FOR LAYOFFS, EXPERTS WARN, the headline reads.

According to Audrey Williams of the *Charlotte Observer*, "Since 1989, major corporations laid off more than three million workers. No industry is pink-slip proof." (3) Especially when the flavor-of-the-month solution is layoffs to make you lean and mean in Wall Street's eyes.

A full-page ad in the *Wall Street Journal* touting a large consulting firm's merger and acquisition assistance shows a matador up close and personal with an angry bull. The caption reads:

"Easy, compared to fending off a hostile takeover."

The ad goes on to describe the firm's dedicated team of merger and acquisition specialists who can help an organization defend against hostile attacks. When a large consulting firm commits this level of resources to this message, it's yet another indication that the experts believe, "We ain't seen nothin' yet!"

Economists predict a positive earnings outlook for the first decade of the new millennium, but seem to agree that it will be nowhere near what we've seen over the last decade. Most of us will agree that the record bull market cannot continue indefinitely. Furthermore, profits will continue to be pinched by factors such as increasing labor costs and pressure on U.S. manufacturing firms to keep prices down in the face of competition from low-cost imports. (That's been a major worry for U.S. manufacturers and displaced workers ever since Japanese autos, economical to buy and to fuel up, blew out an arrogant American auto industry unprepared for the SHIFT from gas-guzzling to fuel efficient brought on by the Arab oil embargo.) So, although the pace of merger and acquisition activity may slow, the amount of reorganization and restructuring activity may actually increase.

As you look to the future, you must consider a growing list of other key challenges, such as:

- Sharp economic swings,
- New competitive pressures,
- Globalization of the marketplace,
- Continued reshaping of business worldwide,
- New technologies,
- Sociocultural SHIFTs,
- Regulatory changes,

- Natural disasters,
- And the ever-changing profile of today's new-generation talent pool.

As the late *Saturday Night Live* comedian Gilda Radner said, "It's always something!"

In an article from *The Futurist*, Stephen Bertman says:

> "Like it or not, we've all been drafted into an army, a peacetime army that fights on the battlefield of everyday life. We wage "time wars" to use author Jeremy Rifkin's term: wars between the slower pace our minds and bodies crave and the faster tempo our technology demands. We are all combat veterans of such wars." (4)

Change has become inherent in the way you do the work you do. It has escaped the narrow confines of the human resources department and has become an issue of personal responsibility. It is part of your daily life, and as a leader you must become a master of the change process. You must start eating change for breakfast, lunch and dinner. You must also help your employees to become change agents as well.

Change in Disguise

What is all this telling us? Well, call it a merger, call it an acquisition, call it 360-degree feedback, call it self-directed work teams, call it cultural transformation, call it sociocultural shifts or regulatory changes. It doesn't matter what you call the new business strategy—whatever name you give it, *it is plain old change in disguise.*

This is the constant. The only thing that stays the same is change! How do you continue to reinvent yourself and your organization to meet and greet change in the flesh or in disguise?

For you to begin meeting this challenge head-on, you must examine how you have personally dealt with changes over the years and how well you have done historically with change in your organizations. So let's look at those two areas.

Personal Change

Do you remember when ice cream was just vanilla, coffee was Maxwell House, phones were just black, sheets were white, lipstick was red, beds were single or double, and stores were closed on Sundays? These days we can't believe the store doesn't open till 10:00 A.M. on Sunday. We want our ice-cream flavors mixed right before our eyes on a marble stone; and instead of coffee with cream, it's a large double decaf latte with skim milk. As you're going through your normal routine, you don't notice how many of these extraordinary changes you have accepted without a problem. It's only when you have a chance to reflect that everything around you is different from what it was five years ago that you begin to notice the volume of change you've been through.

"I was so happy to get my first VCR," recalls co-author P.J. Bouchard. "I loved the 'time SHIFTing' it allowed. Now, I could tape a show that, before this feature, would have zipped into the ether if I weren't home to watch. What a great SHIFT! It was easy to accept—and a whole generation felt the same way, judging by how many VCRs there are out there—because we were already sold on the TV shows and movies that would be the primary source of VCR programming. However, I doubt I would have stayed happy long if I had bought a BETA VCR because they became virtually obsolete so quickly."

The many memories attached to an old car may make us cringe at the thought of trading it in; but on the other hand, most of us enjoy the chance to own a new one. Why else would "new car fragrance" be so popular at the local car washes?

Obviously, certain types of change are more welcome than others.

Did the changes mentioned above threaten you, or did they easily become your norm? We would guess that these changes probably became the norm for you. Why are these changes so much easier to accept than others? The common thread to these changes is that they offer more options and convenience to us as consumers. As we progress through this chapter, we will talk about the tougher changes that you experience in your life, both personally and professionally, and analyze why they are so difficult. Maybe the difficulty lies in something as simple as viewing the change or changes as out of your control and, thus, blinding yourself to the options.

The Many Faces of Change

Now, take a moment to complete the following exercise.

▼ **Draw a picture that best illustrates you and change**

[drawing space]

▼ **Draw a picture of how your organization responds to change**

[drawing space]

Where are you going?

No skipping down to here without drawing the pictures!

What do these pictures tell you? (Other than you should have taken that elective art class your senior year). Probably something about how you felt when a specific change took place.

Happy—sad—worried—excited—relieved

Whatever the emotion or feelings, just remember that everyone has feelings about change, and they are strong ones. If you drew yourself with your hair standing on end or surrounded by sharks, you're not unusual. Case in point: The pictures on the following pages were drawn by business leaders attending a change workshop. They were responding to the question, "Would you please draw (from your emotions) what it's like to make changes in your organization?" The drawings are good examples of some of the deep-rooted emotions we carry about change. We've used this exercise with many of our client organizations. It is a powerful approach when trying to get people to talk about how they think and feel about change. We suggest you use it in your own organization to get the dialogue going around change.

Drawn by an executive from a high-tech company: "You're given the okay to make changes, cheered on by the Executive Team, but are hampered by lack of resources and authority to make the changes."

Drawn by a middle manager of a hospital: "We manage the heck out of our budget, we're very lean and efficient, but it's always the guy who doesn't manage the money well that has the resources to implement change. It doesn't pay to be efficient in our organization."

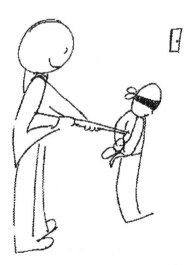

Drawn by a supervisor of a manufacturing firm: "We might as well have a gun to our backs. We're never included in the process (hence the blindfold), we go into it with no idea of goals or how we're supposed to contribute."

Drawn by a senior executive in an HMO: "Change is like trying to move a stubborn elephant, almost impossible. Note the end of the elephant we are trying to make it move."

Drawn by a manager at a high-tech firm: "We almost have to get on our knees and pray outside the boardroom in order to get resources to implement change."

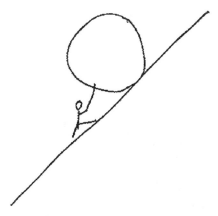

Drawn by an executive from a health care system: "In a system you might as well be Sisyphus rolling the rock uphill. You hardly ever succeed unless you or your boss is connected."

Track Record

Next, let's examine how well you have done historically in your attempts to implement change in your organization. Think about a change initiative that has occurred in your organization over the past three to five years and answer the following questions:

1. What was the change?
2. Was it successful and did it survive the test of time? If yes, why—if no, why not.
3. What did you learn?
4. What would you do differently?

This is one of the first steps in preparing to conduct a cultural assessment and shifting your culture. Once you have answered these questions, a very useful exercise would be to have other members of your organization answer them as well. This exercise will help you and your organization relive the change experience and allow you to compare notes. Some will feel that it was a very positive experience; others will feel it was negative; and still others may think it was neutral. After you relive the experience using "20/20 hindsight," you can apply what you learn to the next change initiative. Also, comparing notes with others in your organization will provide you with differing perspectives that will be helpful as you move toward your next challenge.

Are You a Change Agent or Change Avoider?

As you reflect on the last couple of sections, are you beginning to get a sense of where you think you fall on the change continuum? Do you think you have reached change-agent status?

Take a few minutes to go through this exercise.

You always feel as if you are in growth mode.	Yes ☐	No ☐
You find yourself relying more than ever on your intuition/gut.	Yes ☐	No ☐
You are thoughtful and yet directive.	Yes ☐	No ☐
You see situations from other perspectives (not just through your own eyes.)	Yes ☐	No ☐
Things don't move fast enough—your level of patience is constantly tested and pushed to the max.	Yes ☐	No ☐
You constantly revisit your own values.	Yes ☐	No ☐
Your frankness with yourself helps you to relate to others.	Yes ☐	No ☐
You truly know who you are and you are congruent in your actions.	Yes ☐	No ☐
Your greatest joy is doing for others, so they can do for themselves.	Yes ☐	No ☐
You understand that you must care for yourself, no one else can.	Yes ☐	No ☐

Total **YES** ___   Total **NO** ___

If you answered yes to three or less—you may want to work with a change coach.

If you answered yes to at least five—you're on your way.

If you answered yes to all ten—you eat change for breakfast, lunch, and dinner.

Your score on this exercise is not a predictor of your ability to change, but it does provide an indication of how comfortable you are with change. It tells you whether you are still serving status quo on your plate instead of a steady diet of change. And just like introducing a new food, your responses to change are:

- highly personal,
- based on previous experiences, and
- fairly predictable unless you make a conscious effort to change.

You may not be a card-carrying change agent—yet, but you are beginning to understand the dynamics of the process and beginning to give this subject serious thought, or you would have stopped reading this book by now!

True Confessions

This story, which illustrates how real change begins, merits retelling. In the middle 1980s, Vaughn Beals Jr., CEO, president, and chairman of Harley-Davidson Motor Co., stepped up to the plate. In an interview, he looked straight into the camera and said: "We tried all the usual solutions—the culture routine, the robot routine, the low-wage routine—and none of them worked. We couldn't avoid the inescapable conclusion. We, the management, were the problem." (5) Prophetic, insightful words born of desperation. At that time, Harley-Davidson appeared to have a one-way ticket to the corporate graveyard. The company had lost market share to the Japanese and was plagued by production-quality issues. But Vaughn Beals woke up one day with this revelation. The fundamental problem was not the competition, not the labor issues, quality control, or the excuse of the week. The real problem was HIM.

This marked the beginning of one of the greatest turnaround success stories.

Beals, along with design genius Willie G. Davidson, a third-generation member of one of the company's founding families, orchestrated the buyout of American Machine Foundry (AMF), which had acquired Harley in 1969. Although Harley loyalists were critical of the HD-AMF relationship, it allowed Harley-Davidson to take some of the bold steps needed to survive the 1970s. Once the company was flying solo again, Beals, Davidson, and a few other top executives focused on product-line improvements and marketing to the growing group of "boomers" who had to have a Harley. They empowered their employees by organizing them into teams and removing layers of management. This was a dramatic turnaround in company philosophy and in the bottom line.

Today, Harley-Davidson once again enjoys a faithful following. The customer base has expanded from the Hard Core Biker group to include the RUBs (Rich Urban Bikers), the RIOTs (Retired Idiots On Tour), and the AHABs (Aspiring Hard-ass Bikers). Although they differ in most respects, they share the commonality of owning a bike from the undisputed leader in big bikes. As a part of the overall organizational shift, Beals led a road rally to Wall Street to attend a ceremony officially admitting Harley-Davidson to the New York Stock Exchange. His willingness to revamp the company from top to bottom gave new meaning to "hear the thunder" as Wall Street and the world saw the Eagle fly again. (6)

It Takes Guts

Would you have the guts to do what Beals did? Could you look in the mirror and say, "The problem is me?" Well, it's show time. It's time to step up to the plate and play some serious ball. If you want the big job, then you have to have the guts and the fortitude to admit vulnerability. It's time to look in the mirror and take personal responsibility for what is occurring in your organization.

Personal Journey

How exactly can you begin this process? Well, over the years we have tracked the behaviors of effective change agents and we would like to share those with you.

- **Know in your heart, and in your head, change begins with you**—There is no cookie-cutter approach to making change happen.

- **Ask for help**—When you don't know the answer, find a resource (teacher, coach, and reference book) that does. A formal education that leaves you believing you know all you need to know for the rest of your life is not really an education, is it? It's a formula for failure. Many leaders today are hiring personal coaches. Take the time for your own personal development. It is the most important step you can take in achieving long-term success.

- **Energize your people**—Get people involved. We are not saying that your organization should be a free-for-all. We are saying broaden the span of control that people have and expand their level of responsibility and authority. This fires people up!

- **Trust others to do the right thing and allow them to make mistakes**—This is a biggie. You really need to learn to let go. You are not superman or superwoman. You make mistakes, too! And, yes, in letting go, mistakes will be made. But remember that people learn through doing. So let go and let them do. *You cannot teach people anything. You can only help them discover it within themselves.* —Galileo

- **Listen and respond with empathy**—Yes, this means sharing in another person's emotions, thoughts, or feelings.

- **Offer praise and recognition**—Feedback, especially positive, is as important as oxygen. We all need it to stay energized and alive.

- **Be clear on key result areas, measurements, and goals**—People need to know that what they are doing adds value and is linked to something.

- **Obtain support and resources needed**—Again, do *not try to make change happen alone*. That is the kiss of death.

- **Work hard to communicate, communicate, and communicate**—Tell employees what you know, and tell them what you don't know. Employees don't expect leaders to have all the answers. What they want from you is the truth.

Work on developing these qualities, and you'll be well on your way to becoming a master of change!

Three Types of Organizational Change

Are there different types of change? We believe so. In our work over the last twenty years, we have seen three distinct types of organizational change.

The first type of change we refer to as *"Don't Upset The Applecart."* With this type of change, you merely calibrate or tweak some aspect of the current system. This type of change is very restrictive in focus and perpetuates much of the old, and in some cases, flawed system. It is relatively low in threat and painless. However, the resulting impact on employee mind-set is very limited. This type of change lets you fall victim to what we've come to call the "gas-pedal phenomenon." You've got the pedal to the metal, and you just can't go any faster. Remember, pushing the pedal harder will not make you go faster, but buying a faster car will.

The second type of change we call the *"Boomerang Syndrome."* This type of change is common in organizations of all types and sizes. It is reactive and responsive to both internal and external forces. This type of change is problem-focused, with very clear objectives and outcomes. Because there is no built-in mechanism for perpetuating the new way of doing things, organizations more often then not fall right back into their old habits and practices. You throw out the old way of doing things, but the old way comes back, just like a boomerang.

The third type of change we refer to as *"Conscious Creation."* This is the most effective type of change. It involves a gradual metamorphosis. Because this is not a superficial process, this type of change typically will cause a high level of pain on the front end. However, the rewards (creating a culture that is resilient and can handle change) will be worth the effort and suffering, because you will create a new culture in which change becomes relatively painless. *"Conscious Creation"* comes about through true commitment and thorough understanding of how each change program (whether it happens at the departmental level or at the corporate level) will affect the whole system. A well-orchestrated plan is crucial and involves all members of the organization. This type of change initiative is significantly broader and has a significant impact on changing the mind-set and behaviors of the entire work force.

When we talk about a cultural-assessment and cultural-shift process like Cultural Due Diligence™, we are talking about whole system change, and the only approach for successful implementation of such change is *"Conscious Creation."*

Slow Dance Partners

Why are organizations so slow to change?

In *Teaching the Elephant to Dance*, James a. Belasco, Ph.D., suggests that organizations are like elephants—slow to change and both learn through conditioning. In an elephant training parable, Belasco tells us how. "Trainers shackle young elephants with heavy chains to deeply embedded stakes. In that way the elephant learns to stay in its place. Older elephants never try to leave even though they have the strength to pull the stake and move beyond. Their conditioning limits their movements with only a small metal bracelet around their foot— attached to nothing. Like powerful elephants, many companies are bound by earlier conditioned constraints." (7)

Belasco really drives the point home that conditioning is a very powerful process, and his insight into the challenge that change presents to an organization is thought-provoking. However, as we began analyzing his view, it hit us right between the eyes that so many of us refer to organizations as the thing to fix, the culprit, a thing that can be managed. Well, an organization, as defined in Webster's New World Dictionary, is "a body of persons organized for some specific purpose." That's right, bringing individuals together is what forms organizations. So the challenge for you as a leader is to learn how to manage at the individual level and not just at the "macro" level. Individuals make up groups, groups make up teams, committees, task forces, etc., and these groups make up your organization. When employees are dysfunctional at the individual level, putting them on teams or committees does not suddenly make them functional. Instead, it creates an even bigger challenge for you.

We have discovered that the "we've always done it this way" syndrome has become a very powerful unattached chain, just like the one described in the elephant parable. In many instances, your personal, long-entrenched patterns of behavior and your very own policies and practices have perpetuated this mind-set. The way to change this mind-set is to reframe the way you look at things. It is not as hard as it seems. Take the example of a woman who was on a snorkeling trip in the Caribbean. She paid $3.65 for eight ounces of "special food" to attract the colorful fish. When she opened up her Baggie, she said to the boat captain, "Hey! You sold me dog food!" He replied, "No, it's only dog food when you feed it to a dog. It's fish food when the fish eat it." That's just a different way of looking at the same thing. Have you seen the hourglass shape that holds within it two faces looking at one another, or any of the pictures that have embedded images? Seeing one thing at first glance, and then making a slight adjustment to see something completely different—that's reframing.

There are also many examples of taking reframing a bit too far. There are consultants out there who will tell you that you must not only have "an adjustment in attitude, but also in altitude." The next thing you know, they have you all sitting on the floor cross-legged to view the most recent slide presentation from the marketing department. Or they have you rearranging all the furniture in your office to face west, and outside the office they have you replace your ringing alarm clock with one that chimes so you can enter your morning with peace and serenity. This, too, is just another way to reframe the everyday things around you.

As you might guess from the previous example, we're not fond of reframing things without a clear purpose. Having always done something in a particular way is not necessarily a bad thing. Take, for instance, the newspaper page. It's always been printed with ink on newsprint. There have been improvements through the years in the grade of newsprint, the presses, and even the ink, which is not nearly as smudgy as it once was; however, the basics have stayed the same. A radical reconfiguration won't come about until the purpose of the newspaper page changes. Although "we've always done it this way" is not a good enough reason to avoid changing the way it's done, changing something that continues to be useful in its old form ONLY because we want to throw out old ways of doing things could be an unmitigated disaster. If at present, doing it the way it's always been done is the most successful course to take, that's the course you should take, just as long as it's a conscious decision and you don't shut out the possibility of making a change when a new, better method comes along. Especially in business, where the stakes of a new method that fails can be enormous, we have to admit that in some cases making minor changes can be less ruinous than an ill-advised complete overhaul.

A CEO from a major ice-cream manufacturer told us that he still has customers who want traditional flavors—you know, the flavors they grew up with. His response to this was to make a commitment to filling the niche market that wants the old flavors. "My customers still want to buy butter pecan and orange pineapple. Cherry Garcia doesn't appeal to them." (8) His customers want it the way it's always been. But as a leader, he is still changing, in the way that he produces and packages the product and in a marketing strategy that focuses on the "good ole days." He is not allowing the customers' mind-set to keep him and his business in the past.

A New Expectation

Change, which was barely acknowledged a few years ago, is now recognized as an integral aspect of an organization's culture. Some companies even select individuals based on their willingness to change. For instance, in a November 1997 interview with *The (Phoenix) Business Journal,* Contact CEO Larry Frazier reported, "One of the things we are good at is change. We tell our employees that our middle name is change and if you can't change, you can't work at Contact." (9)

Simply demanding that an employee be willing to change is not necessarily a good thing, though. You don't want obedient puppies. Employees who are change agents have ideas and thoughts about the organization and the way that it does things. Employees who are change agents offer input. They don't parrot management's sentiments.

In some cases, when we hear leaders say that employees must be willing to change, the only change they're talking about is the change they order, their hero projects. When the day is done, the organization is the leader's pyramid, and the employees are just slaves hauling stones to erect a monument to his or her glory.

This mind-set is reflected by the compensation, which is the only thing that really matters in some businesses: executive bonuses, stock options, equity, money, property, and position. We are not saying this goes for all big businesses, but let's agree that executive salaries at most big organizations dwarf the general salaries by staggering amounts.

When some leaders argue that change must be a part of each employee's portfolio they sound as though they don't want to hear the word "no," as though they believe that a dissenting opinion is a sign of unwillingness to change. For them, "willing to change" becomes another code phrase, like "team player," for "someone who won't rock the boat." This is not at all what we mean. Successful, sustainable change is NOT about orders for change that some big kahuna hands down from an ivory tower. We are talking about creating a culture that expects employees to not only be receptive to change, but also expects them to take part in organizational changes and to actually create change initiatives. And as a leader you must think of ways to help each individual contributor be more effective.

How do you accomplish this? Talk to your people and listen with both ears to what they are telling you. Provide them with the tools that they need to better understand themselves and how they deal or don't deal with the change process. There are many tools out there today that can help individuals to better understand themselves and how they view the world. Talk to an industrial psychologist, pick up catalogs that contain self-improvement tools, use psychological assessments like Myers-Briggs Type Indicator. Remember that individuals make up groups and groups make up organizations. Treat the individual, treat the groups/teams and you are treating the organization as a whole.

Resistance: Another Crippling Shackle

According to a study of more than 100 companies from twenty different countries by ProSci, a Colorado business research and publishing firm, *Employee resistance to change is the most pervasive problem faced by change sponsors.* (10) "Resistance to change" is a phrase with which we are all too familiar, but the study proves only one thing for certain: the belief in "employee resistance to change" is pervasive. And we contend THAT BELIEF is the problem. Employees at all levels, in all types of organizations believe that resistance to change is the biggest obstacle to change. We think it's a hobgoblin with very few teeth.

Back in the 1940s, Kurt Lewin (one of the founder's of field theory, action science, group dynamics, socio-technical science and organizational development) introduced the term "resistance to change" as a system concept—a force that affects managers and employees equally. However, many other researchers and authors have taken the term out of its original context, using it as model of behavior that describes employees alone. This creates an unnecessarily adversarial approach to change and a destructive, self-fulfilling prophecy.

Think about your organization and its approach to change strategies. What's one of the first things you talk about? Employee resistance? We think that employee resistance is not an important factor until managers, who believe they must overcome resistance, act on that belief. The belief turns into a self-fulfilling prophecy that can be the *kiss of death when trying to implement a change.*

We're not saying that you should be naïve enough to think that resistance doesn't exist. Articles and books have been written about this topic, and we've come up with a sizable laundry list of why people resist change. However, it's our belief that resistance to change is in reality a symptom. In fact, it's not only a symptom, it often serves as the scapegoat for change efforts that have failed.

Why do people resist change anyway? Pick up any article that talks about resistance to change and you will find recurrent themes. No matter what the business focus is, or who their leader may be, people are just plain people, and they have the same fears and concerns.

One of our interviewees, a training manager, summed it up this way: "Most people still resist change. They have a career stability mentality." (11)

You may have seen it called "collect a paycheck" mentality or entitlement mentality, but it is all the same thing—a need for security and a cry for more control over their own fate. This feeling has been repeatedly confirmed by our experiences. It underlies a number of the recurring theories about why people resist change. This manager went on to cite Maslow's Hierarchy of Needs. The teachings of this social scientist emphasize that an individual must first feel safe and secure before being able to achieve a state of self-actualization that allows a person to embrace change more readily. One of the solutions—as we will discuss later in more detail—is to involve employees in the change process. This gives them a sense of control.

Here's a list of these recurring themes that we can all relate to:

- It means I have to *give up* something.
- It threatens my *security.*

- I like clinging to the *past*. It's *comfortable* and *familiar*.

- I like maintaining personal *stability*.

- I like to feel more in *control*.

- Uncertainty is *scary*.

- I fear *losing status* or my job.

- If I *allow* this change to happen, who knows what will happen next?

- My manager doesn't really *believe* in this change, so why should I?

- Last month it was chocolate, this month it's vanilla. Who knows what flavor of the month will be next month? I'll just wait for it.

- I'm already *burdened* since the downsizing. How can I take on any more?

- I need to *protect* myself.

- I am *emotionally tied* to the way we do it now. This is my baby.

- It is the *tradition*.

As one of our interviewees, Patti Saathoff of Cigna Healthcare, put it:

> "People do not resist change so much as they resist being
> changed. It follows that individuals will cope much better
> with change if they have a hand in creating it." (12)

Our hypothesis was confirmed in the ProSci study as well. According to the executives who were included in this survey, employees resisted change because they often did not know what was planned and did not have a part in creating it. (13)

We see these reactions to change more as **symptoms** rather than as the actual cause of the problem. Experience has taught us that these reactions are symptoms created by lack of involvement, lack of safety, lack of support, and an overall lack of focus by leaders to remove the obstacles that create the resistance in the first place. We are seeing increasing evidence to support this conclusion. In his book, *Breakaway Planning*, corporate consultant Paul Levesque presents a strong case for "sharing with the entire employee population the specific nature of the change effort they are being asked to help implement." (14) Levesque also believes that leaders must be ambassadors of change and that "the greater the leader's anticipation of success, the greater the likelihood of achieving it." (15) Like Levesque, we believe that employees must understand and believe in the goals for change and see some benefit for themselves related to the change. Therefore, when you are thinking about conducting a cultural assessment and making a cultural shift, make sure you involve the work force.

A case in point: We worked with one client who wanted to change the way projects were managed. Management was interested in moving from the individual-contributor concept to multidisciplinary teams. So they hired a consulting firm to come in and implement their program to expedite the product cycle and tie in the manufacturing process. The consulting firm jumped right into the tasks, designed the teams, identified the players and began team meetings. The consultants did not take into account the organization's culture or current climate. Let's just say it didn't fly. The new expectations and team structures enraged employees. The human resources department could have used the deli-counter ticket system to handle the onslaught of complaints from the work force! This resistance again was symptomatic of the many challenges that the organization faced, but they were not the real cause.

The factors that the outside consultant did not take into consideration included:

- This was a biotech firm where most positions were technical and filled by individual contributors who wanted to work with bugs, not people.

- The organization had recently folded one of its divisions and had just gone through a massive restructuring, so many individuals were already performing extra tasks that had been performed by workers who were recently let go.

- The organization had just awakened to the fact that it no longer had a monopoly and that it would take five years just to catch up to the current competition with the development of a new product.

- Tensions were running very high, and the work force feared another downsizing.

If these, along with other factors, had been considered (as they would have been if the leadership had conducted a cultural assessment), the consultants would have recognized that the company was not ready to tackle a major change initiative. Major prep work was needed. By the time we were called in, the work force was pushing back, and the resistance wave had begun. And the price tag just for that outside consulting firm up to this point? A mere $1 million for a program that did not work.

By getting the employees involved and tying the change initiative to a strategic business goal, we were able to gain credibility with the work force. They not only accepted the new team process, but many went to human resources and asked to be tapped when the next wave of teams formed. This experience reinforced our belief that people really do not resist change itself. They resist attempts *to be changed* and really resent change initiatives that don't involve them and don't explain why the change is under way.

All Hands on Deck

People want to do more than just show up for work!

So what do people really care about?

Strategic business futurists Roger E. Herman and Joyce L. Gioia cited a 1998 survey by Response Analysis of Princeton, New Jersey, in an article entitled "Making Work Meaningful" that appeared in the December 1998 issue of *The Futurist.* In their discussion of the survey, they reported the following statistics: *Of the 1,600 people responding, 52% wanted to be responsible for their work and the results it produced, 42% wanted acknowledgment for their contributions, and 39% wanted their tasks matched to their strengths.* (16)

The authors assert, "Today's worker is no longer willing to work in an authoritarian and dehumanizing environment. Workers want meaning in their work and balance in their lives. Given the amount of time people spend at work, they want opportunities to contribute and to know how their work contributes to the organization. They also want to be valued as individuals with goals and aspirations, not just replaceable drones in the hive." (17)

Employees respond positively when they are given clear goals and the authority to make things happen. This kind of exchange can only survive in a culture built on mutual trust. Now, this process does not take away accountability. It does, however, focus on objective results, and it creates an environment for continuous feedback and improvements. Successful businesses develop and measure feedback systems, and all employees are held accountable for their actions.

General Electric Corporation (GE) has been described by many people as a model for successful organizational change. Why? Because, back in 1980, CEO Jack Welch recognized what needed to be done and took action. He revolutionized the structure and processes of GE, which was not an easy feat because it involved laying off more than 170,000 people. That's a lot of people, nearly three times the number of Americans who died in Vietnam. Welch decided these drastic actions were the only way to revitalize this former sleeping giant. For those of us who have never been involved in such a far-reaching initiative, it's hard to grasp the extent of this change. But this well planned and well executed change initiative, dubbed, Work-Out, is still in use twenty years later. The major elements of eliminating unnecessary work, empowering employees, building trust, and creating a boundaryless organization continue to be effective guidelines for change efforts today.

In the book *The Boundaryless Organization: Breaking the Chains of Organizational Structure,* authors Ron Ashkenas, Dave Ulrich, Todd Jick, and Steve Kerr cite GE as an excellent example of a company that successfully adopted boundaryless behaviors. These authors do not advocate elimination of all boundaries, but suggest that organizations adopt permeable rather than rigid structures and processes. They take a biological view of organizational boundaries, comparing them to the structure of a living cell whose permeable membrane lets nutrients, oxygen, and chemical transmitters move in and out. In their opinion, in the boundaryless organization, "information, resources, ideas, and energy pass throughout the membranes quickly and easily so that the organization as a whole functions far better than each of its separate parts." (18)

Welch did a good job of planning for his change initiative. He recognized the challenge of changing the minds of thousands of people, and he knew he couldn't accomplish this alone. He surrounded himself with people who were passionate about changing the culture, individuals who saw the value in involving the entire system.

The Boogieman

Involving employees helps reduce the *fear of the unknown, or fear of what's out there.* Fear of the unknown or fear of what's out there goes back to childhood. We are sure you can remember segments of your childhood. Yes, for some of us this will be a little more challenging than for others; however, let's go there together. Remember the big day when your parents/guardians told you that you were going to sleep alone in your bed, in the dark[*]—without the night light or having your bedroom door open. You thought, "I'm ready for this"—and then they closed the door. Some light was still coming through the crack under the door so that was OK, but then they went to bed and all the lights went out. Then it really hit you. You were alone in the dark. The boogieman was definitely in the room. So you moved quietly and gently to the middle of the bed, not making a sound so the boogieman wouldn't hear you.

---

[*]Recent studies have demonstrated that children who regularly sleep with night lights have a much higher incidence of nearsightedness as adults. So those of you who were in the dark, Mom did you a favor!

You knew the boogieman was right under your bed or in the closet. Oh, and what about the vents? Boogiemen definitely came out of there at night. You even saw the monsters: long dark shadows with green eyes and big teeth. You exaggerated what was out there, maybe. You wanted to move but were too afraid that something might get you.

The same applies to us today as adults. We still fear what's out there. It's like walking or driving across a bridge. We will not venture out if we don't see or know that the bridge connects to land on the other side. How many of us look down before getting into an elevator? We know we want to see the floor before stepping in.

Fear can be seen as a very positive thing. Stephen King, the Czar of Fear, has even coined an acronym for FEAR: **F**ace **E**verything **A**nd **R**ecover. Help your employees to interpret fear in this more positive light, and help them to face everything and recover.

It's unrealistic for you to take a blind leap of faith, and the same is true for your employees. Therefore, as a leader, **you must** try to remove as much of the mystery as you can. It is up to you and no one else. Our biggest challenge stares back at us in the mirror every morning. As Michael Jackson sang, world peace begins with the "Man in the Mirror," so does every challenge you face.

In working with organizations of all sizes and in all industries, we have come to realize that change is even difficult to implement from a technical standpoint. When introducing a new technology or software program in today's high-tech environment, things can easily run amok, cause a heck of a lot of damage to your organization, and even threaten the viability of the company as a whole. Yet, it's the emotional component that is the greatest threat to the success of a change initiative and an area leaders pay very little attention to.

As a leader, you must first address these emotional responses. The Boogieman, real or perceived, must be identified and defined. Only if you are empathetic to your co-workers' concerns will they be inclined to view the change initiative the way you do. It's got to be the same give-and-take relationship that cements friendships.

If you go back to that list of why people resist change, take the time to analyze the words we've italicized: *give up, threatens security, stability, control, uncertainty, losing, burdened, protect, emotionally tied,* and *tradition.* These words have emotion written all over them, and most of them point to fear of the unknown. In fact, what we have found consistently through the years is that fear is a significant barrier in the change process. It is another shackle.

Many of these negative emotional reactions to change can be modified or eliminated if you are willing to play a critical role as a leader and see yourself as an instigator of change and coach to any change process, at least initially. Once change becomes a way of life and employees' minds have shifted, your role becomes more advisory. As a leader, you must come to the realization that you will not be able to fundamentally change your way of doing business without the people you employ—all of them. They must be fully involved; they must support your goals and objectives; and their fears must be addressed at every level, from top management right down to your building custodians. That is the epitome of "cleaning up your act."

Once fear's presence and negative effect are openly acknowledged, you can begin to take steps to isolate and reduce it. Along with involving employees, you must learn how to stop abrasive and abusive behavior too often displayed toward your employees.

Your **attitude** as a leader is more critical than the change itself. You must be people-centered, positive, and supportive. Looking again at the ProSci study, we see that a list of "management behaviors not supportive of change" accounted for 33% of what respondents considered the greatest obstacles to managing change. Being unsupportive was seen by the study participants as the single "biggest mistake" change sponsors could make. (19)

Look Who's Talking

Communication is also a critical aspect of change. It must be direct, not understated. You must share accurate and honest information with the work force on an ongoing basis and help workers explore and express their true feelings towards the change. The operative words here are "accurate" and "honest." If employees do not **trust** the information that is being shared, all the communication tactics in the world will not help the situation.

What we are talking about here is changing human behavior. Some heavy stuff. And as you know, human behavior is controlled by the mind. So the only way to get the change you want is to change people's minds. Now, how easy is that? Co-author Lizz Pellet's grandfather, an exceptional auto mechanic, used to say, "You know, I can change a tire on a moving car, but I can never get that woman (grandma) to change her mind." Our point exactly. Once someone's mind is made up, it develops the ability to wall itself off from influence, and penetrating or circumnavigating the wall takes much more effort. We might as well say this now (and we probably will sometime again): "Some folks ain't never gonna change!" As hard as that is to accept with all of our insight and creative management techniques, it's a fact. How do you deal with it? If someone refuses to consider change, then change the person (replace him or her).

Probably one of the toughest decisions that you must make as a leader is deciding that one of your employees must be let go. You must begin to recognize that part of your job is to address the people issues (something that many leaders just aren't good at yet). In "Why CEOs Fail," an article by Ram Charan and Geoffrey Colvin featured in the June 12, 1999, issue of *Fortune,* the authors address this very subject. As they explored the reasons CEOs "blow it," they found that CEOs fail "more than any other way, by (their) failure to put the right people in the right jobs—and the related failure to fix people problems in time." (20) When you analyze what Jack Welch has done over the last ten-plus years, one thing that jumps out at you is that he did address and continues to address people problems. That's part of your job, too.

As leaders, one of our biggest misconceptions is that we really think we can change people's minds. People must change their own minds.

And how exactly do you accomplish that (getting folks to change their minds and believe that it was all their idea)? Certainly not by an edict from the ivory tower and certainly not by Ye Olde Management Speech. The edict, the speech, and all of the persuasion in the world **will not work**. Beware of the *"Hey! We're all in this together"* speech. You know, the one where you give them facts and hope they agree with you. The one where you hope they'll see things differently after the meeting and act differently. The one where you talk about the change by telling them that it won't be easy, but you have a plan. The one where you tell them you have confidence they can do it. The one you play louder and louder, over and over, hoping that it will have a bigger impact.

Why doesn't The Speech work? Think of your audience. Those who have already bought in need no persuasion, they're already convinced. The rebel rousers have their arms folded and are saying, *"Here we go again!"* And, don't forget about the WAS (Wait And See) group. They will do things the same old way and wait to see if this thing really sticks. So, basically, no one who attends that meeting and hears that speech will come out with a changed mind.

All employees affected by the change must have a thorough understanding of the change and its implications. You must pay as much attention to the emotional dimension as you give to the informational aspects of the change. Remember, employees cannot be mandated to a SHIFT in mind-set. They must be positioned to change their own minds by engaging them in the process. You must engage their egos. Another point worth reiterating is that employees (individuals) make up organizations; therefore, if you change people's minds, you change your organization.

The Ego Has Landed

An important element that we have not talked about up to this point is ego. Ego plays an important role in change. When you are pushing toward a new way of doing things, you imply that the old way or mind-set is wrong, and even though the new way might be better, ego creates rationalizations to defend the old way. All of us have found ourselves doing this at one time or another.

Think about the ego. There will be far less damage to the ego when employees make their own choices. There is ego satisfaction/reward in coming up with their own good ideas that give them permission to let go of old ideas. Being part of the change process allows them to experiment and practice as they go, rather than being handed a finished product that is very foreign to them. Remember the case of the process improvement team. They didn't include the subject matter expert and that contributed to the failure of the project at a cost of $250,000. Now, how productive is that?

As we have stated, people resist for many different reasons.

Think about a time when you have personally resisted a change. What was occurring? Who was involved? No matter what position we may hold in an organization, we are all subject to the tyranny of a boss saying, "I want this changed, and I want it done this way and now." How would that make you feel? Think back to your college or high school days when the teacher didn't really care what you thought, and your experiences and notions were not important. How did that make you feel? How did you react?

Think about personal relationships you've had that were ended by the other party. Have you ever had one end like that and then realize that deep down inside you had been trying to figure out where the escape hatch was yourself? Despite that realization, you likely didn't breathe a sigh of relief at being freed. You probably became enraged, hurt, or devastated. (Maybe all three.) Why? Because something was being DONE to you. You had no control. You had no say in the matter. Often when people are powerless, they resist.

One recognized leader in the airline industry understands the importance of employee involvement and the need to relinquish some management control. In an article from *Leader to Leader*, titled "A Culture of Commitment," Herb Kelleher, chairman, president and CEO of Southwest Airlines, says, "If you create an environment where people truly participate, you don't need control. They know what needs to be done, and they do it." (21)

He goes on to admit that he is likely to be a step behind the employees, who typically know more about what's going on in their area than he does. This attitude has allowed Southwest employees to be vitally involved in the changes within their organization and the industry and to become a success story of participative management.

Rebel Rousers

Workers sometimes resist workplace innovations for legitimate reasons. So, before treating resistance as a problem, check to see if they are right!

As we mentioned earlier, do not kid yourself into thinking that removing fear and involving employees is 1) a piece of cake, or 2) the end-all, be-all answer to your change challenge. This is not the case. Not everyone will jump on the change bandwagon, so you must learn how to work with the resistance that your change initiatives will create. One of the benefits of doing so is that you can use the power of the resistance to help you achieve your goals. Involve your biggest cynics, your biggest resisters. They are typically some of the most influential people in your organization, especially if management is not trusted and/or feared. Because they are anti-establishment, these are the folks that many employees listen to. Therefore, getting them to participate in making the change will have a positive effect on the change you are trying to implement. Involving them will increase the success rate and can actually speed up implementation and continued commitment to change.

Show respect to the resisters because sometimes there is a valid reason for their resistance. Find out. Ask the question. Showing respect to these individuals can actually build strong relationships that can positively affect future change initiatives. Also, working with resistance can even increase the likelihood that everyone can meet at least some of his or her goals.

It is still crucial that you recognize that after all is said and done, there will still be resisters who will continue to try to derail your change efforts. Watch for them, and take immediate action. Employees can resist change through:

- Open opposition and hostility, shown by the very vocal folks who are also very influential in the organization
- Reduced work output.
- Developing 101 reasons "why this won't work."
- Agitating others, constant quarreling.
- Denying that change is really necessary, sweeping problems under the carpet.
- Withholding information.
- Foot-dragging.
- Apathy (apathetic people won't confront you, but they won't produce much, either).
- Not attacking a solution, but not supporting it either.
- Over-complicating the new way.

Let's face it, we know how employees have reacted to change initiatives historically. In the mid-1700s, English hand sawyers destroyed the water-powered mill. In the 1800s, French and English textile mills were sabotaged. Early 1900s teamsters in the United States destroyed the first oil pipelines. Today employees are creating viruses that literally destroy entire IT systems and others are leaving companies and taking proprietary information with them. This is sabotage at its finest. Don't kid yourself into thinking that it has gone away. The work force today is very clever and attempts at sabotage are far less obvious, much more passive, and far more destructive than those of old.

One such example of subtle resistance is a movement we call "The Dilbert Phenomenon." You know the symptoms: cartoons tacked up at almost every cubicle, stuffed animals, the black eyeglasses, and Dilbert paraphernalia everywhere. This is a very unsettling trend for many organizational leaders. It was cute at first. "Let's poke fun at corporate America and those idiots at the top." The joke should be over.

Dilbert and his pals are a parody of the very worst of American businesses. Dilbert is a symptom of the problems that you face as a leader. A large health-care provider called us in when they were adding a new facility. They wanted us to assist them with the development of a plan to combine new and existing staff and to make sure the additional staff would fit in with the long-established culture. One of the first areas we needed to review was compensation. For several weeks, we tried to contact the "comp guy" to no avail. He returned no phone calls or e-mail. We brought this to the client's attention and asked for some help in getting the information we needed. The response was frightening: "Oh, that's just the way he is." That's just the way he is! We were under such a tight deadline for the information, which was vital to the project and, by the way, they were paying us by the hour (not cheap)! "That's just the way he is" should not cut it in any organization.

We decided to take matters into our own hands and staked out his office. He always had his door closed, so we waited for him to come into work one morning. When we saw him arrive, we pounced on him. "Hey, Joe! How are you coming on that information we need?" (We tried to be casual and not let him see our desperation and frustration.) When he opened his office door, we followed him inside. As we entered into his office, we suddenly knew what we were dealing with and why we had not received our information.

His whole office was a Dilbert shrine. Everything imaginable, right down to his coffee mug, was "Dilbertized." This was a director in the organization. He was quietly saying that he thought management was the bad guy, but **he was management!** Your goal as a leader should be to make Dilbert extinct and remove the need for employees to continue to poke fun at management.

So how do you begin to eliminate the symptoms that are causing or perpetuating this trend of resistance? Some ways to begin to eliminate the symptoms are:

- Involve the employees throughout the entire change process. This is the real key!!!
- Make the nature and depth of the change very clear. Tell them why you are changing, what the change is, and what role they will play in the change process.
- Have management serve as coaches throughout the change process and allow for mistakes.
- Show the link to the company's mission and, more importantly, its strategic goals.
- Make sure there is a legitimate reason for the change and that it is for the good of the whole.
- Communicate, communicate, and communicate **honest** information.

The key message here is *involve* employees. Is it more work? Yes. Does it take more time? Yes. Are the results long-lasting? Yes.

INVOLVE

I ignite employees' spirit.

N nurture their ideas.

V value their input.

O open all lines of communication.

L level with employees, tell the truth ALWAYS.

V validate and acknowledge their concerns. They are real, just like yours!

E encourage risk taking.

So, how do you go about preparing the organization for a change like culture shift? We've developed fourteen questions that will assist you in preparing for change.

Preparing for Change—
The Top 14 Questions

1. How flexible are your managers and employees? List specific examples that support your feelings.

2. What can you do to help them progress along the flexibility continuum: provide education, rewards, recognition, etc.?

3. What steps can you take to hire more flexible people?

4. How would you describe the relationship between the board, CEO, top management and middle management? Are their values in sync?

5. How does your organization currently handle change?

6. What requires change? Why? You definitely need to determine if the change is truly necessary. Don't fall into the trap of changing for the sake of change.

7. What are leadership's motives for initiating the change?

8. What are the reasons others may support or resist the change?

9. Who in your estimation will support the change and who will resist it?

10. What resources in the organization are you willing to devote to the change process?

11. How will the leadership team convey the purpose and the extent of the change?

12. What are the potential barriers that could hamper the implementation of this change and what can you do to remove them?

13. How can and should you involve those affected in planning the change?

14. Once the change has begun, what do you need to do to stabilize and maintain it? In other words, how do you keep the energy levels high?

These are very important questions that need specific answers. Going through this exercise will provide concrete evidence and support as you move forward. It helps eliminate the "shoot from the hip" reaction that is so typical when you are faced with decisions involving change strategies.

Change is never easy; but if you begin to make it a way of life—view it as an ongoing, lifelong process, and see change as a positive SHIFT in direction—you will create a healthier organization. Remember to meet **FEAR** head-on and, as Stephen King would advise, **F**ace **E**verything **A**nd **R**ecover. If you can accomplish this, as a leader, you will experience greater personal and organizational success.

Tracking Success: The 14 Signs

When dealing with something so intangible, how do you know when you're on the right track? We have identified fourteen signs that tell you that you are, in fact, changing.

Fourteen Signs That Change is Taking Place and Becoming a Way of Life

1. **No Excuses Here**—People live up to their commitments and keep their promises rather than developing the old laundry list of the top ten reasons *I didn't get the job done.*

2. **20/20 Vision**—There are no big surprises, good or bad. The organization's vision is clear to all employees regardless of their position in the hierarchy.

3. **No Whining, Please**—*Meaningful* business-related suggestions for improvement and change are being generated on a daily basis. The days of gum wrappers and petty complaints filling the suggestion box are gone. Actually, once you reach this point, there is no longer a need for the suggestion box. Suggestions for change are shared openly.

4. **Community Allocation**—There is an actual sharing of resources rather than the usual hoarding that takes place between departments.

5. **Real Innovation**—Employees are taking risks. They are asking for forgiveness, rather than permission. They have moved from the creativity phase (merely thinking about good ideas and approaches) to making things happen, even if they are risky.

6. **Next Project, Please**—The product-development team is trying to sell a great new idea after experiencing the unsuccessful launch of the previous product. The days of hiding in the vending area until the dust settles are gone.

7. **SHIFT Gears**—Constant reinvention is occurring. The plan is always being revised, and the revisions are welcomed.

8. **Talking Heads**—More listening and less telling on the part of the managers and supervisors. Open communication has replaced those long voice-mails and e-mails that people used to hide behind.

9. **Eat Change for Breakfast**—Change is no longer talked about as a negative thing. It is viewed as an opportunity, and people actually want to talk about the changes taking place.

10. **All Encompassing**—Employees at all levels talk about "we" as a whole and not "we" as a department. There is a true concern for the good of the whole.

11. **Out With the Old and In With the New**—When the old way of doing things starts to rear its ugly head, employees will push back and say, "That's the old XYZ Company." *We don't want to go back to that.*

12. **Open Forum**—Employee meetings are very interactive. Employees aren't afraid to ask the tough questions, and management isn't afraid to tell the truth.

13. **No Parking, Please**—The reserved parking spaces for a select few have disappeared. Parking is now on a first-come, first-served basis.

14. **Accountability at Last**—Performance has been tied to compensation. Results are measured and fiscal accountability is assigned. Actions are taken for successful accomplishment of goals and objectives, as well as for missed opportunities.

Can you add to this list? These are some of the telltale signs that we have seen emerge as organizations become more comfortable with this thing we call change.

As you embark on your change journey remember these 7 truths.

Change Truth #1
In order to have movement you must let go of one trapeze to grab hold of the other. Every shift involves movement—no matter how frightening. **Grab the next trapeze.**

Change Truth #2
The curtain drops so the stage can be set for a new scene. Every shift begins with an ending. **Move on to Act 2.**

Change Truth #3
The more you leave behind, the more room there is to discover something new. **Get rid of the old baggage.**

Change Truth #4
Pain and distress is not a sign that something is wrong but a sign that a shift is taking place. **No need to call the doctor.**

Change Truth #5
The only way to get rid of the fear of change is to sail directly into it. Confront it head on. Remember *the doing it* comes before the fear goes away. **Open up the Sails.**

Change Truth #6
Feeling inadequate is a universal response to change and is a natural response to the learning process. We call this **Growing pains.**

Change Truth #7

Recognizing that change is here to stay, it is better to confront the change rather than living the emotional roller coaster and negative consequences of resistance. **Drive the change bus.**

Pulling It All Together

Throughout this chapter we have provided you with a number of strategies for achieving higher levels of success during any type of change strategy. As we wrap up we would like to summarize the steps for moving forward and share with you our suggested principles:

Suggested Implementation Principles for Change Initiatives

Leadership—you must drive the change bus and support the change effort through your actions. Remember to *walk the walk* then *talk the talk*.

A plan—make sure that you develop a clear plan for moving forward. Outline who is responsible for what and hold people accountable—including yourself. Provide the workforce with order/structure—do not confuse control with order.

Systems, processes and structure—don't forget this very important piece. This is why so many change initiatives fail. You must change your systems, processes and structure to support the new state. If you leave this piece out behaviors will not change.

Employee Involvement—remember the involve acronym? Also, recognize that moving in this direction does not mean a free for all. The new expectations must be tied into performance standards. Employees must see their involvement as *part of the job* and not *in addition to*.

Communicate, communicate, communicate—you can never do enough communicating. Remember what we said earlier, tell employees what you know and tell them what you don't know. All stakeholders need to know what the change is, know what to expect, what is happening and how it will affect them.

Jargon—make sure that you use language that is not intimidating, but is friendly and can be understood by all employees. Don't try and sell the change, remember—Ye Olde Management Speech—it doesn't work. In fact, doing so would be a sign of regression. Begin to use words like, *partner, involve, discover* and *create together.*

Measures of success—develop a scoring mechanism that everyone agrees to. This should be developed in advance and made clear to everyone involved. During implementation on-going and frequent communication should be published letting all stakeholders know "how it's going". Otherwise, the rumor mill will create its own evaluation and serve as a barrier to your progress.

Educate, educate, educate—all your employees. Employees not only need to know why they are doing what they are doing they must also be given the appropriate tools to operate in the 'new world'. Also, remember that people need constant coaching and encouragement through all the unexpected ups and downs.

Go after barriers and constraints—both internal as well as external. Facing these during the planning process is far more effective than stumbling over them during implementation.

Celebration—any change initiative you undertake is always a longer road than anticipated. Employees will tend to get frustrated and energy levels will suffer. So, celebrate the successes no matter how small. Think of forming some type of employee group that can serve as cheerleaders for the rest of the workforce.

Compensation strategy—develop mechanisms for rewarded the newly expected behaviors and get employees involved in developing these programs.

We hope that these principles provide you with a clear road map for moving forward.

In closing, please remember that requiring people to change their workplace values (values that have been acquired and reinforced over their entire working lives) can be as terrifying as requiring them to change their moral convictions or religious beliefs. We do know that in this situation, the highest level of management (whatever that may be in your organization) must enthusiastically and visibly lead the change in values and culture. In an editorial on change management from "Management Review", Barbara Ettorre suggests that "managers are beginning to understand that they cannot simply delegate the work of managing change to others. They must become instruments of change themselves, inspiring the troops and becoming deeply involved in the effort." (22)

To create true and lasting changes in workplace values, everyone involved must know and believe that top management truly believes in and wants the change. Commitment, NOT compliance, must become a leader's mantra. And change must be planned and controlled in order to be most effective. Anyone who has driven through Palm Springs, California, has marveled at the expanse of windmills that generate electricity for the region. Anyone who has witnessed the damage of a tornado is awed by the destructive force of that same wind when it is unexpected and uncontrolled. Don't let your organization be the victim of uncontrolled forces that can lead to its destruction.

Can We Talk — CEO to CEO?

By Andy Riddell

Role of the CEO

Call it a merger. Call it a new marketing strategy. Whatever the change is, as CEOs, we are expected to set the tone for change in our organizations. As presented in the preceding chapter, "The Change Game," making change happen is not an easy task. Many of us become irritated or go off the deep end if there is a simple detour on our normal, everyday route to work. If we can become disturbed and upset by something as small as that, think about how affected we are by layoffs and terminations, acquisition of our company, or, God forbid, a so-called merger!

This is all change with a capital C. The following account of a major, capital C change initiative provides some insight into the challenge that this holds for us as leaders.

In 1994, my employer, AtlantiCare Medical Center (AMC) in Lynn, Massachusetts, was faced with some very serious and complex decisions. AMC was on the way out of pseudo-bankruptcy (all the facts and ratios said we were bankrupt, but we never filed for bankruptcy protection), when the marketplace began a downward spiral. Hospital revenues were feeling the impact of legislative changes that restricted reimbursement. At the time, AMC included an acute-care hospital, a nursing home, and a psychiatric hospital with fifteen hundred employees. Financial analysis suggested that if the then-current trend continued, AMC would run out of cash by 1998 and be forced to close all of the facilities.

The senior management team recommended, after additional study, that the nursing home and psychiatric hospital be sold to preserve cash, improve the balance sheet, and get back to the core business of acute care. We would try to institute more cost-management practices while simultaneously continuing to improve patient care. We would strive to deliver top-notch customer service. Our aim was to prime the organization for merger or acquisition. It was an extremely complex process that was traumatic for all of us, to say the least.

The first step we took was to co-create the Ten Commandments of Reorganizational Design. When our management team finished their review, I shared the commandments with the Board of Directors, the Medical Staff members, and all staff members at Town Meetings. People could quickly reject these as unattainable, pie-in-the-sky ideas. If they did so, it would probably become a self-fulfilling prophecy. But if people agreed to accept them in principle, we had a chance to survive this ordeal and emerge intact.

Ten Commandments of Reorganizational Design

"It doesn't matter how many pails of milk you spill, just don't lose the cow." In other words, in any major change you'll make mistakes. To minimize this, you need to develop **gu**idelines to be utilized as a sentinel to be sure you live up to your values.

"Therefore, organizational Redesign will:

1. be compatible with AMC's ethical principles and values and consistent with the Sr. Mgmt. Team's Mission;

2. maintain and/or improve quality and customer service and reduce cost;

3. facilitate quality leadership principles, including:
   customer focus, continuous improvement, management leadership, teamwork, data-driven analytic approach, AMC's ethical principles and values;

4. focus on the needs of the organization as the first priority;

5. seek to reduce the work force through attrition and job reassignment; layoffs will be a last resort;

6. define leadership's role to oversee services that transcend conventional departmental boundaries by focusing on service provision to customers versus increasing the leader's span of control;

7. encourage the empowerment of employees;

8. organize the Hospital to meet the needs of both their distinct and common internal and external customers;

9. offer flexibility to allow AMC to respond to expected changes in the external environment, e.g. Integrated delivery system;

10. eliminate and/or avoid creating duplicate services."

When we shared these commandments with our employees, we received feedback and information that helped us shape a more humanistic approach to the changes that were required. As an example, when looking to reduce the size of the work force, we learned that nearly 120 employees were working primarily for the health-care benefit and would be willing to retire if provided with coverage until Medicare eligibility at age sixty-five. Once we developed a plan that responded to that concern, 37 people immediately took advantage of it and retired early. In time, nearly all of the other people retired early.

Here is perfect proof that the job at the top, CEO, doesn't have to be lonely!

When implementing a change as major as a cultural shift you must talk to your staff. In his book titled *If I Knew Then What I Know Now*, Richard Edler shares some insight from Bill Flately, who served as Director of Advertising at *Forbes Magazine.* When describing what he had learned in his years at *Forbes,* Flately responded, "Good people come in lots of different packages. I admire those who have been able to deal with people from every walk of life. Malcolm Forbes was an example to me." At his funeral there were ex-presidents and bikers from the Hell's Angels, both calling him friend. Celebrate diversity and use it to your advantage. (1)

In business, 95% of the intelligence in an organization is often several layers below management. The shipping clerk can tell you how to fix a problem. Your secretary knows what's really going on. The receptionist hears what customers really think of your firm. If you would only ask. It's OK to talk to strangers. Some people may be offended by the use of the word "strangers." To many of us, that's exactly what our employees are.

How **Not** to Make Shift Happen

Why do I believe in involving/empowering employees and talking to them?

Early in my career, I experienced change in a big way as Senior Budget Analyst for a small, but profitable, analog computer Company in New Jersey. I was offered the opportunity to become Controller in our Graphic Instrument Division, thus spring-boarding me into the "Executive Level" of management at the ripe old age of twenty-eight. My wife and I were expecting our fourth child and planned to buy a house (our first) and get a bigger car to lug all the kids around. After four weeks of interviews (a long and tedious process), I was officially offered the job. I accepted the position and was scheduled to begin in three weeks. In the meantime, my wife and I made the decision to close on a new house and purchase a new car—all based on the career move.

I reported to work on a Monday and went to the employee cafeteria around 10:00 A.M. to get a cup of coffee. Up until that time, I was busy meeting people and learning my way around the office. Just outside the cafeteria door, I noticed a newspaper with this headline: "Graphics Division of XXX (my employer) to be sold to Company YYY in California." Do you know how I felt? My old Marine Corps instinct nearly made it to the sensory/action part of my brain. I was ready to do battle with whomever, the VP of the Division, the President of the Company, anyone in power!

Needless to say, the entire plant was in an uproar. But I had been told NOTHING about this. For the next three days, no one in a management position, including the VP (my boss) could be found. Then, the scenario was repeated on Thursday when there was another report in the paper. This time, we were being sold to a company in New Hampshire.

Here was change with a capital C. This was not just a detour on the road to work. This was a major roadblock in the path that had been presented to me. I tried to rationalize that some level of secrecy was required in light of stock-trading issues. But to avoid all discussion of the matter after the announcement was made was extremely unsettling and disappointing. By the way, this was how the employees and I (a new member of Senior Management) found out about this major transaction. I had been offered a position as a "trusted" member of the executive team, and yet was not given any information about the impending change that directly affected me. Now, I had a new house and a new car and a new job that might not be there when it came time to make the mortgage and car payments. My wife and I had made some personal decisions based on our trust of their word, and we now felt deceived. We were definitely not a part of this change initiative and, not surprisingly, had difficulty embracing it.

I began immediately searching for a new job, even though both deals fell through. I wanted out! Six months later I accepted a new position.

I decided to share this story for two reasons:

One, it is etched in my memory as an experience I'll never forget; and two, the ultimate responsibility for the failure of this change initiative was in the hands of the CEO. In this situation, he chose not to empower his employees, including the top management team. He was not an effective change agent. He was unauthentic and incongruent.

And getting a chance to talk about what makes an effective change agent was exactly what excited me when I was invited to contribute to *Getting Your Shift Together*. "Now I'll have a chance to have that 'talk'— CEO to CEO—with a lot more people than I would ever encounter in my life," I thought. As a CEO in five organizations over a twenty-nine year period, I had a lot to talk about! A piece of cake. Just find the time to sit down and record all of my experiences and what they have taught me. Sounded easy. About as easy as being a CEO these days, I discovered. So many things to consider in a never-ending set of scenarios with too little time and resources. When I finally finished the chapter, it was with the same sense of accomplishment that I've experienced with the multiple major change initiatives that I have led. This has been an exciting and challenging learning experience, one that has provided a closure to my CEO experiences and the initiation of a new role: helping people like you find ways to "walk the talk."

CEO: A Place Too Far?

CEO—Chief Executive Officer. When defined as separate words, each one suggests someone powerful and in charge. A triple whammy when the words are combined. Literally defined, a CEO is an elected or appointed person empowered and required to lead the organization to successful attainment of organizational goals. Figuratively, the title usually suggests the sole, ultimate authority responsible for all activity and operations in an organization. The pedestal that we are often put on lets us tower over others in rank, salary, and prestige, but makes us an excellent target for criticism by staff, board members, and customers. The proverbial "you're damned if you do and damned if you don't" job.

The image of a CEO in today's world is not great. On the following pages, you'll view the results of a question I pose whenever presenting a workshop or keynote speech, or teaching grad school or leadership sessions. I'll ask one to three questions and have members of the audience volunteer to draw on acetate their view of "What is the CEO's image in your company?" I have been doing this for over six years now, and sad to say only one drawing presented the CEO in a positive image! Guess what? The one positive image was drawn by a CEO!!

Take a good close look at these illustrations, and try to picture how your staff, employees or board would present you via markers and acetates.

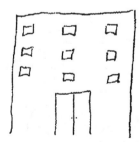

Drawn by a middle manager at a Midwest hospital: "CEO is very well dressed, drives a nice car, expensive suits, hair is never out of place. Spends majority of his time away from the hospital. When he returns, he always tries to make up for time away, does not provide the leadership necessary to bring the organization and team together."

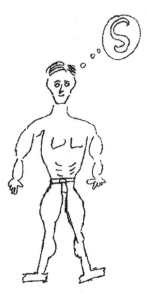

Drawn by an HMO executive: "CEO thinks he's Superman, doesn't delegate, takes on too much, doesn't include his senior team in decisions, hence we take twice as much effort and time to get things done."

Drawn by an insurance company executive: "CEO is the driver, thinks everyone is on board, there are 'yes' people (windows), there are people being run over, people getting on and off, in other words, chaos."

See no evil

hear no evil

but Lots of talk

Drawn by a middle manager in high-tech: "CEO is full of talk, but doesn't have a clue as to what's going on in the organization."

Drawn by a COO of a high-tech firm: "I was hired as COO to make the organization more efficient, cut layers of fat, etc. This is my CEO whenever I make recommendations. The stick people are those to be downsized, he always has an excuse for not reducing staff. The 3 chins represent the fat in the organization that I haven't been able to get rid of!"

The term CEO was popularized in the 1960s when there was a distinct management trend that favored creation of administrative layers. As organizations increased in size and complexity, division directors were appointed to oversee discrete areas of service. Product-line management emerged as an approach to organizing and directing the diversified aspects of a business. The company President or CEO became the leader and was often assisted by a CFO (chief financial officer) and/or COO (chief operating officer). This senior management team increasingly relinquished responsibility for overseeing day-to-day operations and focused on "visioning," strategy, and communicating with the Board of Directors.

In many ways, this development put us beyond "arm's length" with our staff, line management and, in many cases, the customer and our community. We were now out of touch with many more employees. For many of us, this distancing in some big organizations was a BIG mistake and the beginning of our demise. Why is this important you might ask? Well, think about this for a minute. In "Why CEOs Fail," from the June 21, 1999 issue of *Fortune,* authors Ram Charan and Geoffrey Colvin offer insight into what they believe is really responsible for the downfall of many corporate executives. In their discussion of the firing of Eckhard Pfeiffer from Compaq Computer, they quote both *USA Today* and the *New York Times,* which basically placed the blame on problems with strategic vision. However, Benjamin Rosen, Chairman of the Board of Compaq, disagreed with those assessments. According to Rosen, who led the coup, "The change (will not be in) our fundamental strategy— we think that strategy is sound—but in execution. Our plans are to speed up decision-making and make the company more efficient." (2) The critical element that slowed down the decision-making and the lack of execution was the distance between the CEO and the people who had to execute the "sound" strategy. Let's face it, organizations aren't looking for CEOs who fail to execute.

CEOs Nurture Change

So how do we—CEOs—, as Rosen advises, "make the company more efficient"? As leaders, we must stay in touch with our business community. We must know what our culture is and ensure that it is one that encourages employee involvement and embraces risk-taking. We must view our role not only as change agent but also as gardener. We must first cultivate the soil and then plant and nurture the seeds into deeply rooted values and culture.

A simple analogy: Have you ever attempted to have a rich green lawn around your house? Think about the effort it takes to accomplish this. Do you just turn the soil and throw some seed? No! It's not a short-term, shot-in-the-dark effort. It takes planning, dedication and discipline to a process (cultivate, aerate, sod or seed, fertilize twice a year, water, mow and repeat the cycle). It takes the same effort, courage of your convictions and discipline to walk the walk with your employees, customers, and board.

In their classic corporate commentary, *In Search of Excellence,* Thomas J. Peters and Robert H. Waterman, Jr. identify eight principles of effective organizational management. When reviewing the track records of successful companies, they found advantage to having a simple form and a lean staff, particularly at the corporate level. Yet they believe this poses a paradox for leaders. (3) How do we take on a simple form when our business is becoming more complex? How do we relate more to our employees when there are more layers of management between us and them? The answers to these questions can be very simple to determine. It's the implementation that takes discipline; it must become a part of the DNA of the CEO and the organization. This chapter will address many situations (using real, not theoretical examples) to act as a guideline for you to customize your organization's culture.

The CEO's Role is...

Before we proceed, let's attempt to examine our role as the CEO. In order to judge the effectiveness of any administration, we must first agree on what role the CEO plays in an organization. The CEO is, in a true sense, the "catalyst." We should be able to see the overall needs and goals of our organization, appoint the best people available to realize these goals, and give them the incentive, guidance, and support to result in the fulfillment of these goals. Our role is to bring all the elements together in an effective working situation. We cannot and should not be the expert in every field. This would automatically negate our role. When we have expertise in one or several areas over which we must preside, we must be aware of the potential for us to supersede the individual judgment[s] of the people in that department. For example, I moved into my first role as a CEO from the controller/business manager's position. When I hired a new controller to replace me, I found myself second-guessing his decisions. I even overruled his decision to bring in a new computer program to upgrade our accounts receivable programs. In retrospect, it's clear to me that we must focus on the big picture, and not on one pet department or the details of running a department.

As CEO we must make the final decisions. We arrive at these decisions in two ways: (1) by seeing the overall picture and (2) by depending upon the level of expertise of the individuals involved.

The results of this approach are twofold:

1. the decisions made operate for the "total good" of the organization, and

2. the individual areas, given the responsibility, are therefore strengthened by their participation in the decision-making process.

"We are at a crossroads, one road leads to despair and destruction, the other—total annihilation. Let's hope we choose wisely."—Woody Allen

While chuckling at this quote, we come to realize that it gets to the core of what we want to avoid in our decision-making process. As CEO we must make sure that these are never our only two choices.

The Catalytic CEO

There are two key words in the paragraphs above: "catalyst" and "total good." The word catalyst is defined as any agent that sparks a process and hastens a result. In short, our actions as catalyst (cause) creates a reaction/change (effect) within the organization. This is not rocket science. We're not breaking new ground with this statement! If we are to become true catalysts, as CEOs we must always be aware of "The Trust Ladder" (see figure 1), created by the physician-leader Christian Amoroso, MD, in 1993. (4) On Dr. Amoroso's ladder there are six rungs that move from Understanding to Agreement to Credibility to Trust to Risk-Taking, and finally, to Results. Dr. Amoroso's point reinforces the importance of trust as presented in earlier chapters. He too sees trust as a very, very fragile commodity that must be constantly nurtured.

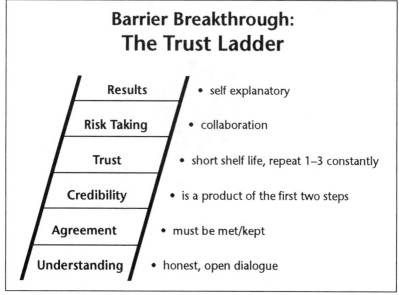

© 1993 by Christian Amoroso, MD

Figure 1   The Trust Ladder

"Total good" of the organization will probably have a different range of relevance depending upon your values/beliefs. Total good means just that! It's not half-total good, just as you can't be half-fired or half-pregnant. Total good is not an amorphous substance, molded to suit the organization's whim of the week! Total good, for the purposes of this chapter, is defined as the combination of an organization's values, mission, vision and strategies. These four add up to create the culture of an organization, which is defined as the integrated amalgam of style, beliefs, behaviors, myths, customs, tastes, and preferences expressed by an organization or group and by which that group is distinguished and defined. In more earthy terms, it's the way things are done.

In further analyzing just who and what a CEO is, here are some of the expectations that I encountered in my CEO experiences. As CEOs, we're expected to be:

© EMERGE 2000

We're expected to:

© EMERGE 2000

And in addition to all of this, we're expected to have:

© EMERGE 2000

There is no doubt that as you read these lists you could add a few more spokes to these wheels. It is like *Wheel of Fortune* in a way. Imagine being Pat Sajack. Your job consists of watching Vanna turn the lighted spoke over and that's your assignment for the day. Ah, the ease of it all, the simple life of the CEO. But, let's face it, you don't get to choose which one you want to work on today! *All of the spokes are lighted everyday!*

Climbing Off the Pedestal

So what does this tell us? Do all of these points fall within the job description of a single position? It finally became clear to me that they can't. We cannot do all of these things alone. We cannot and should not be placed on a pedestal in relative isolation from the rest of the organization. If the board, employees, and others insist on keeping the throne/pedestal image alive, in my opinion, it becomes a very disastrous situation. The CEO becomes nobility, and we all are or should be familiar with the effects of nobility, for there are two sets of rules, one for the CEO (the king or queen) and one for the rest of the organization (the peasants).

What did I do about it? In 1990–1996, my ID badge read: "Customer Service Representative." At the time, we were implementing an organizational focus on customer service. This helped make the point that I was committed to the program.

It also had a more far-reaching impact, one that I could never have predicted. I was Chairman of the Board of a charter group of executives of an organization known as the Lynn Business Partnership (our goal was to improve the socioeconomic state of our city). We would hold meetings at the hospital, and I'd wear my ID badge. It was interesting to have conversations with the people who stared at my chest! In addition, two of the editors of the local daily newspapers kept asking me, "What the hell is that all about?"

Eventually, conversations were eyeball to eyeball, and they all (executives and editors) took us seriously at AtlantiCare Medical Center.

In 1996, once again I changed my name. No, I'm still Andy Riddell. But the CEO part didn't make sense. I was not the Chief Executive Officer— I became the Chief Empowerment Officer.

I must admit that the change came in part after completing an internal Malcolm Baldrige Assessment (the Malcolm Baldrige Criteria for Performance Excellence are the basis for organizational self-assessments, for making awards, and for giving feedback to applicants). In addition, the Criteria have three other important roles in strengthening U.S. competitiveness. They are: 1) to help improve organizational performance practices and capabilities; 2) to facilitate communication and sharing of best practices information among U.S. organizations of all types; and 3) to serve as a working tool for understanding and managing performance, and guiding planning and training. We used the Malcolm Baldrige Criteria for Performance after we had finished working with the Kodak Company implementing their Quality Leadership Process (QLP) at the center. The QLP program helped us focus on the customer and on making improvements in our delivery of services to both the external and internal customer. Using the Malcom Baldrige Criteria for Performance gave us an opportunity to strive to reach breakthrough levels in our organization.

As an organization, we were fighting for survival, coming out of a pseudo-bankruptcy we had to place Request for Proposals (RFPs) on the market for all three of our business lines in order to improve our balance sheet and attract a merger-acquisitioner for our businesses.

So for us, the Malcolm Baldrige Criteria for Performance was the natural next step in our self-assessment and examination. We didn't need to know how to incrementally improve our organization. We needed to know how to break through to levels of excellence, and this assessment would help us determine how.

Included in the summary was a tool we used to measure how well we were doing in living our culture, Our Ethical Principles and Values as shown in Figure 2. The tool measured bureaucracy, achievement, empowerment, and power. Although we, the management team,

Ethical Principles and Values

People
We will:

- recognize that people are our most valuable asset:
- encourage consistent behavior that reflects values of honesty, compassion, consideration for self and others; excellence in effort, desire for personal growth, concern for our institution, society, mankind and our planet;
- encourage each person to reach their potential and honor their achievement.

Communication
We will:

- always tell the truth as truth is the cornerstone of trust;
- carefully listen to our patients, medical staff, employees and community in a thoughtful, respectful manner;
- strive to preserve every person's privacy and confidentiality;
- promote and achieve informed consent; every patient has a right to know their diagnosis, treatment, risks and alternatives;
- promote a lively sense of humor that will bring perspective and balance to our work.

Economic Viability
We will:

- develop, maintain and communicate a business plan that is flexible, up-to-date, and visionary, resulting in efficient resources for current and future needs;
- develop and maintain the highest operational standards;
- positively contribute to our community being an exemplary organization recognized for the highest standards of performance.

Service
We will:

- recognize and accept a commitment to excellence in the services we provide to our internal and external customers;
- promote constant examination of our services through peer review, quality assurance, patient satisfaction surveys, patient/customer focus groups;
- respond to the changing needs of our customers.

Quality
We will:

- take great pride in our work;
- constantly improve our care by utilizing honest and vigorous peer review to examine and improve our performance;
- promote collaborative practice and employee teamwork to provide the highest quality to our patients;
- stay on the leading edge of technology.

Figure 2 Ethical Principles and Values

thought we were doing pretty well with empowerment, the employees did not score the leadership team as highly as we expected. This made me realize that it was my responsibility, as CEO, to empower the members of the organization. After all, if they were empowered; and, if the leadership team were truly sharing information with them, they'd know what a good job we were doing, wouldn't they? The new title, Chief Empowerment Officer, was no less powerful. In fact, my power was perceived as greater than ever because I now had the whole army working with me rather than against me.

Let Out Pent-Up Energy

If we look back at the spokes of the wheel depicting what we are expected to be, what we're expected to do, and what we are expected to have, one thing is clear: We need assistance!! In the five turn-arounds that I led, my career as a turn-around CEO would have *been over* from the start if the energy and commitment of the employees in particular were not realized.

One Friday evening, early in my job at AMC, as I was leaving the building, there was a wheelchair in the doorway. My CFO was walking out with me, and I said, "Arnie, that chair is going to be right there when I return on Monday." Guess what? It was!

What did this say about the organization? The chair had a clear ID on it, "property of emergency room," and yet not one soul saw fit to return it. How many of you upon entering a hospital or an office can tell if people are empowered or not? Have you ever wandered aimlessly through the halls to find that no one, but no one, makes eye contact— let alone, tries to help you! This is the behavior of the unempowered. These small, but telling signs explain why you must become a CHIEF EMPOWERMENT OFFICER!

Let "Empowerment" be Your Middle Name

If you choose to accept this assignment as Chief Empowerment Officer, you risk great danger and threat to the traditional role and relationships you've had with others.

Mission: Impossible? Not at all. But to become Chief Empowerment Officer, you must accept that your previous status as independent Agent 007 will be erased and your relationships with fellow agents (employees, etc.) must change.

As Chief Empowerment Officer, you must lead your employees by demonstrating your true belief in their existing powers and their capacity to release that power and energy in a productive way. If we have successfully empowered our employees and instilled in them the importance of top-notch customer relations, the dedication to customer service will be felt by everyone who interacts with the organization. For example, when I assumed the reins in my latest turn-around, customer service and retention was in the tank! Our first customer survey, while panning almost everything, illustrated some hard, cold, final facts! Of those surveyed, 71% did not want to return, nor would they recommend us to anyone else! That meant only 29% had a positive experience. How would you like to be CEO of any company that had this feedback about products and services?

Less than two years later, that 29% rating was transformed into a consistent monthly overall rating in excess of 95%. We maintained that level and increased it to 97% in 1997. How did we do this? It certainly wasn't by posting cute little smiling faces that said, "Have a nice day!" Instead, we began a concerted effort to engage the hearts and souls of our employees, otherwise, the program would be the butt of jokes in the cafeteria, hallways, and in front of patients.

How did we engage them? Not by my writing a memo about customer service, or by my declaring at a managers meeting that "ve vill have improvements in customer service!" Instead we prepared a "Blueprint for Customer Service Focus." See Appendix A for details.

Honor Thy Customers—Inside and Out

As Max DePree, former chairman of famous furniture maker Herman Miller, advised in his book *Leadership is an Art*, you must listen to your employees—all of them. He described it as "abandoning oneself to the strengths of others." (5)

As Chief Empowerment Officers we must view our relationship with our customers differently as well. With external customers, we must demonstrate the same commitment to collaboration and service. We must empower our customers to have input into our product or service delivery by going after feedback—all of it—the positive as well as the not so positive. Then, once we've gathered that data we must respond. We must take action.

Our governing boards are no exception to the empowerment process. Whether active or advisory, board members typically view the CEO as their link to the organization they serve. In most cases, we are viewed as the top tier in an organization's hierarchy and must be responsible for organizational success as defined by the board and its shareholders. Despite the duality of the role, there is often not much empathy for the CEO's position. As Chief Empowerment Officer, particularly in the private, non-profit arena, we must educate the board and empower them to feel ownership of the organization as individuals and a collective body. They must share in the sense of accomplishment and responsibility the CEO has and must faithfully represent the organization to all of the other people that they encounter in their personal and professional relationships.

So, are you up for the mission of Chief Empowerment Officer? Can you bring your values to life? Can you make the shift from a life of aloofness and incapacity to one of powerful execution through empowerment?

Of all the leadership traits and characteristics identified in this chapter, I believe that the most important one for the Chief Empowerment Officer is to be a **master of change.** So we must be card-carrying change agents. We must be able to recognize change, communicate it, embrace it, learn from it, and understand the importance of having the right amount of control over it. We must also be green-thumb gardeners. Our job in the change process is to cultivate, aerate, and fertilize the soil of our organizational culture, in order to create a healthy environment that will mobilize the entire work force and turn all members of our organizations into card-carrying change agents.

The days of the CEO riding in on the white horse are over. Will this require a shift in our mind-set? Absolutely. Will it be easy? Only you can answer that, for it's up to you! One example that comes to mind was reported by Jenny C. McCune in the May 1999 issue of *Management Review*. In her article, "The Change Makers," McCune relates that CEO John Sunderland of Cadbury Schweppes PLC found that his key change challenge was to move his soft-drink (Ginger Ale) and confectionery (Cadbury chocolates) company towards a *"Managing for Value" strategy to compete on a global level against such rivals as Coca Cola, Mars, Nestle and Pepsi-Cola.* The key tool he used to succeed was a *new profit sharing and stock-ownership plan that encouraged employees to manage the business as if it were their own.* (6) Talk about ultimate employee empowerment. According to Sunderland, "The company also put 4,000 employees through a value-based financial training-program. And it put 'square pegs in square holes' by conducting an audit of 150 top managers and 'changing the responsibilities of about half of those managers, some sideways, up or out.'" (7)

He was able to do this by educating and rallying the troops. His advice to others undertaking such a mammoth change is communication is essential. "You can't communicate too often", he says. "But at the same time," he warns that "exhortation alone is wholly insufficient". (8) Everyone must understand what is being asked of them and be given the tools to do what is requested. Now we know this is no easy feat, but it can and has been done. Driving the change bus is a must in times of radical and swift developments.

We Want Control

Do we embrace change? This is a question I ask at many training sessions, and the majority of people say, "NO! We do not embrace change!" It is quite the contrary. I have found through twenty-nine years of turn-arounds, and as presented in "The Change Game," that people do embrace change ONLY IF THEY ARE PART OF THE CHANGE! If they are not in control of change, the most likely reaction is resistance. Many times, the resistance comes about because the new thing is different, unknown, and unfamiliar—most probably, because we, as leaders, did not see fit to involve people or communicate to them the reasons for the change *in advance.*

This is a key premise that the CEO or any leader in an organization must clearly understand and appreciate. Human beings must feel that they have participated in and understand the decision to institute change no matter how big or small, before they will totally commit to the project. Remember the ego discussion in "The Change Game"? It is the Chief Empowerment Officer's responsibility to facilitate this process. This is absolutely essential when we are talking about streamlining our decision-making process and improving our ability to execute our business strategies. As pointed out earlier in this chapter, the inability to execute our strategies has been cited as a significant pitfall for us as leaders.

Talk to People and LISTEN

Remember my story about not being let in on the possibility that our company was talking with potential buyers even though I was taking a top management position? The total lack of employee involvement was a failure on the part of management. Was my experience unique? Of course not. Have I had other change experiences like that one? Of course!

As CEOs, do we all face the challenge of change every day? Absolutely, and that's why we must strengthen our organization's ability to change by communicating honestly with employees.

If there is any doubt in your mind, remember the statistics:

In 1998 in the United States, there were 7,809 deals totaling $1.192 trillion—an 81% increase over the prior year. (9) Mergers are usually "assembled" by corporate, legal, finance, and investment-banker types who do not focus on the so-called softer side of the deal. The human capital and cultural aspects are usually brought onto the scene (if they're brought on at all) after the blue sky, hard data has been revealed—or when many things go astray, i.e., people are leaving in droves, productivity falls through the floor, and equity value plummets. In fact, the realities are: 75% of mergers and acquisitions are ultimately considered to be disappointments or outright failures. (In health care, as of February 1997, nearly 70% of mergers and acquisitions in the previous five years had failed, which would mean only 30% succeeded, according to Russ Coile, a futurist who is the Senior Vice President of the HealthCare CEO Roundtable.) In addition, only 23% of all acquisitions earn their cost of capital, and companies' stock prices actually rise only 30% of the time.

As pointed out in "The Change Game," change of great magnitude is taking place in commercial, educational, and health-care organizations as you read this book. It takes many names and guises: reorganizing, reengineering, rightsizing, downsizing, open-book management, cross-training, knowledge management, relocation of facilities, to name a few. So what, specifically, is causing the extremely high failure rate for change initiatives? Is there something that we are overlooking when it comes to leading our organizations through change?

Absolutely. To echo what was presented in "The Change Game," many of my fellow CEOs and I are finally starting to *get it*. We are recognizing the importance of the "soft" side of the organization. The soft stuff is the hard stuff and don't kid yourself into thinking anything differently.

But the soft stuff doesn't have to be hard. With all the external pressures CEOs face, it's no wonder that we tend to focus on bottom-line issues—all of the tangible, measurable factors that can be examined and reflected in reports. We are after quantifiable data, not qualitative. If you cannot encapsulate the information into a five-to-ten-minute PowerPoint presentation, then it ain't gonna fly. But we are finally seeing the consequences of this oversight. We are beginning to see that a cultural assessment like Cultural Due Diligence™ must be added to the financial and legal due-diligence process that is routinely performed as part of the change-impact analysis.

Power to the People!

The people part of change has to do with the organizational culture, which is best described as the way the work gets done. We must start paying attention to not only our results but also how they have been achieved. If how we achieve results flies in the face of our stated core values as a business, then we become incongruent. With incongruence come deception and chaos. When there is a change in one's culture, whether through internal policy and procedure revisions or merger with another organization, there is a loss of identity and typically, resistance to change, and even sabotage. Especially in situations where little or no information regarding the change is given to people before the fact, the "culture shock" can be severe.

So how do we become effective change agents? We must view ourselves as extremely influential in our organizations. People watch what we say and don't say, what we do and don't do, and respond accordingly. Any of our actions have the potential to affect the entire organization, so we act cautiously. Using the scientific method, we collect and analyze information. We'll do anything, except turn to our best resource—our people.

As leaders, we must stimulate the process by giving authority and responsibility to the individuals who will work together to effect the change. The CEO should be the spark that ignites the power in the individual contributors. As commented in the "Call to Action": *We must be implementation instigators!* Execute, execute, and execute. And how do we best achieve that? Through people power!!!!

CEO = Chief Empowerment Officer

Now, we've talked about a new name and a new game. It's time to talk about how we meet the challenges and expectations of the Chief Empowerment Officer.

In a 1997 presentation at the annual meeting of the Institute for Health Care Improvement, I offered an acronym to describe the empowered CEO: PIONEER. I suggest you try it on and see how it fits.

P = Push fear out of the organization.

I = Initiate and maintain a culture of trust, ethics and honesty as its soul and backbone.

O = Obligate the organization to embrace innovation as its staff of life.

N = Navigate the organization by establishing a clear vision of the future.

E = Engage the organization to hold the customer as Number One.

E = Expand the word "customer" beyond the end-user to internal functions.

R = Reinforce and recognize behavior that mirrors the organization's culture/values.

In choosing to be a Pioneer CEO, we have to make a commitment to connecting with all levels of our organization. One of the most dramatic and powerful methods is to establish a set of values for the organization. Don't just print them in annual reports and employee brochures—make them LIVE! They must drive your organization.

Values Have Value!

For example, in my most recent tour as a CEO in a complex, near-bankruptcy turn-around situation, we established a set of values that were developed by a cross section of people, including doctors, nurses, secretaries, laboratory personnel, human resources personnel, and managers. We established the values as our mantra to move forward. Everything we did, everything we said, and every decision we made was passed through a screen of these values. We even tested the final operational objectives.

The CEO Can TYPE

One of the tools that I found extremely helpful from a personal standpoint was the Myers-Briggs Type Indicator. This instrument provided me with incredible insight into my own personality and behavior and really put things in perspective.

The Myers-Briggs Type Indicator (MBTI) is an assessment tool that helps individuals understand their most basic preferences. The applications for the MBTI results include individual coaching, career development, team building, management training, and organizational development. The MBTI reflects individual preference for energy (Introversion and Extraversion), information gathering (Sensing and Intuition), decision making (Thinking and Feeling), and lifestyle (Judging and Perceiving). So what type am I? Well, surprise, surprise, I fall into the 80% CEO population. I'm an **ISTJ**. You're probably saying, "It's nice that you have other letters after your name, but how does this really affect me as a leader?" Quite frankly, it means that for those of us who are ISTJs all this "soft stuff" (the people stuff/culture stuff) can be a real challenge.

Let's face it, many of us achieved CEO status because of our hard work and insatiable appetite for success. We are driven by accountability, productivity, and the infamous bottom line: **Just the facts, Jack!** Our world is made up of facts and tangible realities, and we prefer to deal with these in an objective way. Our days are driven by structure, schedule, and order. And our introversion makes us appear somewhat cool and aloof. We tend to think to speak as opposed to those incessant talkers, the "extraverts" ("extraverts" is the instrument's coinage for extroverted people), who speak to think.

We tend to be slow to change, but once we see practical value in making a course correction, we can be quick to implement it and often become zealots of the new way of thinking. We can tend to drive others to the brink, and we can inflict severe damage on ourselves. This comes partly from our combined control and compulsiveness, which can lead to an attitude of "If you want it done right, do it yourself." (Sound familiar?) We can also get tripped up by our high need for privacy and low need to express ourselves. Without saying a word, we can give off an aura of being impatient and even disapproving when that isn't necessarily the case. As a result, there's an unwitting "show me" or "prove it" stance to our demeanor. Show me how it will be cost-effective; prove to me that you're right.

Our no-frills style can lead to a workplace that is plain, austere, conservative, and very slow to change. The good news is that, with good direction (rules and regulations) and checklists, we can change. If we make saying "good morning" part of our checklist, then we will do it every day until it becomes an integral part of our managerial style. However, not everything can be scripted: for instance, things having to do with the big picture (intuition) and coping with interpersonal dynamics (feeling). The big picture represents the unknown to us, and the unknown is often more bad than good.

Subjective, feeling decisions are another area in which we can be found wanting. The entire world of interpersonal dynamics is difficult for this ISTJ type because it is not predictable and cannot be controlled.

As a result, we would rather avoid, or even deny, the existence of seemingly "touchy-feely" situations, even though these could include such innocuous encounters as saying, "Thanks for your help," or discussing some work project as a team, or having a beer with the troops after quitting time. These things can actually frighten us because they can include so many unknowns and a high risk of losing control.

Compounding all of this is that it's inevitable that we will end up managing and working with at least a few Feeling types. "Yes," you are probably thinking, "my Human Resources and Organizational Development Director is exactly that." Well, we need to do a better job of listening to these people. These individuals respond to a whole different array of motivations—fun, harmony, happiness, personal fulfillment, and social responsibility, among others—things that might make introverts cringe. The more we can understand and accept these differences, the more we can realize that we needn't control or deny such seemingly unacceptable behavior, then the freer we will be to let others behave true to their own personality type, with greater productivity the inevitable result.

The same problems that trip us up in the workplace can trip us up in the marketplace. Not understanding that half of the buying public is driven by such intangible things as appeal, looks, image, and just plain feeling good. We can overlook the personal appeal that the Feeling side of preferences brings to a situation.

What can we do about it? Recognize this potential blind spot and equip ourselves to overcome it through greater self-awareness or by surrounding ourselves with other types who can fill in this missing dimension. We should look at this as just one more aspect of our lives that we must manage effectively.

The CEO as Change Agent

When we were working on cutbacks at AMC, my conversations through Town Meetings (see Appendix B) helped minimize the trauma the organization would feel. There is a word of caution here, if you do not have a track record of consistently being out there sharing pertinent information with your employees, initiating Town Meetings only to share negative information won't buy you a cup of coffee, much less the understanding and commitment of your employees.

Don't let these thoughts enter into your mind: "What are we to do?" "Don't we appear to be weak when we seek advice, particularly from our own employees?" "How can I converse with them?" "What do we have in common?" "I'm the leader; they're the followers!"

Don't believe any of those things! We must learn to feel comfortable outside the comfort zone of being the all-knowing, all-powerful CEO.

The Culture Vulture

W hat the heck is this thing we call organizational culture? Is it fact or fiction? Is there really something to this culture stuff? These are questions that have hounded both of us over the past fifteen or so years. We've come to the realization that many of us continue to talk about organizational culture in the abstract. When asked about culture, many of us respond by saying, "Oh yeah, I know what you mean," but then have a very difficult time describing it.

In order to describe it, the first thing you need to know is where organizational culture comes from. Organizational culture has its theoretical origins in sociology and anthropology. These sciences are critical in helping us to understand and make sense of society or societal groups. They also help us to understand why people act the way they do, because culture has a significant effect on human behavior.

What comes to your mind when you think of culture? Many of you probably think in terms of national cultures. The United States has one culture, France has another, Ethiopia another. Some of you may also think of it as something a well-educated person has. And still others may think of pearls or marble. Culture, in fact, means all those things, and more.

Culture is defined as a set of beliefs, values, customs, and behaviors that members of a society use to relate to their world and each other. It is also defined as the norms that we live by, the commonly held meanings and actions for a specific human gathering. In many respects, our values and beliefs are determinants of our behavior. Social scientists from many different disciplines apply somewhat different interpretations to culture, but virtually all agree that the concept of culture is an important one in the understanding of human behavior. The culture of a country, community, or organization is the common denominator that makes the actions of individuals clear to the members of the group.

There are also subcultures within cultures. As a citizen of the United States, you are part of that American culture that generally values civil liberties, a democratic government, and education. If you live in a rural area, you are part of the non-urban subculture, which is quite different from the subculture found in a major metropolitan area. City folk are surprised that people in small towns still leave their car doors unlocked when they are parked on the street. Country folk have trouble believing that city folk might have bars on their apartment windows and multiple locks on their doors. Within each of these subgroups, there are many more subcultures based on groupings by occupation, education, religion, gender, and age, to name only a very few. It is not surprising that many of us have difficulty at some time or another with our understanding of just which culture or subculture we are a part of at any given moment.

Culture is thought to be a learned behavior that is primarily transmitted through language. The training in one's culture is often referred to as "socialization" or "enculturation." As a member of a particular society, for example, you may be taught by your parents to respect your elders. Parents and teachers instill the values of honesty, integrity, and the need to play fair. You may adopt your religious and moral beliefs from interaction with your clergy or fellow parishioners. All of these experiences help you to learn the culture, to know what is expected of you as a member of that group.

As a member of a culture, you also learn that when you behave outside of what is labeled acceptable or legal, there is a consequence that often involves a sanction or punishment. Although the threat of an unpleasant outcome serves as a deterrent to inappropriate behaviors for many, people in every society break the rules to some extent. Tolerance of actions that fall outside of the cultural expectations seems to vary with the number of people who violate those expectations. For example, when you are driving in a clearly posted 45-mph speed zone at 45 mph, but everyone is passing you, suddenly you notice that your speedometer is showing 51 mph and it seems OK. In fact, once you start going 51 mph and pass someone going the speed limit, you may even think there's something wrong with the other driver's behavior! The outcome in this case, a speeding ticket, is not universally applied because the police can only catch and ticket a fraction of the people who are speeding. In time, the posted speed limit might actually be changed or speeders will be ignored.

In the case of other variations from the norm, such as the antisocial behavior of a serial killer, the cultural values are so strong and widely held that such behavior would not become an acceptable aspect of culture unless the society suffered a total breakdown. As reported in several studies, our cultural values against child molesters are so strong that, when imprisoned, many of these criminals face injury or death from fellow inmates who, despite their criminal backgrounds, still cling to the belief that such crimes against children are never acceptable.

Without culture or this shared sense of reality, there would be utter chaos in our world. Many people look at human behavior in our society and believe that part of the cultural glue that holds us together as a group is coming undone. Using another example that we are all familiar with, think about the number of people who seem to ignore traffic signals. At one time, people wouldn't have thought of running a yellow light. Today, people think nothing of running red lights. In metropolitan Phoenix, intersection accidents are the leading cause of traffic fatalities. When a group begins to ignore aspects of its culture that can seriously affect the health and welfare of others, it is time to reexamine the values and perhaps look for solutions that will encourage people to do the right thing. In the Phoenix area, there are now cameras at selected intersections that photograph red-light runners and send them their tickets in the mail. Many people object to this approach to law enforcement, but it has decreased the number of intersection accidents in the short time it has been in use. Police have even begun hiding cameras in the cactus to catch unsuspecting motorists.

We have presented this brief discussion of culture because it is critical in understanding organizational culture. The beliefs, values, and behaviors that are a part of an organization affect the individuals in that organization, the product or service that organization provides, and the organization as a whole.

What is Organizational Culture?

What we have found is that many of us use the term "corporate culture" when referring to organizational culture. From our perspective and for purposes of this book, we prefer to use the term "organizational culture." Our rationale for this is that in studying different types of businesses in all industries, we have determined that they all have their own unique culture, yet many have no corporate structure. In other words, cultures don't exist just in large corporations, they exist in places you might not have thought of, such as your neighborhood, your club, and your church. If you play on a football team, you have a culture. If you own a business of any size, you have a culture.

When you think of your organization it is helpful to think of it as a country. Doing this will help you understand what organizational culture is, subcultures and all. With all of the talk about organizational culture, including dozens of current books, it would seem that we should have a clear understanding of what it is and that we would have no trouble describing it. Yet when we asked our interviewees to describe their current culture, they had a very difficult time and they used a range of references. Most people focused on one or two aspects of the culture, such as leadership style or management practices. Without exception, they believed that knowing something about their organizational culture was important. Most indicated, however, that they did not have the tools and/or experience to really assess their culture in any quantifiable way.

As leaders ourselves, we believe that this inability to define culture leads to a high level of frustration for you as a leader. How are you expected to manage something that you can't always identify or define, let alone measure? For many of you, it's as elusive as trying to nail Jell-O to the wall. And when you think about it, culture and Jell-O are somewhat similar. Jell-O has a form that is defined by the space it is in and can change its shape and form as the conditions change. It is really hard to get hold of and parts of it stick to you more than others. Different people think it tastes different, and ingest it in different ways. Some people even wrestle in it.

In their book *The Character of a Corporation: How Your Company's Culture Can Make or Break Your Business*, Rob Goffee and Gareth Jones maintain "...most organizations, in their many parts, are characterized by several cultures at once, and it is critical that leaders and individuals understand where these different cultures exist, how they work together, and how they clash." (1) However, Goffee and Jones go on to say, "Culture comes down to a common way of thinking, which drives a common way of acting on the job or producing a product in a factory. Usually these shared assumptions, beliefs and values are unspoken—implicit." (2)

When they talk about the unspoken and unwritten assumptions and the hidden culture, they are absolutely right on. This is a valid description of how many organizations operate today. However, as a leader you must stop perpetuating *the same old way of doing things* and rather than managing these two worlds, you must strive to eliminate the unspoken, hidden culture. The answer is NOT to learn how to manage the unspoken culture, but to eliminate it. **Why?** Because living under both the spoken and unspoken "law" gets very confusing for your work force, and it gets in the way of achieving profitable results.

The good news is that conducting a cultural assessment will allow you to examine these two worlds. Through such an assessment, you will not only be able to identify what your unspoken assumptions are, but also learn how you can create the right type of structure and culture to begin to combine these two worlds, the hidden and the overt and ultimately eliminate your hidden culture.

At this juncture, it is important for you to understand how assumptions are formed. "Why?" you might ask. Well, assumptions play a critical role in forming our cultures. Think about this for a minute, when people act a certain way, it generates a specific reaction. For example, in one organization an assumption held by employees could be "even if I work hard I will not be recognized or compensated, so why bother?" This assumption is based on reality. Because, the story goes, everybody gets the same amount of increase no matter how well he/she has performed. In this particular situation, there is no distinction between an employee who produces at maximum capacity and one who shows up when he feels like it. Now, in order to change that assumption, you must change your actions. Once you begin rewarding the high achievers differently from their less-productive peers, the story will change, the assumptions will change, and so will your culture. Therefore, what we are saying is, *management's actions translate into the story that is told. People then make assumptions from the story and these assumptions determine employee behavior. Change the story, and you change the assumptions!*

Changing the assumptions changes people's behavior and therefore creates a more congruent or incongruent culture. This applies to all areas of your business not just compensation or pay practices.

Some authors and experts see organizational culture as a concept that is exceedingly difficult to grasp. Up until recently, we would have agreed with them. However, we have come to realize that it is not that difficult to grasp. Instead, it just needs to be laid out in simpler terms so that you, as a leader, can understand it in your own language. A cultural assessment is the only vehicle that can help you reach that understanding. When conducting such an assessment make sure that you examine what the unspoken assumptions are, why they exist, and how you work with them. The double standards that you continue to perpetuate in your business must stop. What you say on paper **must** reflect how you act. Your **WORDS** must equal your **ACTIONS.** Agreeing wholeheartedly, one of our colleagues added that in his experience "many of the people in management don't know what words actually mean, they are so used to looking at the 'big picture' that DETAILS, like the meaning of their words, are just an annoyance." (3) Do not let that be the case in your organization; otherwise, as mentioned earlier, you will create confusion and mayhem.

OK, that was a mouthful. Now what are we talking about exactly? Let's work with some concrete examples. You have a company policy that clearly outlines how RFPs (Requests for Proposals) are processed. However, in talking with employees, you discover that they haven't followed that procedure for two years. Why? Because it's cumbersome and their reaction is *we'd never get anything done if we followed it.* Or, you have a human resource policy that states that all positions will be posted internally before going to the outside. Yet, everyone knows that a number of positions were filled that were never posted, or worse yet, positions were posted after the external recruiting process had begun. These are blatant incongruencies between formal and informal policies, between the visible world and the hidden world. These incongruencies not only cause confusion in the eyes of your employees, but also cause high levels of frustration and anger and definitely begin to eat away at your trust level.

So what does this have to do with bottom-line results? Lots. Excluding culture from your calculations is like ignoring warning signs you get from your doctor. Culture tells you **how** you are achieving your results, positive or negative. It tells you why you're in the red or why you're in the black. When you have a healthy bottom line and healthy profit margins there is no reason to examine **how** you are achieving such great results. Or is that really true? Well, guess what? If you don't have a basic understanding of **how** you achieve your results, then it becomes virtually impossible to replicate what is working and modify what is not working. Baselines must be established for any and all processes that you use in your day-to-day operations, and your cultural process is no exception. If you don't understand what *is* and *is not* working from a quantifiable perspective, you will just be shooting in the dark. And you know that as rapidly as businesses are moving today, you must be able to hit the target on the first try, by knowing what the target is and where it is.

It's sad to say, but most of us have to be hit with bad news before we wake up and realize that something must be done. Think about it. It is really no different from being told that we have high cholesterol and that we must change our lifestyle. We start off gung-ho, eating less fat, exercising more and reducing our intake of alcohol, but how long does that last? After a couple of months, we see no positive results so, for many of us, what happens? We revert to our old behavior. Our lifestyle doesn't seem to matter, until that day the ambulance takes us to the hospital. Yes, the chest pains have started and now the signals are far more apparent and more life threatening. Now we are paying attention and praying. (No matter what our denomination, we all at one time or another grab onto that life jacket.) And what do we do during this state? Oh, we promise to do all the right things, if only we can have another chance.

Not paying attention to your culture can have the same devastating impact on you and your organization. Later in this chapter, we will talk more about why we need to pay attention to culture, and we will give you specific business examples that show that culture does matter.

Let's continue to define this thing we call organizational culture. Organizational culture can be referred to as the glue that keeps an organization together. It can be the silent code of conduct, it's *more about **how** things get done than **what** gets done.* It can also be referred to as white noise, the background static that may affect you but goes unnoticed. When a new employee is *learning the ropes,* he/she is learning the culture.

It is very important for you to remember that culture is not a thing. It's not something an organization has or doesn't have. Culture is something an organization *is.*

Organizational culture has been likened to DNA. (Dolly the cloned sheep has taught us that even DNA can be altered.) Your organization could be assessed today, and you would be able to define your culture in very specific terms and even identify subcultures. The challenge for you, as a leader, is to recognize that it does exist, and it molds reality for those who work in your organization. Your job is to ensure that the culture does not become dysfunctional. When this happens, culture, especially if it's a strong one, can be a liability. A cultural assessment will allow you to continuously examine your culture and to determine how healthy it is. It will identify where your incongruencies lie, determine what effect they are having on your business, and help you develop a plan to rectify the situation.

Let us not confuse organizational culture with national culture. When conducting a cultural assessment you must include national culture as one of the key organizational characteristics that must be considered. If two merging organizations have distinct national cultures, an additional layer of complexity is added to the equation. Do not be fooled into thinking that you can just blend one with the other and come up with *one* new culture. Customs, rituals, and beliefs in this case will play a key role in how you integrate the two businesses. The same holds true for international companies that are attempting to implement a new business strategy, whether it be marketing, human resources, or financial.

Despite the universal acceptance of Mickey Mouse and friends, EuroDisney fell far short of initial revenue forecasts. Some cultural differences may not have been obvious to the theme park planners. For one, the French were not inclined to see the theme park as a destination resort as Americans do. Their visits were often limited to a single-day ticket. Additionally, European visitors did not purchase costly food and souvenir items after paying the hefty park entrance fee. Disney developers did not consider that many Europeans take their own food when traveling, which significantly affects vendor sales. Although the theme-park development did not involve a true merger or business combination, it was a joint venture involving two distinct cultures that was impacted, initially, by some of their cultural differences.

The merger of auto giants Daimler-Benz AG and Chrysler Corporation provides another example of how national cultures can affect international business combinations. Although this marriage was viewed favorably by industry analysts in terms of product-line blending and management philosophy, workers from the United States and Germany are reluctant to relocate from one country to the other. So the new corporation continues to function as two separate entities with executives shuttling back and forth between Auburn Hills, Michigan, and Stuttgart, Germany. Cultural considerations play a large part in this scenario. Most Americans do not speak German and are reluctant to leave their large homes for expensive city apartments. Also, since Chrysler was primarily a domestic manufacturer, working abroad was not part of its culture and was not necessarily a requisite for advancement. A task force is now charged with developing a program to entice employees to volunteer for jobs abroad, something that was probably not thought to be an issue when the merger took place.

Cultural considerations are not limited to international combinations. There are many examples here in the United States like one where an East coast manufacturing company acquired a West coast biotech firm. The East coast firm was interested only in the technology that the smaller West coast company had to offer. It was quite evident from the start of negotiations that the Eastern contingent wanted to own the technology. The Easterners hoped to have the current employees from the West coast stay on board through the technology transfer, but after that, it was anyone's guess what would happen. The Easterners' leadership team sat around the boardroom table convincing one another that the Westerners would be "chompin' at the bit" to have job offers here: "Who wouldn't want to work for this great company and live here on the East coast?" Answer: No one. At least, none of the West coast employees wanted to move. In fact, none of them even wanted to commute back East for a few months to complete the technology transfer. The Easterners' assumptions would be their demise. Although management and HR representatives went out to the West coast to woo the employees there and educate them on how wonderful the East coast was, no one bit. In fact, the Westerners so resented the tactics and games that the East coast leaders were playing, they began to refuse to communicate openly, or at least, they were not forthcoming with all of the information that was needed to make a smooth transition. In its infinite wisdom, the East coast management team missed two very important components: human motivation and quality-of-life issues. Most people live where they live for a reason, be it family, regional cultures, logistics, school systems, or other similar reasons. Most are where they are because they choose to be. If you do not realize this important fact going in, then right from the get-go, you misunderstand what motivates people and the important role that culture plays in everyone's lives. The end result was less than positive. The Eastern firm did buy the technology, but its inability to understand the technology put the Easterners at a clear disadvantage in the marketplace. As a result, there was a sixteen-month delay in product launch, which negatively affected market share.

Cultures have many different characteristics that can affect the degree of influence on members of the group. There are many contemporary examples of organizational cultures as described by James Collins and Jerry Porras in their book *Built to Last*, that are almost cult-like. All of the examples come from "visionary companies," which the authors define as premier institutions in their industries, widely admired by their peers, and having a long track record of success. Although they caution that "we're not saying that visionary companies are cults," (4) they suggest that some of these companies utilize techniques that might be found in cults. Specifically, they found that some of the visionary companies:

- had a lengthy indoctrination to company policy and procedure. Example, Disney's requirement that every new employee attend Disney University.

- demonstrated a "greater tightness of fit." Example, Nordstrom's is recognized for its commitment to outstanding customer service, and it is reported that 50% of new hires leave because they just don't fit the organization. The employees that stay on are referred to as "Nordies".

- showed more elitism (sense of belonging to something superior and special). Example, Proctor and Gamble describes itself as special, full of the best people, and unique among the world's business organizations. (5)

We are sure that you can think of other organizations where the culture literally exudes from the walls as you walk through the door. The greeters in Wal-Mart convey Sam Walton's commitment to serving the underserved community as soon as you meet them. The "suits" in the elevator at any of the Big 5 public-accounting firms are the first sign of their corporate culture, which values attention to detail in every respect.

And anyone who has ever been a patient at one of the Mayo Clinics will tell you that the Mayo organization views itself as a premier provider and employer. The Mayo way of doing things is part of a culture that has been sustained for more than 100 years; and it starts with the organizational mantra "the best interest of the patient is the only interest to be considered." This mantra has become a standard against which every decision is measured and has made Mayo a premier health-care provider, especially in the eyes of the patient.

After spending nine months with the Mayo Clinic Scottsdale developing and implementing the education and orientation plan for their new hospital in Arizona, we can attest to that strong culture. From the day we came through the front door, we could feel lots of energy, a positive charge that hummed throughout the building. Some of the old-timers told us right up front that as outsiders we would have to be "Mayo-ized" in order to be accepted in the system. They were right. Mayo's culture was described by Paul Roberts in the April 1999 issue of *Fast Company,* which said, "The process is so exacting, and the culture so distinctive, that it usually becomes clear right away whether a trainee has the right attitude." (6) We found this to be true. Employees were evaluated not only on their technical skill and experience, but also on how fully they adopted and applied the Mayo philosophy in their work.

Culture, as you can see, may be defined in a number of different ways. *We define organizational culture as the mechanism that truly defines the organization for the employees and the customers: how things really get done, how people interact with each other.* Organizational culture represents a common understanding held by all employees. *It is a system of shared meaning.* What we mean here is the guiding culture of an organization. This guiding culture expresses the core organizational values that must be shared by the entire employee population. In addition to this guiding culture, large organizations will have many subcultures (departments or divisions). These subcultures typically reflect common problems, situations, or experiences that affect members of that particular department or division. This doesn't mean that the subcultures supplant the guiding culture. However, keeping them from supplanting the guiding culture is the challenge of many organizations today. The subcultures are not connected to the guiding culture/the core organizational values, and they must be.

The guiding culture should be what governs the behavior of each and every employee. It should embody the core organizational values that all employees must live by. The subcultures should be merely an adjunct to the macro culture.

When we say this, you should know the assumptions that govern our thinking. We see the guiding culture like the tablets of the Ten Commandments, a force that everyone (in that culture) should live by. However, we have made a huge assumption that the guiding culture (or core organizational values) are wholesome and full of integrity. We believe this will be the case when the guiding culture is defined by all levels in an organization, and not just by the people who live in the ivory tower. From our point of view though, the guiding culture tells you as a new employee what is expected, even if all that's expected is that the bottom line comes before ethics. In this situation, a new employee has to decide whether he or she wants to work for such an organization. The employee has to make a clear choice, and that's the important point. The guiding culture's rules and expectations, whatever they are, should be clear, congruent, and apply to everyone, so that employees will know where they stand and how to act in the company's behalf.

Along with these definitions come key determinants that contribute to and define organizational culture. A cultural assessment should enable you to examine these key determinants in a comprehensive, structured approach. They should include:

- Physical Layout—Do private offices exist? If so, who has them? Are there offices or conference rooms set up as think tanks or are the departments filled with floor-to-ceiling cubicles?

- Interactions—How do employees get along with each other, with the customer, vendors, etc.? How do they communicate with each other? Is face to face expected or is e-mail acceptable?

- Language—Is there a common language? What is the jargon that is used? What about acronyms? How are people addressed? Are formal titles used?

- Dress—Is there a formal or informal dress code?

- Rules of the Game—How do things really get done around here? Very important for newcomers.

- Group norms—What is acceptable practice? Is it the norm to arrive fifteen minutes late to a meeting? Do people rationalize that lateness by saying, "That's OK! Our watches are set on (fill in your company's name) time"?

- Values—What are they, and how are they practiced?

- Relationships—How does the board interact with the CEO and vice versa? How does the work force as a whole interact? How many people actually showed up to the last company social outing/gathering?

- Self-image—Tough or caring? Environmentally responsible?

- Structure—Is the organization hierarchical, matrixed, boundaryless, etc.?

- How do decisions get made?

- Do you have a formal or informal leadership structure?

Knowing exactly what these determinants are in your organization start you down the path of a true cultural assessment. We will cover all the areas that should be assessed in much more detail later in the chapter called "The Cultural-Assessment Process."

Values Create Cultures

Why talk about values? Well, if you want to change your organization's culture (personality), you must first start with your values. Values determine the definition of good and bad. Values are at the heart of culture. They form the culture. They are the lifeline of an organization. Values are to organizational culture what blood is to your tissues and organs. Without this vehicle to transport the information throughout the organization, departments or divisions can die. Just as impaired circulation results in tissue necrosis or death, an organization can cease to function as a whole if the values are not coursing through its body.

Think of an avocado, once you get through the tough and rough exterior, you begin to see the real meat, or the fruit. Peel back the meat and in the center is the lifeblood, the pit, the core, without which the avocado will not grow. If that pit does not germinate well, then the plant and resulting fruit will never be that good. It all stems from the core. Values are like that core, an influence that gives real life to an organization.

Values state what is important to you as an individual and to your organization. In other words, values are what you stand for. They reflect who you are, which in turn affects what you do and how you do it, which is your culture. When you think about values, take a moment to reflect on your behavior and the types of decisions you have made. Do you always act in accordance with the basic beliefs that you hold? Has there ever been a situation in which you had to compromise your values in order to do what you were asked to do by someone else? How did this make you feel?

For most of us, when our behavior is in conflict with our values, we experience frustration and sometimes pain. This ultimately affects what we do and affects our organizations.

Think about a company's expense-reporting policy and practices. You know that you must follow the guidelines requiring receipts for all transactions. But what do you do when you turn in your report with a smaller amount of "claims" than others apparently submit, and the area supervisor calls you and says, "Are you sure you didn't spend more than that? Don't worry about the receipts"? You value fairness and honesty, but a part of you wants to revise that report. The actual practices are in conflict with both your values and those of the organization. You experience frustration with whatever you decide to do. Leave the claim the way it is and you will feel *cheated*, but change the claim and you will feel you are *cheating*.

This is a type of dilemma that your employees face each day in conducting business. The company says it values honesty and fairness and that it abides by its formal policies, and yet the director of finance has taken it upon himself to administer the policy according to his standards. Herein lies the problem. You now have an obvious incongruency between your formal policy and your informal practice. Can you see what a tempting and compromising situation you have put your employees in? Remove the temptation and the confusion by having formal policies that reflect what you do across the organization. If the policy no longer makes sense, then change it. Don't create a "work around" because then you have started to create a bigger, hidden world.

Values guide us. They give us direction. Let's look at an analogy. Suppose you wanted to arrive at a specific location in central Dallas. A street map of the city would be a great help to you in reaching your destination. But suppose you were given the wrong map. Through a printing error, the map labeled "Dallas" was actually a map of Chicago. Can you imagine the level of frustration?

What could you do to rectify the situation? Well, you might work on your attitude. You could think more positively. You still wouldn't get to the right place, but maybe you wouldn't care. Your attitude would be so positive, you'd be happy wherever you were. The point is, you'd still be lost. Being lost has nothing to do with your behavior or attitude; it has to do with having the wrong map.

In business, employees need maps as well. If they don't have clear direction, the best attitude in the world isn't going to rectify the situation. In most of our businesses, we have two types of maps: Maps of the way things *really are, our reality,* and maps of the way things *should be, our values.* We interpret everything we experience through these mental maps. When there is a disconnect or an incongruency, we struggle to reconcile the difference. As we noted earlier, this is a major challenge for you as a leader. There should be a clear set of directions for reaching your organizational goals and your destination. When there is a need for any of your values to change then let your people know. Otherwise, they will definitely be headed down the wrong street. Our values map must be our reality map. When these two conflict, it becomes very confusing for the work force, and they become lost. They packed their boots to go two-stepping, but ended up needing a warm coat for the Windy City.

Why should we be concerned about these incongruencies? Culture can actually become a liability when the core organizational values are not embraced and **practiced** by everyone in the organization. This breakdown can interfere with your organization's ability to reach its goals, and this can cost you money.

This point was brought home to us during a consulting engagement with a successful international medical-device company. Being ethical was at the core of what this organization stood for, and the belief was that the company should show *fairness and integrity in its dealings with employees, customers, and the overall marketplace.* When product failures started becoming an everyday event for this company, employees wanted to publicly admit to the problem, but the leadership had an attitude that it was *no big deal.* By this time, consumer safety had become a very real concern and adverse effects of the product were starting to hit the press. There was actually a time when you couldn't pick up a newspaper without seeing something negative written about this organization.

Rather than seek the truth, the organizational leaders immediately took a defensive posture and denied what the evidence clearly told them. One lie grew into another and yet another and yet another, until everybody in a leadership role believed that they were right and the

FDA and everybody else was wrong. The truth of the matter was that they were not living up to one of their core organizational values. Integrity had blown out the window along with market share. Actually, their arrogance (not an articulated value) was stronger than their integrity, and it drove their actions. This division, which was once the front-runner in this market and had held 100% of the market share, was now facing criminal charges and had reached the bottom of the heap. Yes, right down to 0%, when they were finally forced to take the product off the shelves. Today, eight years later, the company is still struggling to recover from this experience and has gained back only 17% of the market.

The story doesn't end there. The great loss in market share didn't come about only because the product was taken off the market, but also because, during the span of the next three to four years, the company lost most of its critical intellectual capital. People no longer wanted to be affiliated with the company. Where did they go? Well, to the competition, of course, and some actually became the new competition. This organization has still not been able to regain its credibility with employees, the community, and the marketplace.

So what do you think the current leaders of this business are focusing on today? Well, ethics, of course. It is at the forefront of everybody's minds and drives every business decision that is made. Unfortunately, as the saying goes, *it's too little, too late*. Why do we wait until someone is hurt or until we get our hand slapped to do the right thing? We really must start acting more with our hearts and not just our heads.

It is a very distressing story. Many people lost their jobs (employees who had been with the company for 10-plus years). All but a handful of the top team members lost their jobs, and some even faced criminal charges and were imprisoned. This is reality! And it can happen to you.

The sad commentary here is that it could have been avoided. If the leaders had allowed their core organizational values to drive their business decisions, they would have made the right decision and pulled the product off the market before they were ordered to do so by the FDA.

Or if they were aware of what values were actually driving their actions maybe they would have acted differently. Maybe in some cases, such as this one, the leaders were not ignorant of what they did but rather they did not understand the ramifications of their actions. Conducting a cultural assessment can assist you in identifying what values actually drive your actions, which can prevent such a situation from happening in your organization.

If these managers had listened to their hearts (people were dying as a result of these product failures) instead of their heads (which feared the financial repercussions of the truth getting out), they would have seen the need to admit the product failures and work to end them. Instead they acted more irrationally than if they'd used their hearts to guide them, and they let their hearts turn black. The makers of Tylenol and the owners of Jack in the Box certainly showed that you CAN turn this type of calamity around if you keep a clear head, be honest about the situation, and let your core values drive your decisions.

Since values are so important, you must not only embrace them but, more importantly, you must act on them. They must be articulated to all employees and your expectation must be that all employees will integrate these values into their day-to-day work. They must become part of everyone's performance assessment. Mort Meyerson, former CEO of Perot Systems, said it very eloquently in the June 1999 issue of *Fast Company:*

> "The essence of leadership today is to make sure that the organization knows itself. There are certain durable principles that underlie an organization. The leader should embody those values. They're fundamental. But they have nothing to do with business strategy, tactics, or market share. They have to do with human relationships and the obligation of the organization to its individual members and its customers." (7)

Not only must your values be well articulated and practiced, your values must be reviewed on an ongoing basis to ensure that you are a) living by them and b) that there is no need for change. We have found that sometimes a SHIFT in values can actually create a windfall. Take the case of Ray Anderson, who developed a billion-dollar international carpet-manufacturing business, Interface, Inc., on the precept that a corporation could comply with the law and still make a profit. In "Profits from Principle," an article by Bennett Daviss in the March, 1999 issue of *The Futurist*, Daviss recounts what happened to Anderson in 1994 when he faced a falling market share and declining stock price. After reading eco-entrepreneur Paul Hawken's book *The Ecology of Commerce*, which describes the squandering of natural resources by industry and presents options for environmental consciousness in business, Anderson recognized that his company was guilty of such abuse by "chewing up more than 500 million pounds of raw material each year and excreting more than 900 tons of air pollutants, 600 million gallons of wastewater, and 10,000 tons of trash" each year. (8) Anderson said that reading Hawken's book was "a spear in my chest." Davis also said it put a spur in Anderson's backside as it led to the decision to make his twenty-six factories on four continents environmentally sensitive in every respect. He moved forward to "recycling everything possible, releasing no pollutants, and sending nothing to landfills. 'We're treating all fossil-fuel energy as waste to be eliminated through efficiencies and shifts to renewable energy,' Anderson said. Idealistic? Definitely. Unbusinesslike? Definitely not." (9)

In Anderson's case, the Shifts resulted in greater operational efficiencies and cost savings. And as a direct result of the new business philosophy, Interface was invited by The Gap, Inc. to bid on the job of carpeting their new headquarters because of this environmental consciousness—the winning bid, we might add. "We've found a new way to win in the marketplace," Anderson believes, "one that doesn't come at the expense of our grandchildren or the earth, but at the expense of the inefficient competitor." (10) Anderson's crusade is one example among countless others proving a new rule in business: Profits and social responsibility are becoming inseparable.

As the Interface, Inc. example shows us, you can make money from a SHIFT in values and a real commitment to social responsibility. In the same article, Daviss quantifies this SHIFT. He cites the growth of the San Francisco-based group Business for Social Responsibility, from 45 members in 1993 to more than 1400 in 1999. He adds that the new members aren't just smaller companies, but that they include Fortune 500 firms and large corporate conglomerates. Daviss quotes charter member Gary Hirshberg, who says, "We don't just have the oddball New Age companies anymore. We've got the suits." (11)

Many people do judge corporations today by their social performance as much as their financial performance. We have become consumers with a conscience. We want to save the planet, keep our environment healthy, and have clean air to breathe, but we also want to be rich, or at least very financially secure and comfortable. There are many corporations, large and small, that are finding that you can have it both ways. For instance, McDonald's has come a long way in environmental awareness, from serving up Big Macs in non-biodegradable, plastic-foam cartons to repackaging its fast-food items in recyclable paper and cardboard.

When conducting a cultural assessment you must consider not only the product or service your organization provides, but you must also look at your company's role in the community. What added value does the business bring to the local and global marketplace? In addition to creating jobs in a community, many companies now focus on filling very specific needs. An example is the University of Phoenix and other universities around the country where the curriculum is designed to accommodate the working professional (especially the commuter), who typically faces some significant time constraints. The Phoenix metropolitan area now has more urban sprawl than Los Angeles, which translates into long drives. In response to this community characteristic, the school offers classes at multiple locations and primarily in evening sessions. Its commitment to making higher education available to more people is an investment in the community.

We are not saying that there is one value or set of values that works for every organization. What we are saying is that values we profess, whatever they may be, must be more than words. They must be widely known and practiced in your organization's day-to-day dealings with your entire community (those outside your organization as well as those within).

Why Pay Attention to Organizational Culture?

Let's first look at the three *Ps* of organizational culture: people, practices, and performance.

People

One of our critical personal beliefs as leaders is that *human behavior has a direct and measurable impact on the performance levels of an organization.* Think about this for a minute: How many of your organization's tasks can be accomplished without human interaction or human dependency? Yes, one could argue that we are in a technological age, where human interaction, once the mainstay of the manufacturing floor, has been replaced by robots and automated plants. We may think that since we're doing work via such high-tech media as the Internet that there is less human interaction. However, this technology has not and will never eliminate the human interactions that must take place in conducting business. Look more closely. Is the task of building a car in a robot plant accomplished by the robot or is it accomplished by the people who designed the robot or program? Crucial human interaction was involved there. In addition, although we may be sitting in front of a tube alone as we use the Internet, we use it primarily for communication, which is human interaction if ever there was one. Sure, transactions do occur in a "virtual" environment more often today than ever before, but there is still a human behind the machine. The way we convey our messages across telephone lines is just as critical as a face-to-face encounter, and face-to-face encounters have not been eliminated, by any means. The people who are left on the manufacturing floor these days must still interact with each other in order to get their jobs done. Employees from one department in a hospital must coordinate their efforts with other departments to deliver the best possible patient care. The bottom line is that humans will always be required to interact with each other at some level.

Therefore, you must pay attention to culture and the people factor (your human capital), because, with the dizzying pace of change in business, people know that they are expendable and therefore they don't have the loyalty and allegiance to their employers that employees a generation ago might have had. It's a big cultural SHIFT. A lifetime career with a single organization is pretty much unheard of today, unless we are looking at the government where long-term service is the rule rather than the exception. However, as pressure on government to act more like a business continues to prevail, the idea of a lifetime civil-service job will also change over time. The Carter, Reagan, Bush, and Clinton administrations all made cuts in governmental payroll. At any rate, the increase in job changing has become a fact of life that affects organizations. We are sure that you can personally attest to the high cost of recruitment, retention, and replacement.

So what do these costs look like? According to a survey by M.H. West & Co. published in *PR News*: "On average a company loses about $1,000,000 with every ten professional and managerial employees who leave. Assuming your company has a 10 percent profit, that's a reduction of $100,000 from the bottom line." (12) There is no doubt that this affects the bottom line.

However, these costs represent just part of the value of human capital. To illustrate the point, consider the story of a tourist who approached a famous artist as he sketched a scene on the street of his town. After watching the old man for awhile, the visitor asked him to draw her portrait. He agreed and quickly finished an incredible likeness.

The tourist was thrilled until the artist told her the price, which was ten times higher than she expected. How can it be so much, she complained, when it only took you a few minutes? The artist politely replied—it has taken me a lifetime to complete. She, like so many of us, failed to consider the value associated with lifelong commitment and experience. Taking that attitude toward human capital today can lead to disaster.

More than ever before, you must recognize the value of your people and the hand they play in creating your organization's culture and wealth. In *Intellectual Capital*, author Annie Brooking suggests that "every time we lose an employee we lose a chunk of corporate memory." (13) Her research into the subject confirms the importance of finding and keeping employees with knowledge and experience. Yet, according to Brooking, "lost expertise is a huge problem few companies have attempted to solve." (14)

If you don't pay attention to this part of your culture, your brainpower (or knowledge asset) will go elsewhere. Take the case of Thomas Weisel, founder of Montgomery Securities. He sold his firm in 1997 to NationsBank Corp. After completing the sale, Weisel stayed on with the new owner for a short time, but then resigned and founded his new company, Thomas Weisel Partners LLC. Although some of the competition is claiming that Weisel doesn't have the resources to effectively compete, in fact, NationsBank's loss might become the company's competition.

This scenario is now occurring frequently, especially in the communications and technology sectors. No one can argue with the idea that Bill Gates is Microsoft or that Michael Eisner is the closest thing to Walt Disney, next to brother Roy. What would happen if these people suddenly left and joined the competition or *became* the competition? Many organizations guard against that possibility with contract clauses that prohibit certain executives and knowledge workers from immediately going to work for the direct competition. Such a loss of intellectual capital would be devastating to the organization and the bottom line. People really do make or break the profits. The number of recent news headlines and book titles on the loss of intellectual capital tells us that this is a subject that is finally receiving some much-needed attention.

We believe that it is extremely important for companies to know where they are in the life cycle of their business so they can know when to make changes. If you and your company are not constantly improving performance levels, your organization will begin to lose ground. However, many companies, when reaching the point where changes must be made, fail to realize that they cannot reach the next performance level without people, without human capital. How many of us have rebuilt, resized, restructured, reengineered, and reorganized our companies to meet the many challenges of the global marketplace? Work processes have been adapted to improve productivity and increase shareholder value. We have fixed the "hard" stuff. However, many of us are beginning to recognize that, in order to get to the next level of performance, we must focus on the "soft" stuff. We must deal with the toughest issue, our people, and, inevitably, our organizational culture. The "soft" stuff really is the "hard" stuff.

Practice

When we talk about practice in culture, we are talking about the way that the values are translated into accepted standards of practice. These are the policies and procedures that, loosely translated, become the bible for organizations. But as we all know, the Bible can be interpreted both literally and figuratively. One person's take on a specific scripture can be almost the total opposite of another person's. It is the same in your organization. You have the literal interpretation of the policy that states employees are not permitted to eat at their work stations, but you have the unwritten rule that says it is OK if there are no clients who can see them and if they do it without making a mess (these unwritten assumptions represent the hidden culture).

You may have a cohabitation or anti-nepotism policy that states that two people cannot work in the same department if they live together, especially if one is a supervisor, but everybody knows a "real nice couple" in the same department. They're breaking the policy, but you look the other way. Once you start to think about it, you may find the list of official policies and procedures that vary from the real practice in your organization is longer than you imagined. These are examples of incongruencies in your organization that over time, slowly, very slowly, eat away at your company's values and ultimately your culture. Why? Because once you try to enforce a policy after "looking the other way" when some employees violated it, you are the one who is caught. Employees will begin to talk about how unfair management is, and the resulting culture will be adversarial rather than one that works together toward common goals. This is counterproductive and eventually affects your bottom line. Remember *actions translate into the story that is told. People then make assumptions from the story. Change the story, and you change the assumptions! Changing the assumptions changes people's behavior and therefore changes the culture.* Plain and simple.

This practice area of your culture becomes especially critical when your organization faces a merger, affiliation, or combination with another organization or is simply undergoing an internal change initiative, or negotiating a union contract. You must pay attention to the policies and procedures, both expressed and implied, so that the employees will have a clear understanding of the expectations. Just as employees must clearly understand your core organizational values, they must have a clear understanding of what the expected and accepted behaviors are in the particular change situation. Many times, we cling to policies and procedures in times of trouble or threat, but they are only as good as the three-ring binder they reside in, if someone in the organization can prove that they are not followed consistently and fairly across the board.

Performance

Does culture really matter when we're talking about generating big profit margins, accelerating growth, or expanding our market share? The answer to that question is an unequivocal **yes.** Today more than ever, there is sufficient evidence telling us that we must pay attention to our culture because it directly affects the third *P*—performance.

In their book *Managing Mergers and Acquisitions*, authors Sue Cartwright and Cary L. Cooper comment on the classic book *In Search of Excellence*, saying:

> "Tom Peters and Bob Waterman presented clear evidence linking organizational performance with a strong, dominant and coherent culture. Although the level of performance of several of the 'excellent' companies has declined in the years since the study, this does not weaken the argument that a fragmented, ambiguous or contradictory culture is unlikely to result in optimum organizational performance. The organizational performance of even 'excellent' companies is likely to decline if they are unable either to continue to maintain a cohesive culture or to recognize the need to change." (15)

When trying to diagnose the cause of the alarmingly high rate of failures (measured in terms of *reported* financial performance compared with *projected revenues*), many people are looking to the cultural issues. In "Preventing Culture Shock," an article in *Modern Healthcare* by Rodney Fralicz and C.J. Bolster, the authors state, "Culture can be a make-or-break factor in the merger equation," which, if ignored or misunderstood, "can almost single-handedly sour the deal." (16)

A classic example took place in the airline industry several years ago when USAir acquired Pacific Southwest Airlines (PSA) in an effort to link its East Coast routes with the markets in the West and Southwest. PSA dominated the California corridor and was one of the first "no frills" airlines. PSA crew members wore casual attire in keeping with the markets they served, and a smile was painted on the nose of each aircraft. In contrast, USAir, formerly Allegheny Airlines, was one of the oldest national carriers in the country, with a concentration in the Northeast. The primary customers were business travelers, and the management focused on that segment. Before the ink had dried on the contracts, the paintbrushes were wet, and employees were busily covering the smiles. Instead of integrating this very favorably viewed aspect of PSA, USAir literally erased it, along with the culture it represented. Instead of promoting the smiles from coast to coast, USAir turned the smiles to frowns, from customers who missed the old PSA. In a very short period, market share was lost to upstart rival Southwest Airlines, which sensed this cultural incompatibility and took advantage of the opportunity to replace the service that had been lost. Eventually, USAir all but withdrew from the Southwest, suffering serious financial losses from the cost of the acquisition and the failure to expand its routes.

The smiles were gone from everyone's face, especially the shareholders'.

In *Organizational Culture and Leadership*, Edgar H. Schein states,

"Culture may be loosely thought about, but it is only after the merger that it is taken seriously, suggesting that most leaders make the assumption that they can fix cultural problems after the fact. I would argue that leaders must make cultural analysis as central to the initial merger/acquisition decision as is the financial, product, or market analysis." (17)

Schein then recounts the story of a U.S. company that was about to acquired by a larger British firm. The company actually conducted a cultural audit and decided the match wouldn't work. The company waited for a more attractive partner to come along. A French company that was **perceived** to be a better cultural match entered the picture. The U.S. company had not conducted a formal cultural audit of this firm. The decision to move forward was based strictly on perception. The U.S. company was purchased by the French firm, and six months later, the French parent sent over a management team that decimated the U.S. company. The situation was far worse than anything its executives could ever have imagined. But it was too late! (18)

In addition to the three *Ps*, you must pay attention to culture because it affects many other areas as well. Some of them include the following:

Technology

Cultural analysis is necessary in helping you determine how new technologies influence your organization. For instance, information technology is having a tremendous impact on how we do our work. It is literally transforming many of our practices. Think about the new challenges since the introduction of e-mail. How many times do you grapple with the ethical issues around the use of e-mail? Are you finding that this technology has at times increased and improved your level of communication, but at the same time has created a safe haven for employees who would rather confront issues through e-mail than through face-to-face dialogue? We are not saying that all issues were addressed in face-to-face dialogue before the advent of e-mail; however, what we are finding in our work is that e-mail warfare among colleagues has become the predominant way of dealing with issues. Our point here is that it must be recognized and dealt with.

That type of behavior arising from e-mail use points to another challenge facing you as a leader. In an article in the February 1999 issue of *The Futurist* titled "The Decline of Conversation," the drawbacks of e-mailing are discussed and John L. Locke's book *The Devoicing of Society* is reviewed. In his book, communications expert Locke suggests "that human voice and gesture provide constant feedback about the speakers' feelings, background, and trustworthiness. 'With no access to our species' social feedback and control mechanisms, there will be nothing to keep misunderstanding, incivility, and dishonesty from creeping into our daily life at unprecedented levels,' he says."(19)

As a leader, you know all too well how easily misunderstanding and dishonesty can spread within your own organization, and the ease with which they'll be able to spread will increase exponentially as you progress through the new millennium. We are not saying that you should think about going back to a pre-technological time; what we are saying is that with this new techno-age come new challenges. Don't ignore them.

Managing Across Borders

Cultural analysis is necessary for management across national and ethnic boundaries.

Merging organizations from different countries adds another layer of complexity. You not only are dealing with integration of the cultures of the two companies, you must also take into consideration the cultural differences on a national level. Do not confuse national culture with organizational culture, as they are two very different things. Remember the examples we offered earlier, such as DaimlerChrysler. We saw these issues firsthand when we worked with a French company that had acquired three American entities in three different U.S. locations. The French chose to make their American base in St. Louis, which left the other two entities part of the new system, but not as corporate headquarters. The French company began to enculturate the St. Louis plant, making changes in decor, style, management practices, and the sacred cafeteria. When employees from the other two locations came to the new corporate offices and saw that they were serving different food and wine in the cafeteria, well you can just imagine the reactions. Letters were written, people were outraged and in this case the grapevine went sour.

Building Walls

Your culture can create a tremendous barrier when trying to implement change. Organizational cultures typically do not change as rapidly as most of your strategic planning processes. Back in 1994, we were working with a division of a large international manufacturing firm. Up to that point, this particular group was the only manufacturer of automated medical devices. That's right, they had a monopoly. That all changed when, in 1995, competition moved in and began to eat away at the company's market share. Top managers pulled the leadership team together, conducted a retreat, and basically told the group that they had to change their way of doing business. The managers discovered that the current culture was unable to support the development and production of a quality product that would ward off the competition. Also, the current culture did not believe in paying attention to customer service. The attitude was, "We'll get to them when we're good and ready. We're the industry leader. People will wait."

Well, the customers didn't wait, and the competition began absorbing more and more of the firm's market share. Finally, the company really felt the pain and took drastic measures. It took the culture approximately three years to SHIFT from an arrogant "I don't care" posture to the attitude that the "customer is number one." In the meantime, the company had lost a significant percentage of the market share. When a customer is lost in this business (capital equipment), there is at least a four- to five-year lag before a company can even think of getting a customer back. Today, four years later, this company's market share is a dismal 48%. It has not been able to regain its position as the industry leader.

Labor Negotiations

Another area of cultural concern is labor relations. Labor unions can be viewed as subcultures within an organizational culture. They are highly organized groups with common objectives that unite employees, particularly on issues related to work rules and employment contracts.

Failure to consider the power and influence of these groups is foolish. In early 1999, the pilots' union orchestrated a pilot "sickout" at American Airlines to protest the plan to integrate the pilot group from recently acquired Reno Air. The action by American's pilots forced the second-largest air carrier to cancel approximately 6,700 flights over an eight-day period. This activity led to revenue losses that wiped out half of the airline's expected first-quarter profit, according to estimates by its parent, AMR Corporation. This "sickout" made everyone sick. Had

American Airlines' management carefully considered their pilots' differing cultural perception of themselves and of the Reno Air pilots, management would have realized that American's pilots wouldn't back down, and that if the pilots took action, the company would lose a bundle. The incident was a reminder that, even in this age of givebacks, unions still have power, and it emphasized that we should carefully consider how we negotiate with them and that culture plays a role in those negotiations.

Common Sense

For those of us who have been in the trenches and have seen companies come and go, paying attention to culture is as natural as brushing our teeth. It has become an ingrained habit that would now be difficult to modify. Yes, it seems like common sense, but you know how the saying goes: "Betty (Bob, Barb, or Bill) is so smart, but she (or he) doesn't have any common sense!" In some ways, it's helpful to think about icebergs: What you can't see CAN hurt you. The only one who might be able to reasonably dispute this is James Cameron, writer and director of the blockbuster film *Titanic*. That iceberg led to a multimillion-dollar triumph at the box office!

Shareholders

Let us not forget the shareholders. Shareholders do not hang on to losers. You must ensure that you have a culture that energizes your employees to produce stellar results consistently and over the long term, so that you don't become a has-been statistic. As a leader, you must be able to define your culture and how it is driving your results. In fact, we predict that in the very near future every company, large and small, will be required to have a type of Cultural Resume™, and it will become part of the annual strategic-planning process. Cultural assessment will become as important as the analysis of our financials. In fact, our research has made it very clear to us that investment bankers will be hesitant to enter into a deal if your proverbial cultural ducks are not in a row. Deals have been called off due to the lack of an integration plan, or when no heir apparent could be identified. So the recognition of culture's impact is certainly spreading to the front end of the deal.

Strategy

We are not saying that paying attention to your culture is **the end-all and be-all**. Without a sound business strategy, it doesn't matter what type of culture you create. Remember the Dallas-Chicago wrong map problem. Changing your attitude wouldn't be good enough. However, there is a key role that your culture can play in creating a more sound business strategy. You must examine your whole approach to "visioning" and strategic planning. If you are not involving a solid mix or cross section of employees from all levels and all areas, your strategy is less likely to be on target. And even if it is on target, the other challenge is implementing the plan, which demands employee involvement. Therefore, involve many employees from all levels within the organization.

We have found that the issue is not necessarily with the development of a sound strategy, but the inability to implement. Once the strategy gets into that three-ring binder, it's put on a shelf, and life goes on. This gives another meaning to shelf life. All we've accomplished is to kill more trees. As we stated in our "Call to Action," you, as a leader, must become an implementation instigator or execution expert. How do you make this happen? That's right, **through your people**. Plain and simple. Isn't this why you hired them and pay them a salary? You must get people at all levels excited and involved in making the strategy a reality.

The authors of the article "Why CEOs Fail," which we mentioned in "The Change Game," contend that the vast majority of top executives who fail do so because of one basic shortcoming: bad execution; "As simple as that: not getting things done, being indecisive, not delivering on commitments." (20) They go on to say that CEOs really blow it when they fail to put the right people in the right jobs and, more importantly, because they fail to fix people problems in time. (21) So, you must get all hands on deck and must create a culture that supports your implementation strategy and actually serves as the catalyst for making implementation a reality.

What we really need are the right specifications, or *SPECS*:

S **Strategy**—Get all the input you can and then do something meaningful with that information.

P **People**—Use your people wisely. Put the right people in the right jobs. Hold them accountable and take immediate action when necessary. Make sure everybody has the right attitude, not just the aptitude.

E **Education**—This means everybody, including yourself. Make sure you and your entire organization have the right tools to get the job done, and if you don't, go out and find them. Remember that one of your most critical tools is communication. Communicate openly and honestly—upwards, downwards, sideways. Encourage experimentation and foster learning.

C **Congruence**—You must ensure congruence within yourself first and then within your entire organization. You must translate your words into actions. What you say on paper must be a true reflection of how you behave as a business.

S **Shareholders**—These specifications will help you achieve a healthier bottom line and help keep Wall Street happy (at least for those who are public) or anyone else who has a stake in your business.

Six Recurring Themes of Highly Effective Cultures

So how do you recognize an effective culture when you see one? Over the years, we have seen some very strong recurrent themes in highly effective organizational cultures.

1. Future-proof

Organizations need to future-proof their businesses to ensure sustainability. In other words, you need to ask yourself, "Do you want to be around past your five-year strategic plan?" Stewart B. Clifford, Jr., in *The Excellence Files*, comments on the success of one company: "USAA is one of the largest insurance companies in the United States. Policyholders 'own' the company and are passionate about 'their' company. It has a customer loyalty and retention rate that is the envy of other insurers in the United States. USAA is aware that they are at the top, but they're not resting on their laurels. They are trying to stay ahead by 'Future-Proofing' their business. How did they do it? At the core, we find three elements: **1) continuous learning at all levels, 2) use of technology that empowers the front line, and 3) a culture that is never satisfied with the status quo.** The mission of every employee at USAA is to strive towards ever-faster, ever-better customer service." (22) USAA's employees are referred to as "members" and that there is an almost obsessive commitment to them. There is a pervasive belief that educated and empowered employees are the key to delivering superior customer service. This vision is still supported today and their success is evident by their continued growth and prosperity.

2. Resilient/Adaptable

This is WHOT radio station with the weather word. Partly cloudy tomorrow, with a chance of showers in the late afternoon. High of 73 degrees. Mostly sunny and warm on Friday. Just in time for the weekend.

We all read or hear forecasts like this every day. Young and old alike are interested in what the weather will be today, tomorrow, or on the weekend. Sometimes the forecasters are right. Sometimes they are wrong—completely wrong. They make their forecasts or predictions based on the best available information that they have. When they make an inaccurate prediction, they don't go home and decide to give up on all of the tools that they have been using to try a completely new way of forecasting. They just modify their methodology and continue to use the information and resources that are accurate most of the time.

They can be assured of one thing that remains constant: The weather is always changing. SHIFTs happen.

Organizations have their own weather systems or climates. Just as the weatherperson tries to accurately predict future weather scenarios, organizational leaders must constantly assess all of the factors that affect their climate and seek to sustain the most conducive climate for the well-being of both the organization and individual contributor.

Changes in organizational climate, which are also always present, can be beneficial or devastating. Just as a higher-than-average rainfall in the Arizona desert can add to seriously low water tables and decrease dependence on costly alternatives, the commitment to offer employee child care on site can positively affect employee recruitment and retention. A hurricane in Florida can devastate people, property, and crops in a matter of hours with an economic impact that may last for years. Similarly, a management decision to delay implementation of a risk-management program can have effects that are devastating in both the short and long term.

Although many of these climate factors cannot always be controlled or changed, they can be analyzed so that our predictions (planning) are more accurate. With reliable forecasts, for good or bad weather, we can better prepare ourselves for any "storms." On the corporate level, these storms can have an incredible economic impact. The complacency some leaders display, by failing to take action or make changes when they knowingly allow practices that are counter to their stated values (incongruencies), can be very damaging publicly and financially. The headlines of big-money settlements against Texaco or Denny's may come to mind. The recent headline news about the Bank of Boston's failure to promote women into the executive ranks is another example.

Winds SHIFT and so do people's minds. What impact does that have on your business? Lots. In *Culture Shift,* author and organizational change expert Price Pritchett says we now have "more people, more tools, and more knowledge. And here's the bottom line: Maybe you think you've seen a lot of change lately, but you haven't seen anything yet. The future promises us more change than we've ever experienced before, and it will come at us faster and faster. The question is, will we give our culture permission to change such that the organization can survive in a world of fast history?" (23)

Pritchett goes on to say, "In years past, we could get by with a slower response time. Change didn't move as fast back then. Competition wasn't as stiff. Also, the world gave us more room for recovery. There was enough space between major change events for people to catch their breath and collect their senses. Many of the 'normal' human reactions to the stress of change worked okay. Our old culture could cope. But those days belong in the history books now. A world of high-velocity change calls for radical shifts in behavior. Specifically, we must think differently. Reorder our priorities. Develop faster reflexes. Give the culture an entirely new set of responses." (24)

3. Fast

You must start collecting speeding tickets. You must not only be resilient and adaptable, you must be fast. Slow **is not safe.** Slow is not only dangerous, it is downright life-threatening. Today, it's instant everything—pudding, potatoes, photographs, you name it. The June-July 1999 issue of *The Futurist* reports an insight offered by Joshua Isenberg of The Food Channel who says, "The *Jetsons*-like fantasy of the self-operating kitchen just got a little closer to becoming a reality." (25) The article goes on to describe new technology that allows appliances to network and process information on line. There is even a new intelligent icebox by Frigidaire that can automatically inventory and restock itself. (26) We have entered a time when automation and speed are expected.

4. Gutsy

You must be nervy and gutsy. Your organization must be willing to take risks; and as a leader you must encourage, foster, and create the right environment to cultivate that mind-set. Imagination + creativity + guts

= innovation. Businesses are scrambling to survive and are constantly worried about the future.

What worked in the past won't necessarily work in the future. In order to thrive in the future, you must constantly create new ideas for every aspect of your business. You must continually generate new ideas just to keep your head above water. Businesses that are not creative and innovative about their future may not survive. In order to do this, successful companies are creating a culture where *innovation, invention, agility, and creativity are fostered* and, more importantly, they are allowing the work force to reinvent the company, over and over again, involving them in future "visioning" of the company. Take the story of three bricklayers: The first says, "I'm laying bricks." The second says, "I'm making a wall." However, the third says, "I'm building a cathedral." The third bricklayer is what you will find in companies that are ready for change. Employees like this are capable of seeing beyond the bricks and want to be contributors in creating the future for their organizations.

The 3M Company has a 15% rule: Employees are encouraged to spend 15% of their time developing new ideas on any project that they desire. This fosters individual creativity and innovation. It also speaks to a company culture that allows and encourages those values, behaviors, and activities. It allows the individual to create and to act as not only an individual contributor, but also as part of a visionary team, where everyone is encouraged to create and dream. The creation of Post-It Notes is an excellent example of the effectiveness of this process. As the story goes, the glue on the back of the paper was a mistake, but the company was open to new ideas, and made the decision to see the "mistake" through the process of product development and production. Well, we all know how that mistake turned out. Most of us have at least one or two packs kicking around the office. In fact, you might even mark this page with one, just to come back to this example. It's no surprise then that, even though 3M has been around since 1902, it continues to prosper.

5. Community Involvement

Some companies are more community-minded than others. Timberland is a good example of a company that values community involvement. As described by Clifford in *The Excellence Files*,

"Timberland is a family-owned company noted for tremendous growth in the competitive world of manufacturing clothes. The company attributes its success to three factors:

- Manufacture of high-quality products,
- Leveraging that quality into brand development and into a wide range of products, and
- Creating an organization that allows people to remain committed to their communities as part of their 'whole person' strategy.

"Timberland calls this commitment 'Boot, Brand, and Belief.'" (27)

The company has created an environment where employees feel more committed to Timberland as a result of its efforts to recognize and support the employees' outside interests and values. This community involvement also delivers benefits in customer relations. Commitment to the employees, to the community as a whole, and to the environment can increase your market share and profit margins. Many individuals desire to work in this type of organizational culture. They support it and commit to it. It is easy then to see why some companies with such strong convictions have an easier time in recruiting and retaining a strong work force.

6. Celebrate Diversity

Successful companies today not only embrace, but also celebrate diversity and have expanded the term "diversity" to extend beyond race, gender, national origin, and religion. In fact, back in 1994, Ed Mickens wrote a book titled *The 100 Best Companies for Gay Men and Lesbians*. This book reports on companies that openly value homosexuals. Mickens believes that "organizations that address lesbian and gay issues demonstrate a willingness to listen and respond to the concerns of all their employees." (28) Individuals want to fit in and often seek out work environments that have values that are the same or similar to their own. People want to work in a culture that values them as individuals and they, in turn, will value the company's commitment to uphold those values.

Is There a Right Culture?

Here is the sixty-four thousand dollar question. Well, there are many schools of thought on this topic. Some insist that all organizations have a culture and that no one set of cultural characteristics is more "right" than others. They are absolutely correct when they are referring to cultural characteristics. Cultural characteristics (our interpretation) are things like assumptions; norms; history; stories; regional, national, and international scope; customs; traditions; rituals; and organized labor groups. These are the things that make each of our organizations unique, and no one culture from this perspective is any more "right" than the other.

However, we have found that there are certain homogeneous cultural elements in highly successful organizations. These factors are more about values than about organizational characteristics.

We have really struggled with the fact that things are improving ever so slowly in organizations today. As we were writing this book we continued to ask ourselves the all-important question: Why? Why do organizational change strategies continue to fail? What's not working? What's missing? It finally hit us like a bolt of lightning. The key element that is typically absent in most of organizations is trust. As described here, lack of trust is a symptom and results from not being honest and consistent in our actions as a leader; therefore in order to eliminate this symptom we must ACT (A+C=T): Authenticity + Congruence = Trust. When your employees see that you are sincere and congruent in what you say and do then they begin to trust you but not before this occurs.

Whether you're considering boundaryless organizations, open-book management, employee involvement, or delegation and the like, none of them can be implemented successfully without a high level of trust. It is the missing link. In your personal life, you trust your partner so you will have a fulfilling and equal relationship, you seek out the trusted auto mechanic so you will not get ripped off, and we venture to guess that **some of you** will not try the new restaurant on the corner until someone you trust has tried it and liked it. This quest for trust holds true in your professional life as well.

In your organization, you must be able to trust each other. You must be able to function with the same values and purpose, count on each other during the rough times, be able to "tell it like it is," and work together with mutual respect. This is where it all begins. This is the glue, not our culture, but our trustworthiness. Oren Harari, author, lecturer, and management advisor, spoke to this in the January 1999 issue of *Management Review,* saying, "Trust is powerful. It is the glue that binds people together as they work in ambiguous, uncertain environments in ambiguous, uncertain times. It is also at the root of a leader's credibility or lack thereof." (29) Without trust, honest communication becomes a self-canceling oxymoron and stated goals of empowering people and pushing authority downward fall far short of the mark. Organizations that are marked by a lot of internal distrust are typically organizations that are in decline.

A few years back, we were working with a client who was very frustrated with his change efforts. It seemed as though every change he tried to implement met with great resistance. His conclusion was there was a *lack of communication.* After conducting a cultural assessment, it became extremely obvious to him, his management team, and us that communication was not the root cause of the problem but rather lack of trust was the core issue. Merely increasing the level of communication would not have rectified the problem because no one trusted the information. The solution? We began to create opportunities for the CEO and the management team to begin to gain the trust of the work force. One of the powerful ways that we did this was to modify the quarterly town hall meetings (meetings with the entire work force). The format originally was very vanilla—each member of the management team stood up in their starched shirts behind a podium and presented the results of their department on slick overheads. The audience was not the least bit interested and certainly not engaged.

We recommended that they move to a more interactive process and start getting at the heart of what the real issues were. The management team agreed and the next town hall was held as an open forum. The entire management team sat in a circle in the middle of the room and received questions from the employee population. Recognizing that there would be much apprehension from the workforce to stand and openly direct questions to the management team, we provided them (the employees) with a safe place for getting their questions answered. The training manager facilitated the meetings and ground rules were shared with everyone. Paper and pencils were placed on each chair providing anonymity for any employee who was interested in asking the tough questions. The question was then sent down to the facilitator who directed the question to the management team.

The first meeting of this kind was very successful; however, 75% of the questions were written, although the dialog was very open. Within six months, the trust level was shifting, so much so, that 75% of the questions were now being verbally presented to the management team and 25% were handwritten. The management team was willing to be vulnerable, open, and honest enough to say that they, as managers, did not have the answer to a particular question. This helped raise the management team's credibility significantly. This alone did not change the trust levels in the organization; however, it was a key intervention that contributed to the improvement. The management team begun to A.C.T. (Authenticity + Congruence = Trust).

In order for you to build trust with your people, you must be trustworthy. This takes time, and it doesn't preclude the possibility that you might have to train and develop people so that their skills can rise to the level of your trust. As a leader, your ultimate task is to develop trust, and not fear, in your employees. We are not talking about a one-time thing. You can't decide to build trust when it's convenient for you, say when a key change initiative is about to occur. Trust must be woven into the fabric of your culture. It's what keeps all the pieces together and makes them work. We talked earlier about assumptions and how they create the stories, which in turn create certain behaviors which then defines your culture. Well, in order to change from a culture of fear to a culture of trust, you must change the assumptions. The way to accomplish this is through your actions—over time. Do not expect things to change overnight. Remember, your actions translate into stories, and the stories create assumptions, and assumptions create behaviors which define your culture. If you want to create a culture of trust, you must acquire new skills, to start building relationships without fear. How many of you have been in a conversation with someone who said, "Let's be honest about this"? What was that person really saying? "Hey! For the last 15 minutes, I have been blowing blue smoke at you, and now I want to qualify that I am about to tell the truth." This tends to put many of us on edge. So you can't, out of thin air, change a culture of distrust to one of trust. As we discussed in "The Change Game," you must be willing to look within and make changes in your own thinking about employees and the role they play in your organization.

Once trust has been established, there are a number of other key elements that we have found must exist in order for organizations to remain healthy and produce healthy profit margins.

- **Authenticity and Congruence**—Successful companies have more than a set of core organizational values that are printed and distributed to the work force. Their core organizational values are in sync with their actions. Their core organizational values are evident in their daily activities, so that no hidden culture develops. Leaders in these organizations tell the truth!!

- **Sociability and Solidarity**—Your culture must strike a balance between the self-interests of individuals and the needs of your organization.

- **Open Organizational Culture**—You must remove the bureaucratic nonsense. All bureaucracy does is create barriers, not clarity. The leadership role must be shared. This does not mean that you should abdicate to the work force your role as a leader. What it does mean is that you must begin seeing your relationship with other members of your organization as a partnership. It also means:

  - Working in collaboration with one another, it doesn't matter at what level;

  - Sharing honest information, quickly disseminating ideas throughout the organization, and pulling teams together quickly to do something with the new knowledge;

  - Encouraging autonomy and entrepreneurship;

  - Sharing in the decision-making process; and

  - Holding everyone accountable for his or her actions, including yourself.

- **Innovation**—Many leaders talk about creativity and innovation synonymously when, in fact, they are very different. Being creative means coming up with the idea, while innovation is taking that idea and making changes. When you are innovative, you are actually modifying how you do what you do. What does this take? It takes a culture that:

  - Views learning as an ongoing process, shares knowledge, and provides the right tools;

  - Advocates risk-taking and rewards it;

  - Encourages people to constantly challenge the process and take steps to create something new; and

- Invites conflict. Innovative organizations see conflict as a very positive and creative process. In this type of culture, perpetual change is a stable element. Intel is a great example of this value.

- **Customer is #1 Focus**—Without the customer, without your fans, you have no business.

The CREW

We'd like to share a story with you about a business owner who has created a very lucrative business by making the customer Number One. Because we both have insatiable appetites for great food and fine wine, you could say we are culinary junkies, we often frequent a local restaurant called Crew An Eat Place. We realized that there was something magical going on in this place. So after the second time we dined there, we started doing more observing between each bite.

What we found—no, actually, what we felt—was that not only was the food delicious, but the service was impeccable. The staff was very friendly, and the manager went out of his way to say "hello" to everyone. Not just the phony, "Hello! How is everything this evening?" but a genuine hello, making reference to the customer's last visit or some small piece of information the customer may have shared on that visit. We always have a wonderful dining experience when we eat there. So, we decided to talk to Jim Petrillo, founder and owner, and find out what his secret was. We also wanted to test our theory and assumptions about key cultural elements on a small, non-corporate enterprise.

He was thrilled to be a part of this book project. "Why me?" he asked. We chose Jim for a number of reasons: a) We knew something powerful was happening at Crew; b) We realized whether one owns a restaurant, or a football team, or an international high tech firm, everyone is striving for the same thing: to make money, and in order to make that money, you have to have return customers; and c) He seemed to have all the right stuff: good food, energized staff, and profitability.

When we met with him, it was no surprise to find that Jim holds the customer in high esteem. The customer is Number One. "Customers are viewed by all employees as guests. Employees view where they work not as a restaurant, but as their own home, and the people who come in to dine are seen as their guests." OK, so that's why we feel so welcomed when we come to dine. The next question was, "How do you get the entire staff on board?"

"Very easy. First, I have created a very trusting environment. My employees may not always like my decisions, but they know that I am fair and consistent or, as you say, congruent.

"Over the years, I have found this to be the most powerful tool as a leader. I involve my employees. Everyday before opening, we have a meeting called 'roundup.' Here, we talk honestly and openly about whatever's on people's minds. We discuss dinner specials and promotions, service-setup issues, number of reservations, staffing issues, Q&A and feedback on any and all topics. Oh, and yes, we spend five minutes food-tasting and, sometimes, wine-tasting. Everybody loves that part."

The next important step in creating the team and solidifying the buy-in is the training program. No one hits the floor without a full five days of training. "It doesn't matter if you used to work at 'chez de-poo-poo,' Morton's, or a local Outback, everyone gets the same amount of training." Then, there are the daily written tests. Not only does the content focus on the area the employee trained in that day, but it also includes questions about the history of Crew, what the photos on the wall stand for, and information about the local area. These are all seen as an important part of the organization. "The tests are pass/fail. If you pass, you move on to the next rotation, fail and you repeat that station the next night." This may seem costly in the restaurant business, but it is only the upfront cost. "This process weeds out the employees who think they are above all this training stuff. It is not about the skill level, it is about the employee's attitude and aptitude. With everyone going through this process, we all start out on a level playing field, and we all have the same expectations of our fellow workers."

Jim went on to say that removing the bureaucratic B.S. really puts everyone on the same playing field. "I have no big office, and there are no levels. We really do share the leadership role, and we all know what the expectations are. This helps reduce the level of frustration and builds confidence. It's amazing to see how many of my crew members have grown up in this organization. Nothing gives me more satisfaction and pride as a leader than to watch others shine." (30)

Jim has really found the formula for creating a high-energy work environment. He teaches, guides, facilitates, and treats all his employees with respect. He is also willing to go the extra mile. His employees love working for him, so much so, that some of his crew followed him from Washington, D.C., to Scottsdale, Arizona. How's that for dedication? We've included a recent ad (facing page) that we feel really tells the story about what he has created. And, as his guests, we get to share in that accomplishment.

Without these key elements your organization will constantly struggle to stay alive. Let's face it, even creating this type of culture does not **guarantee** your ongoing success. And, as a leader, you have choices, and you can either learn lessons from those who are experiencing positive outcomes, or you can continue to go down your own path ending up with the same old, same old.

If you stop and think about it, there are many lessons that you can learn from your own childhood. As Robert Fulghum puts it in his famous book, *All I Really Need to Know I Learned in Kindergarten: Uncommon Thoughts on Common Things:*

"Most of what I really need to know about how to live and what to do and how to be I learned in kindergarten. Wisdom was not at the top of the graduate-school mountain, but there in the sand pile at Sunday School. These are the things I learned:

"Share everything.

"Play fair.

"Don't hit people.

"Put things back where you found them.

the crew that cooks
together stays together

People in a relationship this close are either very
disturbed or embrace a common vision.
We happen to embrace a common vision: that of
cooking good food and serving it
in a nice environment. We did it for years
in kind of a hep place back east.
Then we traveled here. In unison. Collectively.
As one. And no, we are not disturbed.

480 488 8840
el Pedregal at the Boulders

"Clean up your own mess.

"Don't take things that aren't yours.

"Say you're sorry when you hurt somebody.

"Wash your hands before you eat.

"Flush.

"Warm cookies and cold milk are good for you.

"Live a balanced life—learn some and think some and draw and paint and sing and dance and play and work every day some.

"When you go out into the world, watch out for traffic, hold hands, and stick together.

"Be aware of wonder. Remember the little seed in the Styrofoam cup: The roots go down and the plant goes up and nobody really knows how or why, but we are all like that.

"Goldfish and hamsters and white mice and even the little seed in the Styrofoam cup—they all die. So do we.

"And then remember the Dick-and-Jane books and the first word you learned—the biggest word of all—LOOK." (31)

Is this tough for you to swallow? Is it oversimplifying your complex and complicated life? We challenge you to take the time to reflect on what Fulghum has said. When you come right down to it, when you think about the type of culture you want to create for your organization, it's about treating others the way you would want to be treated. It's about mutual respect and trust. It's about telling the truth. It's about standing up for what you believe in, whether you are in a boardroom or out talking to the masses. It's about being authentic. You must pay attention to your people. They are the culture. They make things happen in your organization, including improving profit margins. So, respect everyone in your organization, for they can all be contributors and together make great things happen—raise that bottom line!

Leadership and Culture

By Lizz Pellet

Once we are convinced that the culture in our organization is important and that a cultural assessment is a must do and a cultural shift is in order, then the next big step is recognizing the key role that leadership plays in this process.

As leaders we must start by being authentic. We need the real thing. We must be congruent. Remember to A.C.T. (Authenticity + Congruence = Trust).

If we say we value employee involvement, then employees must see that in our actions. Organizational cultures begin with us—the leaders. Therefore, the real challenge for us as leaders is to be able to step outside ourselves. We need to recognize the influence we have over organizations and develop a mechanism for constantly testing our own beliefs, values, and assumptions.

The development of an effective culture will require our undivided attention. In fact, Edgar Schein states: "Leadership is the attitude and motivation to examine and manage culture." (1)

Managers must also be involved in the creation and evolution of cultures, but sometimes they spend an inordinate amount of time destroying them. Watch for those individuals, and take immediate action.

We believe that the values held by the leader of an organization reflect the values of the organization—and those values create the culture. Or is it vice versa? Does a leader typically embrace the values of an organization as his or her own? When we asked leaders, "so what are your values?" we heard many answers. Often, we heard about honesty, teamwork, and employee involvement. When we asked about the values of the organization, we heard the same words. However, sometimes the people we talked to really didn't seem to have a clear sense of their personal values, yet they believed that they and the company had "shared values" (or values in common). Wait a minute, now. How can you share something that you do not have? And what does that expression "shared values" really mean? Does it mean you shared thoughts when developing them? Does it mean you and other members of the organization agree in principle on how the company goes about doing business? Does it mean one value for you, one for the organization, another value for you... and so on?

We're not sure what some people mean or what they think they mean. But we know that what we, as leaders, believe in and value creates the culture of our organization. Although some contemporary psychologists claim that the corporate world is driven by unconscious, destructive, and unresolved emotional processes, we believe that most leaders simply are not in touch with their personal values—what some people are calling "authenticity." Evidence of this theory can be seen in the rising trend toward *self-discovery* in corporate America. In "A Leader's Journey," an article for *Fast Company,* author Pamela Kruger interviews Paul Wieand, founder of the Center for Advanced Emotional

Intelligence (AEI). After a devastating experience in the banking industry, Wieand decided to rethink his approach to leadership. As a result, he started AEI. "Its goal," according to Wieand, "is to turn ultra-achievers into 'learning leaders'—people with enough self-knowledge and emotional security to remain true to their authentic selves and also to grow from criticism." (2)

This concept is catching on. "Congruence" and "authenticity" are no longer words used strictly in psychological circles. They are finding their way into the inner offices, outer offices, and boardrooms. Authenticity is a critical factor in leadership. "The truly authentic leaders are open both to their gifts and to their underdeveloped qualities. People who understand who they are tend to have a more powerful voice— and to make a more profound contribution to an enterprise." Kevin, founder and CEO of Leadersource, suggests, "Get in the habit of asking yourself two crucial questions: 'Why do I pursue the work and the life that I do?' And, 'What do I act like during the most fulfilling times of my life?'" (3) We can all heed this advice.

One thing to remember about being authentic is that many times people can see through you when you are not. They can see when your actions do not match your words. They can hear it when they overhear you discussing a sensitive issue with someone and they hear you give this other person the exact opposite story from what you had told them earlier. "Let's be honest here." You hire a lot of smart people to work with you, and these smart people can see right through the smoke and the mirrors. If you put on a show long enough, these smart folks will tire and move on.

When I was working as a line manager, the one thing I always told my management team was: "Say what you mean, and mean what you say. This is the only way to be real, to be heard, and to be understood." I was giving them straight communication and being authentic. Forget the sugar coating, forget the hard charge, forget the power trip—speak from your gut.

Notice I didn't say, "Speak from your heart"—that would be too touchy-feely, but it would be correct. The reason why many of us as leaders cannot tell people what they feel is because most of us are Thinkers, not Feelers. As mentioned in "Can We Talk—CEO to CEO?" 80% of all leaders (CEOs) are ISTJs in the Myers-Briggs Type Indicator (MBTI). Introverted, Sensing, Thinking, Judger. No F there.

Differences are a Plus

P.J. and I are opposite types according to the MBTI assessment, with the exception of being classified as "Extraverts" (MBTI's spelling, not ours) because we both love to talk and both get our energy from the outside world. But all of the other preferences are opposites. Imagine working in a shared leadership position where you and your business partner have opposite preferences—not so much styles, but different ways of processing information and relating to the world. One individual is creative, involving, full of new ideas and endless possibilities, nurturing, and understanding of other people's feelings and emotions. This type is the life of the party, eternally optimistic, and starts way more projects than will ever be finished. The other individual is focused on the sequence, terminally serious, opinionated, tuned into the facts, justice, and the pursuit of order and power. These types are life's administrators—driven by results and hard charging. Observing a strategy meeting between these two types could be like watching a "T-bone" car wreck at an intersection.

Fortunately, we understand the differences and use them as strengths for our professional partnership instead of viewing them as a challenge. It's a lot like the ability to see the glass half-full and half-empty at the same time; the chance to make lemonade from lemons, even in the off-season; the chance to open your mind to new and different concepts; the chance to see things as they really are.

It's all a matter of choice. The reality is that there are multiple points of view on almost any issue. As leaders, we can choose to see the glass any damn way we want. However, what we choose to see isn't an absolute truth, but a reflection of our training and preferences. Conversely, listening to people gives us a chance to see another aspect of reality. Their points of view have validity and shouldn't be dismissed out of hand. So, the secret to making the best choices is to surround ourselves with people who see all sorts of things, and then to be open enough to feedback, new concepts, and feelings to allow them to seep in. Moving to this style of leadership may be a big SHIFT for some. It may be like moving through sludge at first—slowly, ever so slowly. But if you allow this type of feedback in, it does not have to overcome you. You can control the flow and the direction that will inevitably affect the outcome.

The Leadership Kit

Too hocus-pocus for you? Of course not. *Fast Company* compiled a great "how to be a leader kit"—a step-by-step approach to making yourself into a good leader. As they say, "Remember leaders are made, not born." Here is a short version of their kit:

- Leaders are both confident and modest. Healthy ego, but strong enough to check it at the door.

- Leaders are authentic. Earn the trust and respect of the people you work with. Who believes in leaders who don't believe in themselves?

- Leaders are listeners. Be curious about other people, watch out for grandiosity.

- Leaders are good at giving encouragement, and they are never satisfied. Always raise the stakes of the game for you and your people.

- Leaders make unexpected connections. They see patterns that allow for small innovations and breakthrough ideas.

- Leaders provide direction. That is different from providing the answer. Reminder: You're not in control, and you're not really in charge—but you are in touch and you are out front.

- Leaders protect their people from danger—and expose them to reality. Don't insulate—mobilize.

- Leaders make change—and stand for values that don't change. Help people identify what habits and assumptions must be changed for the company to prosper and... which values and operations are so central to our core that if we lose them we lose ourselves.

- Leaders lead by example. They use small gestures to send big messages. Remember: You are always under a microscope.

- Leaders don't blame—they learn. Even the smartest business people around make mistakes. The right mind-set is an experimental mind-set: Try, fail, learn, and try again.

- Leaders look for and network with other leaders. Stop playing the role of the Lone Ranger! Look for allies, and help others.

- The job of the leader: Make more leaders. That is the ultimate task. (4)

As you can see, the underlying theme of the list is being real (or authentic) and open to change. This means allowing your true self—the one who usually only speaks to you late at night when the covers are up around your nose—to be heard, to be felt, to be released without the fear of embarrassment or humiliation. To achieve a flexible yet resilient identity we have to look inward, that's where it rests. To be a truly great leader, we must look inward, that's where the real person, the self, is located. We need to identify and accept our limitations, be willing to explore and be open to change.

'I Can' Beats IQ

Psychological research has shown that by the time we reach our mid-thirties, our identity solidifies, making change intolerable. For instance, I (ESTJ) entered a fellowship program at Johns Hopkins University to study organizational change. I was looking for a cookie-cutter approach to change. The program was designed to teach leaders about change and how to apply that change in organizations, which sounds easy enough. What I found was a program that focused on "self" and on how you cannot begin to effect organizational change without understanding **yourself** and how **you** deal with change.

Let me tell you, I wanted to quit after the first weekend. I had no intention of sitting around for eighteen weekends with twenty-six strangers, standing naked in front of the mirror with everyone watching me. I could hardly stand to look in the mirror when I was alone, so who needed an audience? I wasn't the only one feeling the pain. As my classmates and I shared stories, I discovered that many other people were experiencing the same feelings: frustration, fear of failure, fear of being discovered, and anger towards the education staff. These were all normal growing pains. You know the saying: "No pain, no gain." This group was feeling the pain in a big way. One individual even likened the experience to torture. However, we had to learn that the program wasn't just about looking at ourselves, which was painful enough. The program was intent on making us discover ourselves.

I began to experience a real metamorphosis. As I participated in the exercises, I began to notice that I felt like an outsider looking in. I was physically in the room, but I was watching myself talk to the group. I knew this person doing the talking was me, but it did not "feel" like me. I have come to understand that whole phenomenon. I had never "felt." You know, that F word. In business, we rarely ask each other, "So what did you feel about that?" No. We're more likely to ask, "So what did you think?" Herein lies the problem with us as leaders: We use only our heads and our guts, never our hearts, so we do not have to feel.

Say you have just broken a bone, and during the diagnostic exam, the Emergency Room doc asks you, "Does that hurt?"—while applying pressure to the affected area. "Ooohhhhhhccch! Yeah, Doc. That hurts," you respond. Now, did you **think** you felt the pain or did you really **feel it?** We so often associate pain with feeling that it is no wonder that we don't want to go down that path.

The Johns Hopkins program, like many "growth" programs that are out there today, helped me view my world differently, helped me look inside myself, or outside myself as the case was. And I saw that what was coming out of my mouth did not connect with my heart. Throughout my life, I had been speaking from my head and dancing fast so that no one could peer through the veil at my raw emotions or that constant lump in my throat. I thought this was what a good leader did: Give the people what they want. Everyone—from the management team to the line employees to the shareholders—always got a dog and pony show. I was very good at it. "That's how you get to be the boss; that's how you get to be at the top of your game," I thought. Although doing that dance may be the only way to go in some situations, being authentic is much more powerful and gratifying—and it does not have to cause you any pain at all.

I completed my metamorphosis with a much greater understanding of myself (and the general concept of "self"). I had to say goodbye to some very ingrained habits. I had to stop acting like I was listening to someone, while I was actually just formulating what I wanted to say next. I had to climb down quite a few pegs before climbing back up again. I had to see that all my life I had been one of the greatest bullshitters to hit the boardroom, and I had to stop using humor as a cover for my real feelings. Everything was not a joke, even though that is how I had played it for so many years. I recalled that back in high school I was chosen "class clown" in my senior year. That made me stop and think: "Man, this stuff goes way back, way back."

Transform Yourself

But there is always an opportunity for change. We just have to be willing to stand still long enough, to take a deep breath, look in the mirror and allow it to happen. We must open our eyes, our hearts, and even our souls to different perspectives, challenges and experts. They are out there, everywhere. They may be sharing the office next door; maybe they have just written a great book; maybe it's the person who cuts our hair; our golf partner. We just have to be open to change and keep our ear to the ground listening for opportunities.

You may want to consider engaging an executive coach to help you through the transformation process. This is a great way to get to the issues in a safe environment: one on one, without an audience. Through successful coaching, personal behaviors can be changed dramatically. A coach can help you get to the roots of your frames of reference and ways of being.

Discovery Can Mean Change

So, what was the outcome of the Johns Hopkins program for me? First, I realized I was in the wrong job. I could no longer just keep on keepin' on. I had gone through this experience of self-discovery, of finding self-worth, and understanding my values, and now I was ready to apply this knowledge to every facet of my life. If I wanted to stay with the organization, then I would have to make a change—and I did. I transferred to another department where I thought my contributions to the organization would be greater.

Not long after my move, some incongruencies began to surface. One example was the issue of diversity. The corporation had just released "New Company Values," and the values did not fit the way some individuals were being treated. You know the old routine: "Well, this is the policy, but we overlook it for some and not for others." As I sat in the "great hall" and listened to the CEO of the whole corporation (who had bestowed his almighty presence on us all the way from head-quarters) give his "Rah-rah! We are all in this together" speech, it hit me. I looked around and saw nothing but blank-void-cheering faces. As I listened to the hollow words, "We value this... We value that... We are one big team who will... blah, blah, blah," I knew I could no longer work for this organization. To stay I would have been incongruent with myself. I would not have been authentic. I would have been like many of the other managers who just turned their heads away from the situation and said, "Ain't that stock doing great? We are sure to split soon." All of a sudden, I felt like a corporate "Stepford wife," a drone who would do whatever was best for the company, everything for the company, regardless of whether it was congruent with my personal beliefs and values.

Soon after this meeting, I joined the ranks of "Free Agent Nation" and set up a consulting firm. Now, this was a huge leap—not of faith, because I knew the business would work out. However, it was a leap into the uncomfortable zone. Remember that I am the STJ. I can't live without rules, order, structure, and loyalty. Leaving an organization without my gold watch was difficult, but the hardest part was the ambiguity of the whole situation. How do you find clients? How do you build trust with someone you have no history with? How the heck do you close a deal? These were all new questions, the great unknown. The only ambiguity I was comfortable with in those days was taking something out of the freezer that I had forgotten to label! Mystery dinner! That's about as far as I would go. No way would I let something so mysterious happen in my professional life. But then I thought back to Hopkins, I wanted the real self to guide my head for a change. So that was the first noticeable change.

Many other things changed as well and not just in my professional life. My new sense of self helped my personal life tremendously. I also ended the ego trip that had started so long ago. I stopped looking at the destination and made a decision to enjoy the journey, wherever that might take me.

Did this affect my leadership style? You can bet your corner office it did! I was no longer worried about impressing people. I was more interested in mutual issues than making sure my needs were met. I was more engaged in listening than in speaking to hear myself speak and make sure I was heard. This has made a difference in our business. People want to work with us because of the values, ethics, morals, and culture of our organization. We have stuck our stick in the sand at times and said:

"No, we will not take the contract. We cannot work with that client. Their values are not in line. They are talking out of both sides of their mouth. They are not congruent." And every time we have turned a client down, there has been another one, a bigger one, or a different one, and it has turned out to be a greater learning and growth experience for both our company and the client.

Lone Ranger's Last Ride?

The other very important change I made was in sharing the power. P.J. Bouchard and I are true business partners and co-leaders. We share the risks, the responsibilities, and the glory. This type of arrangement is not meant for everyone. Again, it's the yin and yang. You have to recognize your own strengths, weaknesses, opportunities, and challenges before taking on this type of arrangement.

What's interesting is that our power-sharing arrangement mirrors a growing trend in corporate America. This is a SHIFT toward the kind of leadership we advocate in ALL situations, not just power-sharing relationships. Co-leadership is based on partnership and commitment to the success of the whole group, not just one individual, or one division, or one function. You can't share power if you're insecure or insincere. And maybe, just, maybe, corporate America is waking up to the value of having authentic leaders who are willing to communicate and share power.

We're convinced that leaders will HAVE to learn to share power, control, and glory—not to mention money. We expect this trend to continue and force a SHIFT in the focus of MBA programs and in management styles across the board.

As sighted in numerous articles, much of this power-sharing trend stems from the increase in mergers and acquisitions, which has caused many shareholders to conclude that two heads are better than one. However, power sharing can't be a willy-nilly arrangement. It requires a very special dynamic, and two strong individuals who must be comfortable with "self" in order to be able to give up full reign and allow someone else to take part in the steering. There also must be a clear and unified vision of where the company is headed, established goals, and a mechanism in place to avoid redundancies in responsibilities, as well as a clear delineation of strengths. Megamergers have married not just giant businesses, but senior executives, creating newlywed cultures, with all their adjustment pains, at such recently merged companies as Citigroup and DaimlerChrylser—and at ExxonMobil.

In the case of a merger, power sharing is the most economical way to integrate the two companies. It comes down to knowledge economy. Why forfeit some of the most important intellectual capital in the company? Years of experience, client relationships, product knowledge, history, executive recruitment, and leadership development cannot be replaced overnight. And when you complete an acquisition, does there have to be one "heir apparent?" Not necessarily.

There are examples of co-CEO partnerships that have worked well. Goldman, Sachs & Co. has had three such arrangements in the past three decades. IBM's 1995 acquisition of Lotus is another example. In an article for *Management Review* titled "From Merger to Marriage," author Jeff Papows describes the integration process:

> "A task force was quickly established of 35 senior representatives form both companies, who made the merger a marriage. Following the departure of Lotus CEO Jim Manzi, it would

have been logical for IBM to quickly put one of its own in charge. But the new IBM was different. Within 24 hours of Jim's departure, IBM named me and my colleague Mike Zisman as corporate co-presidents, thereby assuring the rank and file at Lotus that IBM had no desire or hidden agenda to make us over in its own image." (5)

Smart move. The rank and file are the ones who move the company—the leaders are only the drivers. Co-leadership means an equal partnership with similar values and vision, and that is what will drive success or failure.

Papows went on to say, "Today, we have overcome the cynicism that greeted the merger. IBM has provided the autonomy and identity we need to do things we could not have achieved as a smaller company. Our success is being built on mutual respect and shared vision of what we can accomplish together." (6)

Citigroup, the Citicorp/Travelers Group merger, is being led by co-CEOs Sanford Weill and John Reed, and is doing quite well as we write this book. There are some experts out there who assert that, without such a power-sharing arrangement, the deal could not have gotten done in the first place. Power players Weill and Reed know the arrangement may not last forever, and they have said publicly that at some point it will be healthy for the company to do a hand-over, where one of them (if not both) will have to go, to prove to stakeholders that the merger is successful.

To succeed, co-leaderships have to tread lightly at first. Co-leadership situations remind me of a couple going into a second marriage and trying to blend their families. They have to be very careful to avoid even the appearance that one side is winning in the deal and the other is losing. Often, this is accomplished by taking things away from both sides.

Although mergers are most commonly called off because of financial considerations, some mergers have been nixed because of the inability to choose a CEO successor or formulate a co-leadership plan.

In 1998, the proposed $165 billion merger between Glaxo Wellcome and Smith Kline Beecham fell apart when the two firms' bosses, Sir Richard Sydes and Jan Leschly, could not agree on who would become CEO. Sometimes it does come down to the financial risks, and sometimes it is the personality and leadership styles of the individual. It is hard to release control when you have held the lead position for a long time. There's an old dog-sled adage about leading the pack: "If you are not the lead dog, well, the view just ain't so great!"

The whole organizational culture begins and ends with us as leaders. We have the opportunity to create, shape, and mold an organization's values, and those values map how the work really gets done. It's our corner of the world, if you will. That is a great responsibility. Just think of all the individuals who work for your company and how much influence you have with those folks. Some would say you have power over them, and that is true. Power may be the infinite game (as psychologists Michael F. Broom and Donald C. Klein maintain in their book, *Power: The Infinite Game,* a good book on organizational power), but we are talking about values and the need to be authentic. It is in values and authenticity that you can find the greatest opportunity to be a true leader and have the greatest influence on many.

Board Hits CEO, Leaves no Splinters

You are probably saying, "I may be the leader and I may have the power, but I report to the Board. They are the governing body in this organization."

That may be true, depending on your organization.

Some boards have more influence, more control than others. In "The Cultural Assessment Process," we map out the CEO-board relationship, identify the keys to success in this relationship, and look at what constitutes a good board. But before we leave this section on values and authenticity, I need to share a CEO-board experience. As I've said, the

CEO is the culture, which really means the CEO embodies the culture. Can the CEO embody the culture if it's not based on his authentic values and self? Sure, the CEO can put on a false face and do the ritual dance of homage to values he doesn't embrace, but sooner or later, he must wake up like I did. The following story of a clash between a CEO and a Chairman of the Board points up the dangers of being inauthentic, and the pain that people can be spared when we clearly understand and act upon our values.

P.J. and I worked with a company that needed a change agent— someone to help the CEO drive change and reshape the company into a learning organization. The company had been working with one of the larger consulting firms, but the relationship did not work out. After a year of consulting services, no "real" change had occurred. The clients had spent a boatload of money to have someone come in and tell them what to do, but could see no tangible results. No major SHIFT in employee behavior occurred, profit margins were not up, and the dead wood they knew they had was still floating through the corridors. When we looked, it turned out the consultant was not the real issue, even though that plays into the story. The real issue was the board-CEO relationship.

At the point we were brought in, the CEO-board relationship and the CEO's relationship with the management team were both very strained. Emotions were running high, and the employee population was confused by the current situation.

We used the following allegory to try to help the CEO to see where this situation was surely heading: "Let's say you (the Chairman of the Board) want a new puppy. Your last dog (former CEO), who was a loyal and supportive companion, died last year. So you decide you need another dog that will offer the same companionship and loyalty, but you decide you don't want an older dog because it might come to you with some bad habits, since it was trained by someone else. You decide you want a puppy with fresh legs, full of energy and excitement. So you go looking for this puppy. Your family (other board members) knows this friend who has a puppy, and they convince you to take a long, hard look at this little guy. You see the puppy a few times, and like the way it runs around the pen, but you are not convinced he is the right one. Your family urges you that he is the right one, so you agree, and think he will work as long as he behaves. (By taking this puppy you are not being authentic, you know he is not the right one for you, but you accept him for the sake of others.) The family was so enamored of the puppy that you knew you just had to bring it home. The puppy (CEO) comes home with you, you set up a long dog run in the back yard, and install a pet door so he can come and go as he pleases. You buy him some new toys and a brand-new, huge pet bed. You think to yourself, 'Now he just has to be a good dog, obey, honor, and do what he is told.'

"The puppy is so happy with his new home (assignment) that he just wants to do all of the right things. He sits by your side in the living room, he carries in the paper like you ask, and he is good with the family. However, he also high-tails it out the pet door every time you are not around. But you think, 'That's why I installed the pet door in the first place, so let him run.'

"When he is out in the back yard, he starts barking. This is cute at first, quiet little puppy barks that kind of sound like a bay more than a bark. The puppy begins to grow, the barks get louder, and he begins to get some of the neighborhood dogs (employees) barking. You go outside and everyone just seems to be having a great time, but now your neighbors (management team) are getting a bit irritated. Your puppy has their dogs yippin' and yappin' at them. 'We want this!' 'We want that!' And your little guy is encouraging the whole thing. The first thing you do is shorten the run. That will teach him! But no! He still goes out there every chance he gets and barks with the other dogs. More complaints from the neighbors. One says she is going to call the police (shareholders). So this time, you bring the puppy in and lock the pet door. You say, 'Bad puppy! You will only go out when I say you can go out, period.'

"So the little puppy just sits by the door and looks out, occasionally letting out a little yip, even when the other dogs are outside barking their little heads off looking for his sound. The puppy hears the other dogs and decides, 'No way am I going to be cooped up in here, that's my team out there. I will be heard!' So while he is inside, he starts barking to beat the band. At this point, you begin to discipline the puppy. 'Bad boy. Quiet down. Stop that.'

"You think to yourself, 'He may just need some help. I will bring him to an animal specialist, an animal behaviorist (consultant).' So off you go to the specialist. You tell the specialist the whole story and explain you are at your wit's end. The specialist gives you three options: '1. Hire me for a year to help him behave. 2. Buy an electronic collar that zaps him every time he barks (disciplinary action with weekly action meetings). 3. Put the little guy up for adoption. (Termination).' These are the only options he presents, and since you know he's the specialist, you wonder what else you can do.

"The situation gets worse. You get so frustrated that you begin to beat (emotionally) the puppy every time he barks, because the neighbors call as soon as they hear one little yip. You beat the puppy so badly, he has no bark left. The neighborhood falls silent. The little guy just sits by the door. He won't fetch the paper or do any of the other tricks he had learned so well. You think, 'Well, one more try!' So you bring the puppy to the veterinarian (new consultant) for one more chance to see whether the dog can be turned back into the good little puppy he once was. The vet looks into the puppy's eyes and knows he's been broken. There is no bark left in him. Not an easy job for the vet, but he knows what to do. The vet persuades both the master and the puppy that they should part ways. He feels they would both be better off with someone else. But the puppy refuses. He knows he can be the puppy you always wanted. 'Just one more chance,' he yips. 'Just one more chance. I will change for you. I will never bark again (incongruence with your values).'"

Ending the relationship was the best thing for the both of them. For the master, no more calls from the neighbors, no more visits form the police. He replaced the puppy with an old dog from a trusted friend, and this dog had all the "right" habits. He was the most obedient dog the master had ever had. The puppy, on the other hand, felt worthless. He had not served his master well. It took a lot of encouragement from the vet and the behavioral specialist to help the puppy get his self-esteem back, but eventually he did. And now he is doing just fine, barking up a storm for a farmer (new governing body) that just loves the sound of his voice. And he plays an important role herding sheep. He gets to be a real team leader.

"What happened to the neighborhood?" you ask. Well, all's quiet on that front. The neighbors are right back into their old routines, no barking dogs to worry about, no added noise to their routines, and no interruptions.

Just the way they like it. It is as if nothing has ever happened. A blip on the radar screen.

The actual company was never able to make the changes needed to grow and become a learning organization. It was all a result of incongruence. It started with the board, which never really was committed to the change. The board members just thought this whole "learning organization" concept was what everybody else was doing, and because it looked like a quick fix, they wanted to follow the pack.

The Chairman of the Board didn't think the new guy could pull it off and never truly supported the CEO. He allowed the management team to circumvent the CEO and listened when they did nothing but complain. So, ultimately, the Chairman knew the CEO would fail, and it would prove that he was the wrong choice in the first place. The Chairman wanted this to happen in order to validate his belief that he should be the one in control.

To keep his position, the CEO was ready to compromise his values. To stay in power, he was willing to let everything he stood for be undermined and ripped away. He did not want to give up his seat. However, with some strong urging from his true supporters, the ones who really believed in him and cared for him, he was able to see that going counter to his values would be wrong. It would have been incongruent for him to keep his position. He would have lost his integrity. Instead, he moved on. He found a better place, one where he has a far greater organizational impact; one where he can be authentic and congruent with this own value system.

The moral of the story?

Be true to your authentic self, and you'll never feel like a whipped puppy.

Due Diligence

Before we dive into cultural assessments in general and Cultural Due Diligence™ in particular, it is important for you to have a general understanding of the due-diligence process. Due diligence is one of the methods used to study, investigate, and evaluate business opportunities. Although the term was popularized in the 1980s, the activity has been a part of business transactions for years. It is basically a well-defined procedure for data collection and analysis that uses audit tools and techniques, including financial tests and ratios. According to Gordon Bing in his book *Due Diligence Techniques and Analysis: Critical Questions for Business Decisions*, the main objectives for performing due diligence are:

- Verification that the business is essentially what it seems to be.

- Verification that an investment complies with investors' criteria. (1)

Historically, due diligence has focused on the legal and financial aspects of an organization and its operations. Attorneys, accountants, and other consultants generally perform this isolated task. It is a critical step in determining whether a deal, project, or research-and-development initiative is worth pursuing.

Due diligence is typically done before major decisions are made or shortly after they are announced to the public. The scope of due diligence determines the length and cost of the procedure and typically varies with factors such as the size and complexity of the organization or businesses that are under scrutiny; the size of the deal; the relative risk to all parties involved; and time and budget constraints.

What is due, or sufficient, diligence varies with every situation. At a minimum, due diligence typically analyzes the following:

- Historical activity (prior five years' worth, if available)
- Ownership and structure of entity
- Management team
- Products and services, including market share by category
- Assets and liabilities
- Information systems and technology
- Organizational culture

In each of these broad categories, information must be collected and analyzed in terms of the stated objectives for due diligence. These objectives should be clearly defined at the outset of the study. Bing provides an excellent list of "Critical Questions for Business Decisions" in his book. (2)

Due diligence is universally conducted as part of the analysis for mergers and acquisitions. Increasingly, it is used when evaluating all types of business combinations or affiliation agreements. However, the focus of due diligence continues to be on the so-called "hard" data.

In a 1998 study by Watson Wyatt, a global consulting firm, 190 top executives from companies representing a variety of industries were surveyed regarding their merger and acquisition experiences. The results confirmed that the most sought-after information during the due-diligence process were financials and market share.

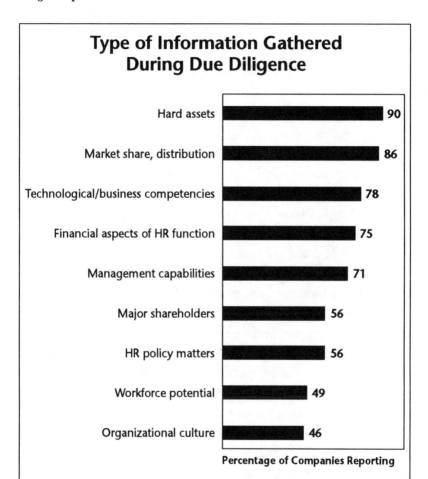

Type of Information Gathered During Due Diligence

Hard assets	90
Market share, distribution	86
Technological/business competencies	78
Financial aspects of HR function	75
Management capabilities	71
Major shareholders	56
HR policy matters	56
Workforce potential	49
Organizational culture	46

Percentage of Companies Reporting

The information most often sought during the due diligence process relates to financials and market share. Information about business competencies is gathered more often for U.S. deals than for others.

Cultural incompatibility was consistently rated as the biggest barrier to successful integration, yet results indicate that this area is least likely to be researched during the due diligence process.

Executive Summary of Watson Wyatt's Worldwide 1998/1999 Mergers & Acquisition survey   (3)

We all perform due diligence to some extent in making day-to-day decisions. When evaluating a job offer, for example, most of us try to learn as much as we can about our prospective employer. We talk with people who already work there, read the latest annual report, or do an on-line search of business articles. Some of us go a step further and secure a Dunn & Bradstreet report on the company's historical performance or consult with an industry analyst regarding future performance forecasts.

The courtship and dating experience is another area where we conduct some due diligence before entering into a long-term relationship. Most people would not consider marriage before they knew something about their partner's health, wealth, and wisdom. Think about those family dinners that reveal a lot more than whether or not Aunt Lucy's gravy has lumps. Observing dinner-table dynamics gives you valuable insight into what lies ahead if you become a member of the family. This is due diligence that should precede any "I do!"

In the case of our health, we would certainly go into an in-depth data-gathering and analysis mode if given a medical diagnosis with several treatment alternatives. Who rushes into surgery without first determining if there is a non-invasive alternative? Who submits to an experimental therapy if a proven method provides comparable outcomes? It is certainly in our best interests to examine the situation at least as much as the doctors examine us!

In all of these examples, we first look at the facts and then try to draw some conclusions. Ultimately, our decisions are based on the hard data coupled with the soft data that is culled from our situation and life experiences: the feelings, beliefs, personality, and behaviors that make up our individual culture.

However, this soft side of personal due diligence still seems to be lacking in organizational due diligence. The accountants focus on numbers, the lawyers look at legalities, management focuses on issues, and investors focus on returns. No one focuses on the culture, the human side of the business. History has shown us that only 15% to 25% of all mergers and other various business combinations live up to expectations. In addition, 25% to 30% are reported to be downright failures, with the acquired entity being sold or liquidated at a loss within three to five years. The remaining 45% to 60% have resulted in little or no apparent benefit to the buyer's shareholders. Perhaps the high failure rate results from normal due diligence's failure to look at the cultures and people involved. There is strong evidence that culture is indeed a critical missed component. In Watson Wyatt's survey, cultural incompatibility was consistently rated as the biggest barrier to successful integration in a post-combination environment. In their analysis, the researchers also stated: "Our experience shows that conducting an early and thorough assessment of organizational culture can help the acquiring company forecast the deal value and manage cultural issues before they become bottlenecks and diminish deal value." (4) Yet many leaders are still not taking such advice seriously.

In a 1997 position paper, J. Robert Carleton, management consultant and senior partner of the Vector Group, says, "Unfortunately, little or no time is generally spent analyzing the nature, demeanor, and beliefs of the people who will be involved in carrying out the business plan." (5) He believes that standard due diligence does not address some of the key questions that must be asked to accurately assess organizational readiness for a major change, such as a merger or acquisition. Even when some of the "right" questions are asked, Carleton argues, they are often limited to brief interviews with key executives, who likely have differing views from the rest of the employee group. The people in the trenches, the ones doing much of the actual work are not even involved. He finds it interesting that "in financial and legal due diligence no such 'act of faith' is acceptable" in terms of the investigative procedure. (6)

Another person who believes that examining the culture should be part of the due-diligence process is Pamela S. Harper, president of

Business Advancement, Inc. In an article for *Channel* magazine, she comments, "Much like a marriage, the success of a merger depends not only on getting two companies together, but also on how well they will get along once that commitment has been made." (7) She recommends use of a "compatibility checklist" to document areas that might need attention.

Are all of these people on to something?

Is it time to redefine due diligence to include a cultural component?

Should organizational-development and human-resources staffs be added to the due-diligence team? Should you at least consider conducting a compatibility checklist before celebrating your success, be it a business combination or a new internal business strategy?

We definitely think so!

Now, we recognize that management often views organizational-cultural issues as somewhat squishy, like cold fusion. They think that focusing on these issues is unnecessary and that everything will just work out. Although we're not saying that culture is the only element that needs attention, we are saying that culture is a major culprit in combination failures and one of the key reasons for the high percentage of change-initiative failures. As Bing points out in *Due Diligence*, "Business deals all too frequently fail because differences in corporate cultures prevent the parties from understanding, accepting, reconciling, or compromising." (8)

What is this telling us? Companies must examine organizational cultures as well as the other key elements. Those that are taking the time to do so are reaping more fruitful and long-lasting results. Yes, due diligence of any kind can be tedious, time-consuming, and costly. However, ignoring a process that promises to turn up significant information affecting the outcome of a business objective or deal looks like negligence in the eyes of the shareholders.

Cultural Due Diligence™: What Is It?

Cultural Due Diligence™ is a cultural assessment. We, along with many others, believe that cultural assessment is the missing component in traditional due diligence. CDD™ is our own mechanism for assessing all the key cultural aspects of your business. The process analyzes key cultural domains that include:

- leadership and management practices, styles, and relationships;
- governing principles;
- formal procedures;
- informal practices;
- employee satisfaction;
- customer satisfaction;
- key business drivers;
- organizational characteristics;
- perceptions and expectations; and
- how the work gets done in your organization.

The Cultural Resume™ puts all the information into a nice little package that shows you the data results and lays out your organization's culture in one clear message.

The bottom line is that you can't just focus on the traditional bottom line!

"Bottom line" always sounds like some kind of object: "Hey, Hal! Hand me that bottom line." "Sue, have you seen the bottom line lately? I swear I left it on my desk last night." Beware of the bottom-line mirage. What you see on paper isn't always what you get. The numbers alone don't tell you what you really need to know. Yes, you still need to assess the hard data that is easily quantified, but you also need to go beyond to get at what other factors affect the results.

For example, as a leader you typically look at the management team's credentials, experience, and length of service with the organization. Basically, more is better in each area. But what about the overall management theme, style, and methods of communication with employees? Do management and staff value the same directives and objectives? When you review policy and procedure manuals, do they really tell you how things are done? You know that informal practices (the hidden culture) often supersede the formal procedures, yet the formal procedures are the ones that typically get reviewed and revised when an organization is facing an inspection, survey, accreditation, or certification.

What about communication? In traditional due diligence, you look at the organizational chart and reporting relationships, you review policy manuals, and you may scan meeting minutes or internal memoranda. But how does information really flow? Is e-mail the main method for making announcements? Do you rely on the company newsletter for disseminating important information to the work force or, does the old bulletin board still serve as the message center?

All of these questions point to areas where cultural incongruencies can exist. Inattention to factors such as these can adversely affect internal change initiatives as well as business combinations of any kind.

Conducting a cultural assessment like Cultural Due Diligence™ provides a factual analysis of where your organization is relative to its culture. It helps you to determine whether your values are in sync with the type of culture you are trying to nurture or create. It answers some key questions about your current culture, and it will give you a good understanding of the potential changes that may need to occur in order to achieve strategic goals and objectives.

As part of our research, we interviewed many business leaders who had experienced a change initiative of some kind over the last few years. Every individual reported that some degree of financial and/or legal due diligence was performed in conjunction with the process. Especially in cases involving mergers or acquisitions, the analysis was often extensive and costly. We then asked each respondent if they were familiar with the term "Cultural Due Diligence"™? Most indicated that they really hadn't heard much about it, but once we defined it for them, they thought it was a great idea. So how many of these folks felt that any cultural assessment, no matter what it was called, had been performed as part of the due diligence? Only 5% had even looked at the cultural issues, and this was after multiple experiences with failed initiatives.

CEO Ben Gill of RSI-Ketchum, a major fund-raising organization, is one leader who did "see the culture light," after RSI acquired Ketchum Inc. in 1995.

Ketchum was going through hard times. The company had forgotten its core focus, and good employees were jumping ship. Ketchum was down to forty employees when RSI acquired it, and, boy, did this acquisition create tremendous challenges for the Ketchum CEO. For the previous three months his time had been spent firing and retiring long-term employees. Now down to only forty employees his challenge along with Gill was to make the acquisition happen without losing the remaining forty.

By mutual consent all forty remaining employees were asked to board a plane for Dallas. While in the air the Ketchum CEO informed them that the acquisition was taking place and that, while they would be terminated from the old Ketchum while in the air, once on the ground they would be rehired by the new Ketchum owners. There was a symbolism here that must not be missed. Suddenly, people who had experienced the instability of the wind down of their company would soon be "on firm ground" once again and enjoy the stability of a strong parent company relationship. That "stability" became the theme of a day long orientation into the new organization.

Was this the best way to accomplish the transition announcement? Who knows, but of the forty employees offered employment once they landed all but four accepted.

The next three years proved to be very difficult. There were cultural differences, and the acquired company felt like a stepchild. Despite RSI's efforts to include the acquired unit in quarterly meetings, the former Ketchum employees still did not visualize themselves as part of the larger organization, and there was a degree of corporate embarrassment. They no longer viewed themselves as successful. In addition, they were very suspicious of RSI, which is not hard to understand when you consider their introduction to it.

Two years into the deal, RSI split those employees back out into their own entity. Even though this was not a cost-effective move, management knew it was the only thing that could get the company back on its feet. To date, there has been a phenomenal turnaround, and the gross revenues are excellent. The former top dogs of Ketchum rejoined the company and are going stronger then ever.

In an interview, we asked Ben what he would do differently next time, and it turned out that next time was already upon him.

"We are in the throes of another merger, and this time, we decided to get professional help. Not just on the investment-banker and lawyer side. We have hired a consulting firm to help us with the cultural issues through the integration. They may be holding our hand, but it is a much smoother transition. Basically, they are quarterbacking the process. We have bimonthly meetings, and at those meetings, we lay out a ten-day plan. At each meeting, we measure our progress and issues are discussed and resolved. This is the much smarter way to go."

We also asked Ben to give us an example of how the consultants helped in the cultural transformation.

"Under the consultants' guidance, we revisited our strategic-planning process. This is something we had not done in some time, and it proved to be very productive. It helped us see where all of the growth is taking place. Next, they had us assess each of our management-team members and conducted an exercise to see if everyone fit in their jobs and where we might have some gaps. The assessment measured personality traits, communication skills, and interpersonal relationships. Many people have been moved as a result of the tests, and it has been very productive for the employees and the company. The main objective of the assessment was not for the company to move the folks around but to have the individual identify strengths and weaknesses and make the decision to shift on [her or his] own. The company doesn't even receive a copy of the results, it goes straight to the employee. Then, it is up to [her or him] to take some kind of action, if necessary."

These actions are helping to SHIFT the company culture. We then asked him whether he felt organizational culture really mattered?

"Yes, culture is something that takes time, and it requires various developmental stages in order to grow the right one. The role of the leader should be to facilitate change as the company matures. I spend 75 percent of my time shepherding that process to make sure the culture we have developed stays intact."

Ben went on to describe an effective culture:

"Integrity, unselfishness, positive motivation, trust, aggressiveness, and non-complacency are critical core components of our culture." (9)

His points were very well taken, and the same theme ran through most of our interviews. When we asked about the success of change initiatives, the failure rate among our sample paralleled that documented in the literature. All of the executives we talked to said that at least 50 percent of the change initiatives and combinations they'd been involved with were deemed failures by some or all of the affected parties. Some of the executives even went as high as 75 percent. Would Cultural Due Diligence™ have helped any of these people in their varied roles as change agents? A resounding "Yes! Most definitely! Absolutely!" was the response of all of our interviewees. Even a purebred CPA financial officer and former CFO for a major health care system spoke to the failure of one of the largest health-care acquisition ventures in history. He admitted: "I'm not convinced that the culture assessment would have been what saved it, but I believe it [culture] is something that should be evaluated." (10)

"So, tell me more about this Cultural Due Diligence™," you say. "It still seems a little vague and ill-defined, a little too soft and touchy-feely." A word of caution here—we are not saying that a cultural assessment such as CDD™ is the end-all and be-all. What we are saying is that conducting a cultural assessment such as CDD™ will provide you with invaluable information that is essential for making sound business decisions. In the case of a merger or acquisition, this process will identify the incongruencies that exist between Company A and Company B. This data will help you determine how the two entities should be integrated. It is the ability to integrate and to be congruent that will reduce the failure statistics.

In the case of an internal change strategy, conducting a cultural assessment like CDD™ will provide you with great insight into your current culture and value system and will help you determine whether or not you have a culture that can support your new business strategy. Again, the goal is not the assessment itself but rather the ability to identify incongruencies in your system and to eliminate them.

Basically, Cultural Due Diligence™ attempts to verify that your business culture is essentially what it appears to be. It does this by going below the surface in the examination. Think about what you do when you are not feeling well. What started out as a cold might have developed into pneumonia. You go to the doctor, have an exam, and probably go for a chest X-ray. The X-ray confirms a suspected diagnosis. Like an X-ray, Cultural Due Diligence™ provides a picture of what is really going on beneath the surface.

Cultural Due Diligence™ can't fix an organization that is pursuing the wrong strategy. What it can do is cut down on informal practices, internal politics, mistrust, resentment, and just plain bad management that might sink the right strategy.

Cultural Due Diligence™ seeks to identify the differences between your formal and informal practices and to nail down your incongruencies. There can be no preconceived notions that the objective is to "find something wrong." If that is the mind-set at the beginning of the investigation, it is likely to dictate the outcome. CDD™ identifies the strengths as well as weaknesses. Traditional audits typically focus on defects, but it is just as critical to examine the positives. Organizations often focus their time and energy on what is not being done right. Let's stop this negative nemesis. This is so exhausting and debilitating for people. Take the time to look at the things you do well. Face it, if you weren't doing some things well, your organization would not exist. Could you improve? Absolutely! You can always improve, but is it total doom and gloom? Absolutely not.

In the case of a merger or any type of business combination, Cultural Due Diligence™ forces you to answer the tough questions about whether these two cultures, these two divisions, these two functions can merge. The questions include:

- Where are the incongruencies within each of the organizations, and what are the gaps between these two distinct cultures?

- Whose culture will win out? Should there even be a winner? Whose values will shape the new organization?

- How do you create an inclusive culture?

- How will you manage the flow of information and people?

- How do they best live together?

- What do they combine? How does the combination flow?

- What can you do to prevent a cultural clash that can negatively affect your financial success over the long haul?

These are pieces of cultural differences that CDD™ seeks to uncover and confront. It also gives you the opportunity to assess up front the challenges and opportunities you will find in uniting the two entities. Let's look at a couple of different examples:

A large manufacturing company made a strategic business decision to combine its sales force and customer-service operation. The thought process was that combining the two would reduce redundancy and improve efficiency. It sounded like a good plan. We began the assessment phase with the typical organizational-chart review, physical-location mapping, and management-styles evaluation. Because the two operations were part of the same organization, we didn't think there would be a need to review formal policies: HR issues such as benefits, compensation, etc. Boy! Were we wrong!

As we entered into the evaluation process, we began to see incongruencies in almost every facet of daily activity. Database information on customers, product lines, and purchasing procedures did not match up. Then, we began to look at management practices more closely. The differences between the two departments were as vast as the Grand Canyon: participatory management versus hierarchical, weekly communication meetings versus quarterly, "order as you please" versus "stay within the budget." The investigation of the human-resources practices turned out to be just as contradictory. Compensation plans were way off track, not only between these two departments but also in relation to the organization as a whole. They did not match company policy at all. After auditing the two functions and conducting Cultural Due Diligence™, it looked as though we'd been comparing two completely different companies. It was amazing that these two functions were in the same business and that they served and supported the same customer base and product line!

What started out to be a strategic decision to integrate the two ended up as a companywide analysis of many management practices and procedures. In the end, we discovered more than $1,000,000 in waste per year, over two dozen redundancies, and several mismanaged policies and procedures. It was a long process and none too comfortable for the management teams, but in the end, the company saved money and did integrate the two functions under one management structure. The results were very positive. Customer-satisfaction indicators rose by 30%, and market share rose by 20% over the next two years.

In addition to mergers, acquisitions, and internal integration, Cultural Due Diligence™ is a must-do before implementing any type of internal change strategy. Before you embark on any internal change initiative, you must first understand your culture. Does it support the new business strategy or not? If not, what do you need to do in order to bring that support about? For example, the decision has been made to implement self-directed work teams. One of the first questions in the due-diligence process would be, "What is your belief system about employee involvement (empowerment)?" As a management team, if you can't agree on or you don't believe in employee involvement, then the move to self-directed work teams is doomed to fail.

Take the case of a large international manufacturing firm in which an edict to move to self-directed work teams was handed down from the CEO to the top management team. About 50% of the management team was committed to the new initiative, and 50% saw it as a nuisance. There was a significant incongruency between the CEO and the top team and among members of the top team. Consequently, the message that went out to the work force was very mixed and caused a high level of confusion, not to mention animosity. Half of the work force was committed to this new endeavor and the other half felt "this too shall pass," and both points of view were reinforced by different managers. The lack of cohesive commitment resulted in increased stress levels, decreased performance levels, and caused the performance-energy levels (morale) to go right down the tubes. Those who never bought in were quick to say, "See, it didn't work. We told you so." The management's lack of commitment was quite obvious to the work force. Although the teams were now "empowered" and self-directed, they could NOT: spend more than $200 on anything, authorize overtime, participate in the hiring decisions for new members of a team, or rate each other's performance at review time. So they were "self-directed" as long as the management still had control. Incongruency? You bet.

What's the lesson? If you don't start assessing and paying attention to the incongruencies that exist within your organization toward values, behaviors, actions, and relationships, your change efforts will continue to be unsuccessful.

Now, let's look at a similar situation, but in this case, the firm took the time to conduct Cultural Due Diligence™ before implementing self-directed work teams. In doing so, the company discovered that its decision-making process was not inclusive and that employees were not encouraged to get involved in decisions that affected the business. In fact, a number of the members of the top team were not even sure how they felt about employee involvement and the development of a participatory work environment.

The group recognized the importance of defining their values to determine whether their current value system would support this new business initiative. The good news is that the top team came to the conclusion that employee involvement was critical to the future success of the organization. Therefore, the organization's value system was modified to reflect this change that, in turn, changed its behavior. The top team made a sincere commitment to the success of this process, and it worked! We are happy to report that self-directed work teams are now, five years later, part of the culture of this organization and seen as a way of life.

Moral of the story—Take the time to understand what you value as a business before jumping into the next sandbox. It just might not be for you.

Why Conduct Cultural Due Diligence™?

The last bottle of Opus 1 has just been opened and the party is about to end. The evening has been filled with lots of laughter and joking. It's truly been a night for celebrating.

The next thing you know, it's Sunday morning and your head is pounding like there's a 30-piece band in it. All you hear and feel are the percussion instruments. Your mouth is dry, your teeth feel like they have little socks on them, and the room is spinning. You know before you even get up that this is not a typical Tylenol headache. This is a bona fide "hug the porcelain bowl" hangover.

As you start to kneel down before the bowl, you begin to reflect on the wonderful celebration the day before. Vows were exchanged. A lifetime commitment was made. The marriage has been consummated. Now, you're asking yourself, "Where do we go from here?" The courtship is over. Reality is beginning to sink in. You start asking yourself, "What do I really know about this person?" One thing that stands out is that together, you have a very solid financial portfolio.

You suddenly realize real-life decisions need to be made. "Do we combine checking accounts? How will we raise our children? How will we make decisions?" You've never really gone there with each other. There are many nuances to your relationship that didn't surface while you were dating. That's because in the dating phase you were on your best behavior. Showing your warts was a no-no, romantic fantasies filled your days and nights, and your fears never really surfaced (at least not openly). This was a highly emotional time. The adrenaline was flowing, and you just couldn't wait to see that person. That's all you could think about.

Combining organizational cultures is no different, just a lot more challenging. Cultural compatibility must be assessed prior to the combination phase. Think about the challenge of two people coming together and working through their own personal beliefs, assumptions, and perceptions. Scads of books have been written in the hope of assisting couples with this assessment and transition. Now, take your organization. We're not talking about two people, we're talking about 30, 300, 3,000, 30,000, or more, who all bring their own beliefs, cultural differences, gender, age, assumptions, and perceptions to work every day. Compound the leadership challenge that represents by attempting to combine with another distinct culture. What kind of picture does this paint for you as a leader? Don't kid yourself into thinking that this will all come together and synergy will be achieved without a lot of hard work. Combining two cultures is probably the most sobering challenge you will face as a leader during any type of business combination.

Now, it's been a year since the deal was made. You continue to suffer from a daily hangover that just won't go away. This is not your typical headache; it is chronic and needs immediate attention. We invite you to step back and think about your current challenges. What are you hearing? Listen to the messages. Read the cues: higher rate of absenteeism, higher turnover rate (Why are people leaving? There's where the real story lies), increases in defects and scrap levels, decrease in market share, rise in customer complaints (in fact, customer retention is dropping), lots of unhealthy competition is erupting within the organization (people are unwilling to share resources), back-stabbing has become the norm, and more and more people are spending time at the water cooler talking about how great things used to be.

If you are reading this and saying, "It's all part of the aftermath, and this too shall pass," you're kidding yourself. If you don't grab hold of this monster, it will take control of you. So what can be done about it? Increasingly, executives seeking to acquire or enter into an alliance are thinking more about cultural issues during the precombination phase (or courtship). There is a simple reason: Those who have lived through the anguish of clashing cultures in unsuccessful acquisitions or disappointing alliances don't want to repeat the experience.

In *Joining Forces—Making One Plus One Equal Three in Mergers, Acquisitions and Alliances*, authors Mitchell Lee Marks and Philip H. Mirvis cite this example: "CEO Ron Oberlander of Canadian newsprint and publication-paper producer Abitibi-Price recognized that a consolidation of firms in the highly fragmented industry was inevitable. Knowing that several potential partners existed, he wanted an understanding of various cultural challenges before making a combination decision. For those firms that passed his company's strategic and financial filters, cultural fit would be used as a criterion in moving forward with a deal." (11)

Our experience tells us that conducting an early and thorough assessment of organizational culture can help the acquiring company to forecast the deal and manage cultural issues before they become bottlenecks and diminish deal value.

In order to do this, it's imperative that you secure sufficient information that tells a very clear story about what is really going on in your organization. Otherwise, you won't be able to write an accurate and defensible prospectus/business plan. In other words, your motive in gathering this information should be to allow yourself to truly grasp the magnitude of the integration process.

Here are some questions you might ask:

- What is it going to take?
- Are we willing to make the investment?
- What are the similarities?
- What are the dissimilarities?
- Do we really need to combine both cultures?
- What are the advantages or disadvantages?
- How much work will be involved?
- What are the resources that must be committed to this process?
- What are our core organizational values?

Integration Can Take on Many Forms

When the decision is made to integrate, you should take the integration process to the next level and co-create a new culture. Integration is all fine and good, but to become a market leader after the merger requires unity of strengths.

In some cases, the cultures may differ so extensively that a merger may not be the most logical and sensible approach. We have seen organizations that have actually backed off from moving forward. However, when they did recognize that each complemented the other in numerous ways, some found a solution in joint ventures, and others formed simple alliances.

An interesting example is presented in an article by Chuck Salter in the April 1999 issue of *Fast Company* titled "We're not blue, and we're not red. We're purple. We're the best of both worlds," which describes the joining of Tivoli Systems, Inc. and IBM. In his discussion, Salter points out the many differences between the two companies. He describes Tivoli staff as playful, but serious about and committed to their work. As an example, a hallway at Tivoli converts to a bowling alley with water bottle pins. This is in marked contrast to the stereotypical Big Blue employee who would be too well-dressed to consider bowling on the job! However, when IBM made the decision to acquire Tivoli, there was, according to Salter, "a clear strategic fit. Tivoli was strong where IBM was weak." (12)

Instead of folding Tivoli into IBM, Big Blue put Tivoli in charge of its entire systems-management business. This strategic maneuver is becoming very popular with large companies and is referred to as a "reverse acquisition." Just because I buy you does not mean you have to lose your identity and be folded completely under my wing. In reverse acquisitions, the opposite occurs. I make you the "guy calling the shots." You continue business as usual, just with a hell of a lot more resources and support. In the IBM-Tivoli case, there is a blending of the power of a large organization with the speed of a small one. The net result is something that neither company could achieve independently. (13)

This type of operation represents the future, not the past. It was IBM's answer to a set of questions haunting big companies everywhere:

Must the advantages of size—financial resources, clout with customers, deep reservoirs of talent and technology—come at the expense of speed?

Must a commitment to professional behavior—clear lines of authority, sound rules for making decisions—come at the expense of agility and flexibility?

Must a proud tradition of success well-honed and a sense of "this is how we do things here" come at the expense of changing with the times and doing things differently?

Does being big have to mean "being out of touch?"

This example shows us that even the big guys are looking for new and different ways of conducting daily business.

What we are saying is that before you can make a decision one way or another on any combination, you must understand the cultures of both sides. Do they blend? Should they blend? A few words of caution here: Whatever you decide, make sure it is in the best interests of the customer. How do you structure yourself and operate in order to achieve knockout results?

Put the M back in M&A

In a true merger, no one culture should win. Having one side be the winner over the other can be the kiss of death. Unfortunately, more often than not, what we have experienced in the merger frenzy are acquisitions disguised as mergers. There is typically an acquirer and an acquiree, and the lead company's culture typically dominates. If you are the lead company in a deal and you are not interested in blending cultures, respect your partner's culture. Respectfulness helps the "merged" employees see what you as the lead company have to offer in the way of structure, processes, and business behavior. One simple way to accomplish this is to ask people how and why they do things. People really enjoy talking about their work. It gives them a sense of pride. Their contributions need to be honored. Pay attention to their culture.

You must recognize that the elements that make up their culture are being threatened, and the status quo or aspects of their way of life may be changed or, worse yet, lost. The first step in managing a cultural collision is to understand the current cultures. You must spend time developing a Cultural Resume™, yours and theirs. Such a process allows you to visualize in detail what incongruencies exist between the two cultures. It prevents you from jumping into a deal blindfolded.

This will also allow you to determine the potential fallout of imposing your culture on your potential partner, which may cause you to have second thoughts about such an imposition. You may even have second thoughts about destroying a culture that is deep-rooted and is very successful. Remember, people join organizations for lots of different reasons. You can readily see the obvious extrinsic benefits, but a cultural assessment will help you to see the intrinsic cultural benefits—flexible work hours, educational opportunities, casual work environment, flexible benefits, the list goes on—that attracted people to your potential partner. Show respect for each other's cultures. They are what brought you to the point of considering this deal.

If you do choose the path of cultural assimilation, be aware that you will encounter more negative force and resistance than if you make an effort to work together in building a cultural end state.

As a leader, you must begin to see what all engaged couples need to see. The marriage isn't the wedding, nor is the merger the moment you sign all the documents to make it official. As a leader, you must change your focus from getting the deal done to making the partnership viable over the long haul.

Once the letter of intent is signed, but before you walk down the aisle together to say, "I do," you must perform an assessment like Cultural Due Diligence™, incorporating it into your in-depth due-diligence process. Understanding how each potential partner thinks and acts is critical not only to the transition phase, but also, more importantly, to the combination phase.

As a leader, you must begin to understand how you can decode, translate, and contextualize the overt messages and publicly available information about your potential partner(s). Unless key players from both organizations learn to read the deeper meanings that the other side's culture communicates, then mutual working relations remain under threat.

You must also develop a prudent, yet aggressive and solid transition plan when it comes to fusing the two cultures. It must be a plan that will generate a road map outlining what needs to occur by when, and who will make each step happen. Good project management is what we are talking about. You must be able to measure and track your progress. This cannot occur when you are relying on your gut rather than on hard-core data. A process, like Cultural Due Diligence™, will provide you with that data.

Positive, long-lasting results are what you must be after.

Be 'For Sale Ready'

With frequent job and career changes being the norm rather than the exception, many of us face the challenge of relocation on a fairly regular basis. As part of this experience, we often need to sell our homes, just as we have finished all of the upgrades and improvements that seem to be an integral part of home ownership. Yet no matter how much we have done to make our dwellings more uniquely livable, there is always a to-do list that must be completed before we put the "For Sale" sign in the yard.

According to real-estate agents, the way to get the best price for your property is to have "buyer's eyes" when preparing your house for a listing. This means that you must view every aspect of it in the totally objective way that a prospective customer would. The worn-out welcome mat at the front door that Aunt Martha gave you as a housewarming gift twelve years ago doesn't say, "Welcome" to a stranger. The loose tile on the kitchen counter top that is just a nuisance to you says, "What else haven't they fixed?" to a buyer. And the inside of the frosted shower door that only you ever see can totally gross out someone who already has second thoughts about buying a resale home. Since most buyers form an impression of the home in the first fifteen seconds of the visit, it doesn't take much to negatively influence their perception of the overall property.

So what does this have to do with organizational culture? What we want to do is provide an approach to objective analysis of your organization that is quite similar to the one that most people follow when selling their home. An in-depth examination of not only what is, but what is perceived. A "buyer's eye" view that is not clouded by emotional attachment or pride of ownership. Both homeowners and real-estate professionals agree that the time and money spent taking care of potential or existing problems more than returns the investment, even if you end up deciding not to sell.

"For Sale Ready" is really a mind-set that you should have when managing your business. Even if you are not preparing for a sale (or purchase or affiliation), it is in your best interest to do the necessary "preventive maintenance." When and if a sale or combination opportunity arises, you will be better prepared to negotiate if you have a thorough knowledge and understanding of your property. Even if you never sell, you will benefit from the "home inspection" that might find areas where small fixes now could eliminate the need for large repairs later.

When we talk about Cultural Due Diligence™, we are suggesting that you examine the nooks and crannies of your organization and perform the "white glove test" on areas that may not have been dusted off in recent times. In some areas, it may require the truly microscopic vision that prospective buyers seem to have, the vision that looks beyond the expanse of polished hardwood floors into the corner where the small spider has lived, undisturbed, for many years. We are sure you could name a few spiders in your organization. We can all think of departments or divisions that might have been similarly neglected!

We encourage you to think with the "For Sale Ready" mind-set. Consider the importance of the "curb appeal" of your organization, both to prospective buyers and prospective employees. Yet remember that aluminum siding or wood veneer can hide significant flaws and blemishes that affect the overall integrity of the organization's structure. Think about the importance of the foundation (core values) and the roof (leadership umbrella) when determining the potential for damage and the associated expense. Employee discontent, like shifting soil, can lead to significant cracks in the foundation. Indecisive or incongruent leadership trickles down through an organization just like water permeates a roof in need of repair. What about the things we take for granted until they don't work, like the wiring and the plumbing? Internal communication tools, departmental policies and procedures, and reporting relationships often need to be "rewired" or "replumbed."

Assessing organizational culture also demands consideration of the external factors that are out of your control. Just as home sales are affected by market conditions, competition, and factors such as the area school system or crime rate, organizations are affected by technological advances, legislative changes, and economic considerations. It is not enough to simply know that these factors exist. There must be an ongoing effort to determine the impact of such changes on your individual organization. For example, just as individual homeowners must assess the need for flood insurance based on their geographic location, floodplain designation, historical flood activity, and overall level of comfort with risk, as an organizational leader, you must decide whether the advantages of installing an updated information system will be outweighed by the increased staffing requirements, requisite facility changes, and the risk of negatively affecting accounts receivable in the short term.

If all of this sounds like a lot of work, IT IS! But failure to consider all of these things means failing to conduct the cultural assessment that is the only guarantee of truly insightful organizational management.

Aside from the importance of being "For Sale Ready," it is important for you to consider the M&A track record over the last several years. In 1998, according to Mergerstat.com, U.S. companies cut 7,809 merger and acquisition deals with a total value of $1.192 trillion. (14) Using these statistics and the historical data that says about 75% of these deals will fail over the following three years, we come up with about $325 billion per year of failed investments. That's not a very encouraging picture. Will Wall Street be kind to these losses? Will the

CEOs of these failures be idolized and immortalized? What will happen to the millions of individuals who will lose their jobs as organizations cut heads to make up for the lost capital? These are very serious questions to ponder. In many cases, failure has meant the company's stock prices fell, it lost market share, revenue and profits dropped, and the end result was a sell-off or another merger or acquisition.

Do some examples come to mind? How about International Harvester? Or maybe American Can? These were very significant losses. One of the better-known and frequently reviewed "buy now, lose big later" cases is Novell. The company's purchase of WordPerfect did not work out, Novell was forced to sell it off and lost $1 billion on the sale price. What's forgotten in most discussions of this flop is that this figure does not take into account all the time, energy, loss of productivity, and other costs associated with combining the organization, processes, and management team. Those "soft costs" are never mentioned. What we see is the red ink that occurs when an organization just has to "dump it" or "shoot the proverbial puppy." It has been estimated that immediately after an announcement of a merger (or, for that matter, any type of change initiative), employees lose an average of two hours of productivity a day for the first thirty days, and one hour of productivity in the next thirty days. So over a sixty-day period each employee has lost ninety hours, or more than two weeks of productivity. This loss takes into account water-cooler rendezvous', cubicle huddles, and sick time used by individuals experiencing high anxiety and emotional uncertainty. Let us look at a hypothetical example: A company with 1,000 employees has an average annual wage of $50,000. At that rate, those 90 hours of lost production time per employee over a two-month period will cost this company roughly $2.163 million. Don't forget, that as far as employee compensation goes, the cost is really about one-third higher than the salaries, because while the employees are busy being unproductive, the employer is still paying for their health benefits, vacation time, and the employer's portion of Medicare, etc.

There is a plethora of reasons for these failures, so don't be fooled into thinking culture is the only element that needs attention and that conducting Cultural Due Diligence™ will save the day. There is a lot of discussion about "synergy," "economies of scale," and "market share." All we are saying is that culture is now being identified as a major culprit, one of the key reasons for the high percentage of failures that organizations are experiencing. As a result of this new recognition, there have been deals that were called off before the final handshake due to the inability to choose a new management structure or to develop a viable plan to integrate the two cultures.

Some suitors have even been spurned because of incompatibility and differences in culture. A case in point. While the Time-Warner merger negotiations were going on several years ago, Paramount stepped in with a cash offer to buy Time, Inc. This offer had greater appeal to some shareholders than the share exchange that was being considered in the Time-Warner deal. However, Time's directors, who wanted to preserve the "Time Culture," did not believe a Paramount affiliation was best for the long-term interests of the organization and so, made a cash and securities offer for Warner. Two Time shareholder groups and Paramount then took action against Time. The courts denied the injunction and ruled that the Time directors had the ultimate decision-making authority for the company and had acted in the best interests of the company, which would also be in the best interests of the shareholders in the long term. So, in effect, the law upheld Time's goal to preserve its culture. It was not about the money. It was about preserving this culture as a "pillar of American society." The courts do not impose their values on us, but they reflect on what they infer are the widely held values of the society.

As an organization, it is very difficult to make choices that take into account the interests of the shareholders, employees, the local community, and sometimes, even the nation. That's why we stress having very strong organizational core values that shape your organization's culture, which in turn becomes the cornerstone of how all of the business decisions are made and how potential conflicts are resolved. Using the score-card approach to values and culture, there is a direct correlation between conducting Cultural Due Diligence™, or knowing your culture, and hard-dollar costs.

Survey Says

Our research has told us that when it comes to any change initiative, organizations are focusing on the wrong things. According to Watson Wyatt: "Around the world, retention of key talent (intellectual capital), communication, and integration of cultures were most often rated as critical activities in the integration plan for mergers and acquisitions. Yet only eight percent of respondents stated that human-resources management issues were a top priority during integration. And, just four percent of respondents said communication was a priority." (15)

In a 1994 survey of more than two hundred companies conducted by Amherst Consulting Group, "a high percentage of these companies reported that changing culture to support change initiatives was critical for success." (16) The chart on the next page indicates the different approaches taken to link culture and change initiatives.

Training was the primary approach to bring about cultural change, encompassing all levels of management. There was an emphasis on executive and leadership development. Cultural change was focused on encouraging continuous learning, fostering empowerment, and increasing communication. (17)

We implore you to not fall prey to the training trap. Training **is not** the answer. We repeat **training is not the answer**. First, we need to agree that you can train a dog or a cat, but you educate people. You can't train someone how to believe in something. What we're talking about is changing human behavior, and as we discussed in "The Change Game," this is no easy feat.

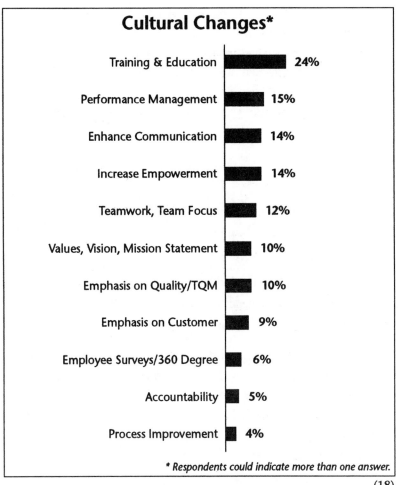

Cultural Changes*

Training & Education	24%
Performance Management	15%
Enhance Communication	14%
Increase Empowerment	14%
Teamwork, Team Focus	12%
Values, Vision, Mission Statement	10%
Emphasis on Quality/TQM	10%
Emphasis on Customer	9%
Employee Surveys/360 Degree	6%
Accountability	5%
Process Improvement	4%

* Respondents could indicate more than one answer.

(18)

Internal and External Shifts

As a leader, you must take a systemic and systematic approach to any and all business change strategies, and you must pay significant attention to culture. Based on the available information about culture's impact on business, to focus strictly on financial statements would be foolhardy. Financial statements **do not** tell us the whole story. Financial statements are results. This is not enough. You must start paying attention to how those results are achieved. Furthermore, financial statements **do not** tell you about some of the most critical factors that affect your business, such as management competence and continuity, potential loss of intellectual capital, and the costs associated with that loss over the long haul.

Here are some equations that financial statements don't spell out for us:

- Increase in waste = $
- Loss in production time = $
- Decrease in employee energy levels = $
- Potential for cultural clash = $
- Rise in employee turnover = $
- Potential for employee sabotage = $
- Effectiveness and efficiency of how things get done = $
- Validation of our organizational purpose = $

In fact, there's a host of other critical elements that affect your bottom line that aren't reflected by the financials. These "non-financial/human" factors determine the future structure and viability of your company. For this reason, as a leader, you must pay careful attention during the entire due-diligence phase and use an assessment tool like Cultural Due Diligence™.

Risk Quotient

What are the risks involved in not conducting Cultural Due Diligence™? There are no satisfactory alternatives to a comprehensive, systematic, and systemic due-diligence process. Risk multiplies when **all** aspects of the business are not objectively reviewed. You cannot rest on your laurels. You cannot rely strictly on results. It is imperative that you begin to examine HOW these results are being achieved. You must understand how your culture is working for you or against you.

Put the Diligence Back in Due Diligence

The bottom line is you don't want to focus merely on what appears on paper. To understand **how** results are being achieved, you must begin to ask questions like: What is the overall management theme? What are the inner workings of your organization? How does information flow? What do you value as a business, and more importantly, are you living up to those values? Do you have informal practices that supersede your formal procedures, and what impact is that having on your performance? What are people talking about in the elevator, at the water cooler, in the restrooms, at lunch, at breaks? This is where you will find the truth, listening to the stories.

Beware

If your desire for due diligence is only perfunctory (in other words, if you are just going through the motions), recognize that. Ask yourself, "What is my intent in doing Cultural Due Diligence™?" If it is not sincere and rigorous, then maybe you need to step back and determine whether it is in your best interest to spend the time, energy, and money.

And maybe there are a few isolated cases when Cultural Due Diligence™ is not advised. For example, if a firm is being acquired only to obtain intellectual capital with no intent to incorporate the people, products, or ideas, why bother? Don't get people's hopes up only to let them down. One of our interviewees told us about an experience where he, as human-resources director, was charged with the responsibility of meeting with the new employees from a firm his company had acquired and to get their thoughts and ideas. "They were all so excited about being a part of our operation at first, because they were facing bankruptcy," he related. "But less than a month after they were on board, I had to meet with them again to tell them that they were being let go." (19) This human-resources director believed that going through the motions of taking them into the fold was cruel and unnecessary treatment.

Play it Again, Sam

So to reiterate, the purpose of Cultural Due Diligence™ is to get beyond your perceptions, to distinguish between your imaginary world and reality, and find the activity that takes place without your knowledge. (There's always some.) You must learn to get below the surface and experience, or at least understand, what is really going on. It is like the first time an individual goes to the Caribbean. Many people get a first look at the water, and see the beauty of it all: the white caps, the rough surf, and the warm, soft sand underfoot. The first time they walk out on a dock or get in the water knee-deep, they see the colorful little fish swimming by. This entices many of them to want to see more, so to the snorkel-rental shack they go. They sign up for mask, snorkel and fins, and they're on our way. Now, they can go deeper into the water where they see more colors, more fish, and coral—a real view of the living sea. They know they are still close to the surface. They can hear themselves breathing.

Many people are satisfied with this view, but some of them, the real adventurers, sign up the next day for their first scuba-diving lesson. They really want to see what is down there. The fish have hooked them! They want to see the shark and the elusive ray.

Like the sea, most things in our world have many, many layers. We just need to make the effort to look below the surface.

As you begin thinking about making shifts in your organization, make sure you look below the surface. Don't forget that the hidden stuff, the "soft stuff," **is** the "hard stuff." Your culture is the toughest thing you will ever encounter as a leader, because you cannot touch it, smell it, or see it. You must begin to assess each puzzle piece of your organization's culture. Dissect it, be curious, and explore the deep, dark ocean of your organization. By careful examination, you will begin to uncover the gaps or incongruencies that exist. Once you begin to identify these elements, you can then begin to create the interventions needed to close the gaps and reach congruence.

The more in-depth your Cultural Due Diligence™ process, the better prepared you will be for the imminent changes that will come your way, allowing you to SHIFT rather than drift.

The Cultural-Assessment Process

What should you look at when conducting a cultural assessment? A thorough cultural assessment should give new meaning to COMPREHENSIVE. Remember that "For Sale Ready" mind-set we talked about in the last chapter? This is where you begin to look into those nooks and crannies that may have been ignored for a long time. This is when you look with "buyer's eyes."

A comprehensive cultural assessment like Cultural Due Diligence™ scrutinizes the many different facets of your organization—governing principles, formal procedures and systems, organizational characteristics, subcultures, informal and interactive practices and external forces—and it creates linkages and bridges to assess where there is congruence and where there are disconnects.

Why is this type of assessment important? As presented earlier in the book, without congruence there is chaos—a lack of clear direction in defining what is acceptable or unacceptable behavior—and in this chaotic state your organization will be unable to effectively implement any type of business change strategy, including business combinations.

The Human Web

Because organizations are made up of a web of people who are required to interact with each other in order to produce tangible results, your cultural assessment must consider all of the many ways that the human web is held together. Organizations are large and complicated systems that are driven by the interconnections among their members, and when one element of the system is tweaked the whole system is affected. Based on this premise, we like to take a holistic rather than a fragmented approach to examining the human web and all its attachments. This is the only way to create healthy, congruent cultures, and we encourage you to do the same.

The cultural assessment you conduct should help you determine the essential steps for creating effective relationships within your organization, and thus enhance your ability to make sound, logical business decisions for both internal and external change. This is especially critical when you are considering any type of business combination—remember culture clash? You need to have a thorough understanding of what your own culture is or is not. You should develop your own cultural profile (or what we call the Cultural Resume™) before you proceed with any external combination, and your potential partner should have a cultural profile as well. With these in hand, you will both be able to compare apples to apples and be better positioned to prevent a culture clash. Taking this step will also speed up the integration process, avoiding costly time delays. Remember, this approach of assessing your culture and developing a cultural profile also applies to any type of internal combination—for example, combining a number of divisions of a corporation or integrating departments such as sales and customer service, or introducing a new HR program or a new marketing strategy.

The Label Frenzy

Many assessment tools that exist today saddle organizations with labels. The goal should not be to put your organization in a box or boxes. Putting people and organizations in boxes does nothing but confuse the situation and cause people to think that one box is better than the other. Taking a systemic approach (as we do with CDD™) helps you uncover very specific details about the condition of your culture. What is your culture? What are the life-giving forces of your business (what's working)? And what are the life-draining forces (what's not working)? For example, rather than a jargon-laden label like "you are a fragmented, high-sociability, achievement-oriented culture," a thorough cultural assessment should allow you to examine the real details of your culture, telling you things like how well you deal with conflict and where the potential breakdowns may be, so that the root causes of any issue can be addressed.

Get Down to Details

You must get beyond the obvious when assessing your culture. As we said before, values implied and expressed lie at the core of organizational culture. As business leaders, we have experienced firsthand how trust and respect are destroyed by organizations with a single-minded desire to achieve high profits. We have experienced firsthand how the trust and morale of employees (and the community in which they do business) are devastated when management places greater value on profits than people.

A colleague told us the following story about being laid off from his job:

"We had no inkling it was going to happen. The company was reporting very healthy profits. So the day they were terminating people, it looked like a war zone in our office. People were crying as though a death wind was blowing through. A manager from another department walked up to me as I was talking to one of the people who was cleaning out his desk.

"The manager asked me, 'How are you doing?'

"'I'm angry,' I told him. 'This is just another example of putting profits before people.'

"He said, 'I've got bad news for you, they want you down in HR.'

"That was fine with me. From the moment they announced the layoffs—a short-term piece of idiocy that was calculated to make their stocks tick up for a moment or two so they'd either meet their MBOs or get bigger bonuses (probably both are tied, no?)—I 'quit' in my own mind. I mean, I hung around to see whether I was laid off and would receive the severance package, but if I did not, I planned to give my resignation.

"I would not work for such untrustworthy, cynical people again, even though I had virtually no savings and no prospects. I would have been the most terrible of hypocrites to stay on after watching good people go down for nothing. I would have been incongruent."

This is a fairly strong example of the trauma caused by excluding people's *thoughts* and *feelings* and *sensitivity* toward each other in the development of organizational solutions to issues of change and growth.

Maybe some vision-statement writers should simply seek permission to write one that reads: "Profit—nothing more, nothing less!" Maybe this type of statement would make it easier for many companies to be congruent. Sometimes it seems as though the people who state the values, vision, and mission of a company would like to tell the truth about their drives but don't because they feel it's their duty to give lip service to higher-sounding ideals.

The interesting question is "Why?" Is it a cynical effort to curry favor with the public by projecting the image of a "good corporate citizen?" An extreme example is the tobacco industry. Will tobacco companies ever admit they knew about the dangers of smoking? There's financial evidence to suggest they'd be better off if they did.

In another recent example, a utility company was fined $10 million after pleading guilty to 25 federal felony counts for lying to nuclear regulators and polluting water near its nuclear station." It was reported that the company lied and then attempted to conceal the violations. The utility company flat out failed to live up to what good and responsible corporate citizenship is all about.

If we begin to see more judgments like this, perhaps choosing profits over principles will be less appealing.

How many movies like *Silkwood* or *A Civil Action* will leaders have to sit through before they realize how easily their own companies could end up on the big screen? Or that the outcome of their actions will cause them to pay a very steep price—not just in the litigation, but in destruction of trust and respect from their employees and the community.

Getting Started

With that said, you may want to know what a cultural assessment should entail and how to go about conducting such a process in your organization. Let's take a look at the Cultural Due Diligence™ and Cultural Congruence Architecture that we follow in our assessments. See Figure 1, next page.

Figure 1 depicts the three primary sections of the model, which are totally interrelated and fluid. As you can see, our approach to organizational culture is all-inclusive. Organizational culture is not just about the organizational characteristics—labor groups, norms, history, and the like. Many other factors contribute to organizational culture, and all of them must be examined.

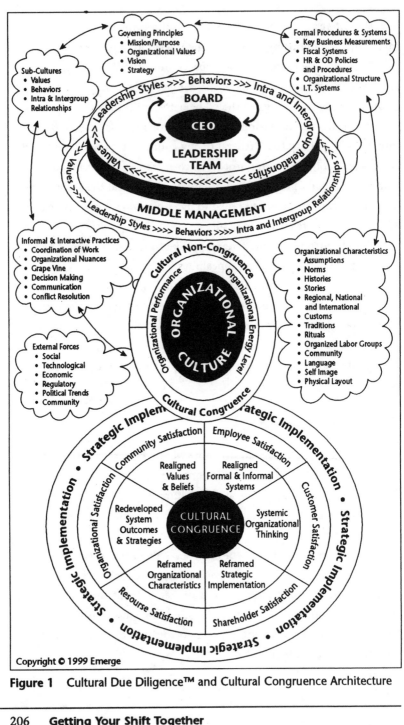

Figure 1 Cultural Due Diligence™ and Cultural Congruence Architecture

As you view the Cultural Due Diligence™ and Cultural Congruence Architecture your initial reaction might be, *"Gee, this is confusing! How the heck do I make sense of it?"* If this was your initial reaction, then you have just experienced your first true feeling of what any change process, including Cultural Due Diligence™, entails. We wish it wasn't so complex, but that's the way it goes. Welcome to the world of organizational dynamics! Because of this complexity we have tried to break the cultural assessment process into manageable chunks.

In Figure 2, you see only the top half of the Cultural Due Diligence™ and Cultural Congruence Architecture.

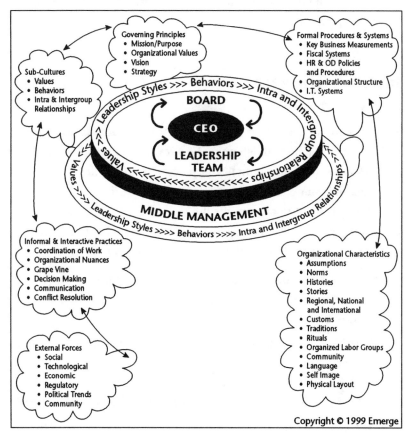

Figure 2

It is the descriptive part of the process. This is **Phase I** of the Cultural Due Diligence™ and Cultural Congruence Process, and we call it **The Dig**. The analysis is extremely comprehensive and requires an in-depth and objective assessment of who you are.

Although all elements are critical, the process of cultural assessment has a definite beginning and end point and a logical movement from one area to the next, as described in the following steps. When reviewing the steps you will also note that we incorporate a variety of assessment tools that collect both quantitative as well as qualitative data. We feel that both types of data are crucial in any assessment process. The numbers are supported by the stories, and the stories you get are supported by the numbers.

Phase I: The Dig

Step 1

The first step in Phase I is to conduct what we call a **Readiness Assessment**. This will help you determine how ready you are to undertake a cultural-assessment and cultural-shift process. It will outline your strengths and your challenges as you move forward. This exercise will also eliminate the "shoot from the hip" reaction that is so typical when any organization starts talking about a new business change strategy.

So take the time to respond (honestly) to these questions.

- Who is driving this initiative to conduct a cultural assessment? What role will the CEO play? Does he/she see himself/herself as the key driver?

- Describe a change initiative that you have implemented in the last year-including any type of business combination. (Describe how the organization currently handles change, i.e., does the decision-making process involve the entire organization or just a select few?)

- Was it successful? Did it survive the test of time? Why? Why not? What did you learn?

- How flexible are your managers and employees with a change initiative? List specific examples that support your feelings. How have they helped or hindered any past change initiatives? Do you have a sense of who your resisters are and who your supporters are?

- How did you measure its effectiveness?

- What did you learn? What did the organization learn?

- As you think about launching a process such as Cultural Due Diligence™ and Cultural Congruence process, what would you do differently?

- Can you define the reputation of the HR/OD Department? In other words, how would their internal customers rate their performance?

- How experienced is your HR/OD department in dealing with organizational culture and change?

- Are they (HR/OD) open to new learning and being on the team vs. leading the team to implement a cultural assessment and cultural shift?

- From your perspective, whom do you need and want to involve in the assessment phase and in the implementation phase? By name and department.

- How would you describe the relationship between the Board and/or Corporate, CEO, top management and middle management?

- Are their (Board/Corporate/CEO/top and middle management) values in sync? Be very specific here.

- What are leadership's motives?

- What are the potential barriers that could hamper the assessment and implementation phase of your cultural-assessment and cultural-shift process.

- Have you ever conducted any type of cultural assessment before? If yes, what was it, and how successful was it? How was it received? Was it done as part of another process? What was done with the information that was gathered?

- Have you ever conducted any type of general employee survey? How long ago? Was it successful? How was it received? What was done with the information that was gathered?

- What resources (financial and human capital) is the organization willing to devote for the assessment phase? For the implementation phase?

- Has a communication strategy been developed or at least considered? How do you currently communicate change initiatives to your workforce? E-mail? Town hall meetings? Memo and bulletin board? Intranet?

- How do you plan on using the information that is garnered from your cultural assessment?

Step 2

The next step of **The Dig** is to conduct an overall assessment of the current culture, which involves all your employees. (Again, this should be done for Company A and Company B when considering a business combination). This will serve as your baseline in determining how healthy your current culture is or is not. This assessment tool should also identify specific key areas that must be examined and potentially modified. The tool we use to accomplish this is called the Cultural Health Index™.

The Cultural Health Index™ is a document that focuses on the need for identifying organizational balance and alignment. The process of alignment and balance is what we term "congruence." Theoretically, management has focused on the critical changes necessary to enhance the organization's structure, operational processes, environments, and policies and procedures. However, the focus has been one-sided. As we have seen throughout this book, the human component of the organization has often been the forgotten side. This instrument, therefore, looks at the health of an organization based on its balance and alignment of people (the human system), organizational structure and operational processes. The instrument focuses on the governing principles, formal procedures and systems, organizational characteristics, informal and interactive practices, and organizational values that frame the direction and actions of organizations. It is not what management believes that drives the effectiveness of the organization's actions; it is the perception and ultimately the action or inaction of employees at all levels of the organization that determine the level of health or unhealthiness of the organization. This instrument is a baseline marker for the "current life" of the organization. It serves as a reference point for understanding what an organizational culture needs to consider as a key "thought process" in the development of present and future actions.

The Cultural Health Index™ provides the baseline and vehicle for decision-making. It allows you to understand the organizational and personal dynamics of the members of your organization, and it allows you to identify the types of strategies that are necessary for intervention. This is where the rubber meets the road when we are talking about a merger or acquisition. Knowing the exact culture of Company A and comparing it to the exact culture of Company B ensures a more systematic and systemic approach to integration and raises the success ratio by 50%. Taking this step will "red flag" systems and procedures that are not efficient, values that are incongruent, organizational characteristics that could create barriers to the integration process, etc. It will also identify systems, procedures, values, leadership styles, characteristics, etc. that are not only efficient but should serve as a benchmark when developing strategies for combining the two organizations. Not performing a formal cultural assessment of the organizations to be combined is like mowing your 1.4 acre lot with a weed whacker instead of a lawn mower (a riding lawn mower of course). Same result? Maybe. But the mower (formal assessment) is much more thorough and efficient.

In any case, the goal is to create satisfaction in the cultural-congruence phase of the Cultural Due Diligence™ and Cultural Congruence Architecture (See bottom half of Figure 1).

Step 3

In Step 3, you should examine your governing principles and, in the case of a business combination, those of your potential partner.

Figure 3   Governing Principles

In other words, what are the standards by which all employees are expected to live, and what is the direction the organization is taking? When you ask these questions, a culturally congruent organization should get the same responses from the entire management team (and all employees, for that matter). Therefore, you must look at vision and purpose/mission. You are probably thinking, "We have purpose/mission and vision statements. What is so different about this?" Merely having these statements doesn't mean that they are reflective of how you operate on a daily basis. A thorough cultural-assessment process should take nothing for granted. It should test your purpose/mission and vision. In other words, it's not enough to have them written down, your actions must demonstrate to the work force that these statements are more than words, that they drive your decisions.

How do you determine that? It's very easy. Ask your people. Ask them whether these statements are more than just words. Ask them whether they understand how what they do supports your organization's vision and purpose/mission. If they cannot articulate that, then either the purpose/mission or vision are flawed or you haven't done a good job of tying what they do to your vision and mission for the organization.

As we noted before, people don't like to just show up for work. What they do must have a purpose. So give them one. We worked with one client who printed the company mission and vision statements on the back of employee-identification badges. This, the management thought, would put the information "close" to the employees at all times, and just in case the regulatory commission might drop in and survey the employees on whether or not they were aware of the company mission and vision, they would have the answers handy. How lame, though, if an employee has to flip over his or her badge to tell someone what the company vision is.

Many organizations that we have worked with have vision and mission statements that are merely a bunch of words that people can't recite or don't even understand. Employees should be able to clearly articulate either of these statements by reflecting on their actions and those of the top team. So again, it is not a matter of just identifying that you have a vision and purpose/mission; you have to take the time to understand how they are being lived.

The same holds true for the organizational values. What is stated in words must be reflected in your actions. To say you value employee development and then to turn around and cut the training budget is incongruent and is certainly not representative of what you say you believe. A cultural assessment tool like the Cultural Health Index™ should serve as a good indicator and base line for where you stand in this area.

As far as strategy goes, having a clearly defined strategy isn't as important as how it was developed and how it is currently being used. More often than not, organizations spend an inordinate amount of time developing foolproof strategies only to have them sit in a ring binder. Developing strategy is such a painstaking exercise that the outcome should govern your day-to-day decisions. In too many places, strategic planning is viewed as a painful once-a-year exercise that everybody has to go through. About the only thing that comes out of it is a sigh of relief from the work force when it's finally over—until next year. And what will next year bring? The "higher-ups" jet off to some mountaintop (remote strategic planning session) and enlist the help of a tribal elder (high-priced consultant) to chant, burn incense, drink lots of very expensive wine, and descend from the mountain with stone tablets. These holy tablets are then transcribed, distributed, and posted in every conference room. How is that for an inclusive culture? Does any of this sound familiar?

How do you go about assessing these areas? Here are some questions that can help you get started:

- Do they—guiding principles, such as purpose/mission, organizational values, vision, and strategy—exist?
- How are they communicated to the work force?
- How are they developed and by whom?
- How often are they reviewed and by whom?
- How are they practiced?
- Are they all well connected?
- Do they support each other? Are they congruent?
- How is strategy set? How does the company take the following factors into account?
  - External customers. What is the company's approach to listening to and learning from the customers and potential customers; customer expectations?
  - Market requirements/expectations, including price, and new opportunities. Are decisions made with the best interest of the customer at the forefront? In other words, are business decisions made that add value for the customer, or are they bottom-line driven?
  - The competitive environment: Industry, market, and technological changes.
  - Risks: Financial and societal.
  - Human resources capabilities and needs.
  - Company capabilities—technology and technology management, research and development, innovation, and business processes—

to seek or create new opportunities and/or to prepare for key new requirements.

- Supplier and/or partner capabilities.

The next critical component in **The Dig** is the assessment of the Board (if one exists) and/or Corporate Headquarters, the CEO, leadership team, and middle management. The purpose of assessing this group is to identify the incongruencies that exist in the inter- and intra-group relations, core values, behaviors, and leadership style(s). See Figure 4.

Figure 4

Step 4

Step 4 is assessment of the Board (if one exists) and/or Corporate Headquarters. You should develop your questions around Board responsibilities, relationships, values, change, organizational culture, and internal capability. The assessment questions should be open-ended, and one-on-one interviews should be conducted. If the Board is a very active one and the values of the Board are not in sync with the CEO, then you are headed for disaster. So start by assessing your Board.

When you are about to embark upon any type of business change strategy, make absolutely sure that your Board has bought in. What we mean by buying in is that Board members must espouse the same values as the CEO. You must also examine the CEO's working relationship with the Board. If it is one of distrust, nothing the CEO can do will be good enough. So you need to figure out how to create a high level of trust between the Board and the CEO. How far apart are their (CEO and Board) management styles?

If you have an active Board, take the time to understand where it stands. If there is no active Board, then you need to recognize the power the CEO has over your organization and its culture. Noted author and organizational development pioneer, Edgar Schein remarks: "Neither culture nor leadership, when one examines each closely, can really be understood by itself. In fact, one could argue that the only thing of real importance that leaders do is to create and manage culture and that the unique talent of leaders is their ability to understand and work with culture." (1) Schein goes on to point out that when an organization's survival is threatened because elements of the culture have become maladapted, it is up to the leader to do something about it. (2)

Without Board influence, the culture in your organization will likely be a mirror image of the CEO. It's kind of scary to think about how much influence and power the CEO has in an organization.

That's why it is so important to begin by examining how values of the CEO are acted out and how they are translated. Why should you care about these elements? Because the actions of the CEO can create a world of reality or fantasy for the entire work force. If the CEO says she believes in conflict, yet shies away from heated discussions and, in fact, discourages such behavior in meetings, then she is not being congruent, she is not living up to her stated belief in conflict, and thus is sending mixed messages to the work force. Therefore, **Step 5** assesses the CEO, as well as the entire management team.

Step 5

As reflected in Figure 4, the management team includes the CEO, top-level executives, and middle managers/supervisors. Although many organizations have eliminated the middle manager (at least in concept), most organizations still have a middle layer, one that separates the work force (subcultures) from the top management team. Therefore, we have made the decision to include them in our analysis. It's just as critical for the CEO to be in sync with these groups as it is for the CEO to be in sync with the Board.

Now, let's look at the working relationship of the management team. Are values in sync throughout the whole group? A process like Cultural Due Diligence™ forces you to examine this aspect of your business. As we discussed earlier, if there are breakdowns in values, leadership styles, behaviors, and working relationships, then any change you try to implement will likely fail. So take the time to understand the similarities and dissimilarities that exist, and discuss how they will help or hinder your ability to implement the tightest of strategic plans. This is extremely helpful when considering some type of business combination. What are the incongruencies that exist in these areas between Company A and Company B?

Here are some suggested questions that you should incorporate in your assessment of the CEO and the management team. We suggest that one-on-one interviews be conducted.

- As a leader of this organization, what are the top three challenges that you face today? (organizational and personal)
- As a leader, in order to meet these top challenges what do you need?
- Consider your direct reports/staff, what resources would be most valuable to them in addressing these top challenges?
- Our organization would be more successful if we: (fill in the blank).
- What I need most right now from my top team is: (CEO only)
- What I need most from my immediate supervisor is:
- What I need most right now from my colleagues is: (senior and middle management)
- My relationship with the CEO is:
- How would you describe the relationship between the Board and/or Corporate, CEO, top management and middle management?

- Are the values of the Board, CEO, and management in sync? In your mind, what are they?

- As a CEO, how could you do a better job of setting examples to promote the values you have committed to on paper?

- As a management team, how could you do a better job of setting examples to promote the organization's values?

- Developing the quality and quantity of tomorrow's leaders here at _____ is a critical component to creating a healthy culture and profitable business. What general suggestions do you have to ensure success in the leadership-development process? Does anything exist today? If yes, what is in place?

- How would you describe your current culture?

- How would you describe an effective culture?

- How flexible are your managers and employees? List specific examples that support your feelings. How have they helped or hindered any past change initiatives? Do you have a sense of who your resisters are and who your supporters are?

- What resources are you willing to devote for the assessment phase: Cultural Due Diligence™? For the implementation phase: Cultural Congruence?

- How do you plan to use the information that is garnered from the cultural-assessment process?

Step 6

Step 6 of **The Dig** is to analyze your formal policies and systems. See Figure 5.

Beyond the governing principles, a cultural assessment like Cultural Due Diligence™ should assist you in determining the level of congruence between your formal procedures and systems and your actions. Is what you say on paper or what you've filed in a ring binder how you are actually operating, or are your procedures outdated, invalid, and

---

Figure 5   Formal Procedures and Systems

cumbersome, thereby creating the infamous hidden culture (see informal and interactive practices)?

In the beginning there was the plan; and then came the assumptions. And the assumptions were without form, and the plan was completely without substance. And therefore darkness was upon the face of the workers.

And they spoke among themselves, saying: It is a crock of crap and it stinketh!

And the workers went unto their Supervisors and sayeth: It is a pail of dung and none may abide the odor thereof. And the supervisors went unto their Managers and sayeth: It is a container of excrement and it is very strong, such that none may abide by it.

And the managers went unto their Directors and sayeth: It is a vessel of fertilizer and none may abide its strength. And the Directors spoke among themselves, saying: It contains that which aids plant growth, and it is very strong. And the directors went unto the Vice Presidents and sayeth: It promotes growth and is very powerful.

And the Vice Presidents went unto the President and sayeth: This new plan will actively promote the growth and efficiency of this company, and in these areas in particular.

And the President looked upon the plan and saw that it was good, and the plan became policy!

An Anonymous Author

Ever see that in your organization?

When assessing your formal procedures and systems here are some examples of what you should be examining.

- **Key business measurements**—Do you have any type of formal quality program? What are your customer-service indicators? Would everyone within the organization know and understand the key business measurements? Or will they answer with broad statements such as: "Marketing will make the difference." "HR just needs to hire the 'right' people for the job." "Managing the money will be our success." "Tightening up the people systems will reduce our overhead, giving us more to work with"? Many times, the answers we get to these questions reflect the impression that one isolated area is responsible for a problem.

- **Fiscal systems**—Is the organization public or private? How is the budgeting process handled? What are the authority levels? What are your purchasing procedures? What are your financial tracking systems? What are your vendor or supplier systems and contracts?

- **Organizational structure/design**—What does your organizational chart look like? Are many of your processes centralized or decentralized? Is your organization structured around teams? What is your system for visioning, etc.?

- **Work environment**—How do you maintain a safe and healthy work environment? How are health, safety, and ergonomics addressed in improvement activities? How would you describe the key measures and targets for each of these environmental factors, and how do employees take part in establishing these measures and targets, etc.?

- **IT (Information Technology) systems**—What role does IT play in your organization? What are the main types of information and data that are collected? How are the information and data deployed to all users to support the effective management and evaluation of key company processes, etc.?

- **Human resources and organizational development**—There are a number of key areas to examine in this realm; they include:

  - **Communication**—How are announcements made? Which communication media do you use: newsletter, bulletin boards, Internet? How often do you communicate? How do you handle public relations? What is your policy on e-mail and Internet usage, etc.?

  - **Career Development/Human Development**—What opportunities are available for career development? What career ladders exist? Do you have a leadership-development program, mentoring program, or coaching program? What do your health and wellness programs look like? Do you have an internal posting program/internal recruitment system, job-rotation system, or job-sharing program? What about you performance-evaluation program(s)? Do you conduct 360-degree feedback, etc.?

  - **Employee Education, Training and Development, and Instructional Systems**—What strategies are used in the education process? Do you use computer-based training? How is curriculum design handled? Do you encourage distance-learning programs? Are your programs offered during work hours or after hours? Do you have an organizational-development function? If yes, to whom does this function report? Is it strategic? How is orientation handled? Is organizational culture part of the orientation? How are new knowledge and new skills reinforced on the job, etc.?

  - **Compensation**—Do you offer alternative pay methods? What do your benefit programs look like? What type of merit, motivational and commission plans do you offer, etc.? How are benefits administered? Do you offer cafeteria or flex plans?

These are a few of the areas that must be examined when you think about your formal procedures and systems. Once you've collected this data, the key is for you to determine how in sync you are with your practices. In other words, are the formal procedures and systems found in your procedural manuals and other written policy documents congruent with how your organization behaves? How do you determine that? Conduct focus groups with your subcultures (departments). This is a crucial step that shouldn't be missed when talking about mergers and acquisitions. Comparing your procedures with your potential partner can really expedite the integration process.

Informal & Interactive Practices
Step 7

The next step in **The Dig** is to analyze your informal and interactive practices (See Figure 6). Is your culture congruent, or are you experiencing disconnects? How does work really get done? Is getting work done based on the formal procedures? Or is it based on whom you know? What are the organizational nuances of your organization? How active is the grapevine? How are decisions made: collaborative or top down? How do you communicate with each other? Is communication formal or informal? And how do you handle conflict? This step is the golden nugget. As you interview your subcultures, you'll begin to validate how effective your formal procedures are. This is where the congruence (or incongruence) of your actions and your words are truly tested. This is probably one of the richest areas for you to assess. This is reality!!!

Informal & Interactive Practices
- Coordination of Work
- Organizational Nuances
- Grape Vine
- Decision Making
- Communication
- Conflict Resolution

Figure 6   Informal and Interactive Practices

Remember you must uncover your hidden culture, define it, and take steps to eliminate it!!!! The more informal practices you find, the greater the need to review your formal procedures and systems. The informal practices tell you what is REALLY going on in your organization. So dig—and dig deep. This is the area that really tells how well you are living up to your word.

Step 8

The next step is to assess your Organizational Characteristics (see Figure 7). All of the elements under this heading offer an immense amount of information about your organization. What are your norms? Are people expected to dress a certain way? What is the history? How long has the organization been around? What are the stories? How does the organization view itself? These are the things that make your organization unique in the minds of your people. How you address each bullet point laid out in the cloud in Figure 7 can both attract and repel your most valuable assets, your people. How you deal with diversity, religious holidays, and celebrating differences is a very important factor, and in light of so many of today's headline discrimination stories, this one can also directly affect the bottom line. What is management's relationship

Figure 7 Organizational Characteristics

with the union? Remember the American Airlines example? This one can be very costly to the organization. What is your relationship to the community in which you do business? This issue may be paramount for some of the work force. Timberland, which we discussed in the Culture Vulture chapter, is a good example of a company that constantly contributes and grows with the community—remember "Boot, Brand and Belief"? An examination of all of these characteristics helps you to further define your organizational culture. Again, this is very powerful when doing a comparison between Company A and Company B.

Subcultures
Step 9

Next we must address the subcultures, your functional departments (see Figure 8). Yes, as we have pointed out within your culture there are subcultures that must reviewed. This is where the true test begins. This is where your values, behaviors, and inter- and intra-group relationships are really tested. The subcultures offer you a great reality check. As a leader, are you really living up to the commitments you've made to the work force? We are sure you can think of a few examples of infighting between departments at one time or another. Such behavior is a great indicator of how cohesive your organization is. In larger organizations, divisions can also be viewed as subcultures that must be assessed. Use this group to validate the findings from all of the assessments that you have conducted, including the Cultural Health Index™.

Figure 8   Sub-Cultures

External Forces
Step 10

The last step in **The Dig** is to analyze the external forces (see Figure 9). What external forces drive your thinking? What are the social, technological, economic, regulatory, political, or community trends that move you into action? Remember the story of Ray Anderson at Interface, Inc.? He was chewing up more that 500 million pounds of raw material each year and excreting more than 900 tons of air pollutants, 600 million gallons of wastewater, and 10,000 tons of trash—not very environmentally conscious. But when he did "see the light" and changed his business process around to recycle everything possible, he became 23 percent more efficient in converting the raw stuff into sales dollars, cutting $40 million in costs, and boosting revenue to $76 million. His company also started winning contracts based on his new and improved environmental policies. If he hadn't stepped back and analyzed his practices, this wouldn't have happened. That's why it's important to step back and analyze your current practices, values if you will, to see if they are truly in line with your belief system, to test the theory of congruence in your daily work.

As you can see, a cultural-assessment process like Cultural Due Diligence™ creates the opportunity for you to seek and destroy the boogieman. It lends you the tools and strength to learn from history (not politics) and to go beyond repeating your history into creating your present and future.

Figure 9 External Forces

Phase II

After you've completed **The Dig,** then comes the assimilation and analysis process—what we call the Culture Connection™. You must assimilate all of the data that has been collected in the previous steps. Then, you should develop an executive summary (what we call a Cultural Resume™), which should provide your organization with a "big picture" overview of the findings. The feedback should also include a detailed report from the interviews and survey instruments that were used. The intent here is to uncover the incongruencies and congruencies that exist and to identify the similarities and dissimilarities that exist (especially critical during a business combination).

Examining congruence and non-congruence in your culture will uncover the points of wellness and the points of dysfunction within your organizational system. As you can see in Figure 10, we have placed organizational culture at the center of our model because it is at the core of change and development. An extensive assessment like CDD™ will help you define how incongruent or congruent your culture is.

You may be familiar with Weisbord's Six-Box Model, the Burke-Litwin Model of Organizational Performance and Change, and other works regarding organizational culture, performance, and change. Although we share some thoughts with many of our fellow OD practitioners, we are unique in our commitment to reflecting culture at the core of organizational change.

As you can see in Figure 10, organizational culture is encircled by organizational performance and organizational energy levels. If you are suffering from a non-congruent culture, then your employee energy levels will be adversely affected and your ability to perform optimally, to implement your strategy and satisfy your customers, will be hampered. All of these factors will contribute to a less-than-healthy bottom line. Note this formula: LEL = PP = LCSL = DIR = **DIE**. Low energy levels = poor performance = low customer satisfaction levels = decrease in revenues = **Decrease In Earnings**. Therefore, a process like CDD™ helps

Figure 10

you to identify your incongruencies and to create a functional culture
that keeps employee energy positive and satisfaction levels high. By
addressing these areas, you increase your opportunity to enhance performance and energy levels, which affect your ability to implement
whatever business strategy you have developed. In the Change Game
chapter, we mentioned a recent *Fortune* article that reported that many
CEOs have failed due to a lack of attention to people problems and
their inability to execute their plan. You cannot execute your plan without a positive energy level in your work force, and you cannot have
that positive energy level without a congruent culture.

Whatever assessment tool you choose, be sure it is one that helps
you collect data that is relevant, allows you to better know your organization inside and out, does not put you in a box, and helps you to create cultural congruence.

Cultural congruence is about believing that everyone must be
involved and that different points of view give you more tools and perspectives to handle challenges, and that trusting such diversity will
achieve positive outcomes.

As illustrated in Figure 11, cultural congruence creates multiple
levels of satisfaction: organizational satisfaction, community satisfaction, employee satisfaction, customer satisfaction, shareholder

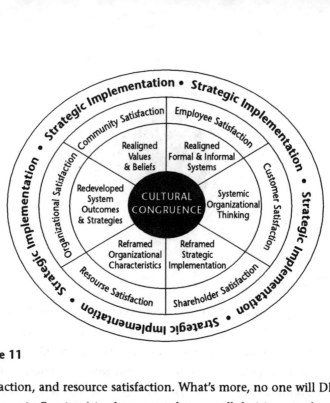

Figure 11

satisfaction, and resource satisfaction. What's more, no one will DIE (Decrease in Earnings) in the process, because all decisions made, all thoughts created, and all actions implemented are based on input from and consideration for customers, employees, shareholders, leaders, community, and the organization itself. We are not saying here that decision-making should be a free-for-all. There is always a need for a level of order/control to maintain balance in a system, but we are saying that the control should be "shared" not "owned."

How do you know whether your organization could benefit from a cultural assessment like the Cultural Due Diligence™ process? Well, ask yourself the following questions.

- Is my organization going through or thinking about a merger or acquisition?

- Are we currently involved in a joint venture or some type of alliance?

- Is my organization thinking about consolidating departments or integrating divisions?

- Are we contemplating a SHIFT in marketing strategy?

- Have we or are we planning to SHIFT to E-commerce as a way of doing business?

- Are we thinking about embracing self-directed work teams? Or a boundaryless organization?

- Could my organization make changes that would increase productivity levels?

If you have answered "yes" to at least one of these questions, then you should seriously consider conducting a cultural assessment like Cultural Due Diligence™.

In making your decision to move forward, you should also revisit the Readiness Assessment presented in Phase I of **The Dig** and take the time to answer those questions.

If your responses to these questions are generally positive, you have a sound track record for change initiatives. Congratulations! If your responses are less than favorable, then you need to seriously think about the barriers that are hampering your change efforts. A process like CDD™ can support you in that endeavor.

Moving Forward

You've decided to move forward with Cultural Due Diligence™. (If you've chosen not to move forward with CDD™, we hope you will do some kind of cultural assessment in your organization.)

As a leader, it is important that you personally experience the due-diligence process before proceeding. Ask yourself the following questions: Am I personally committed to the process? Do I believe that it is a good use of time and resources? Am I just going through the motions because it is the latest fad?

If you are having butterflies about doing it, or if you want to find out whether the benefits are worth the effort, you might also ask yourself: Who can I talk to that has gone through this? Remember, you don't have to tackle this alone.

Your personal commitment to the success of this process is critical. Without your explicit support, this initiative will be viewed with disdain and you won't get at the truth of your organization. Don't allow yourself to fall into the compliance trap of thinking that merely changing policies will be enough to comply with environmental, labor, workplace-safety and equal-opportunity regulations. This unauthentic action will be found out because practices won't change without your commitment. For the same reason, don't fall for the flavor of the month—it just won't stick. Our intent in developing CDD™ and in urging people to do cultural assessments was to **not** have the process be viewed as a fad or the latest flavor of ice cream. Conducting a cultural assessment must become a part of doing business and must be viewed as important as preparing your financial statements.

OK. Now that you've determined that you will be moving forward with a true commitment to the process, we suggest you refer to the Readiness Assessment that can be found in "The Cultural-Assessment Process" chapter. We encourage you to go through each of those questions before you proceed with a cultural assessment process.

The next critical step is to identify an internal culture specialist. This is an individual who will serve as project manager during the entire CDD™ process, including the Culture Connection™ (or implementation) phase. Before making that decision, ask yourself the following questions: What internal talent do we have? Can they lead this new business strategy?

We would venture to guess that your initial thought is probably to put the human resources (HR) department and/or the organizational development department (OD) in charge. This approach may work when you are talking about an internal business-change strategy. However, even then these individuals are too close to the situation and emotionally attached. This could cloud their ability to make objective business decisions. The individuals must be able to detach themselves from the outcome(s). Through our own personal experience, we have found that any large business-change strategy drains the internal staff, no matter how competent or experienced—especially in the case of a merger or acquisition.

In working with a number of highly competent HR and OD professionals, we have found that many of them did get emotionally caught up in the change and many became concerned about how the change initiative would affect them. When we asked these individuals if they were to "do it again" what they would do differently, many responded by stating that they would prefer to work with an external, neutral partner to support the cultural-transition team. They had a number of different reasons for this preference. Some wanted an individual like a designated driver, one who would not become intoxicated by all the difficult decisions or paralyzed by emotional entanglement in the outcome. Others wanted to go outside to find an expert because of their sheer lack of experience in initiating a large-scale change effort.

So often, HR and OD professionals are expected to work their magic and make things happen in organizations, all while still performing their daily functions. Well, before you demand that of your people, make sure that they have the requisite skills to be able to succeed; otherwise, you've taken the first step toward failure. This is a trap too may of us fall into, assuming for the wrong reasons (e.g., because we really like the person or because they've been so successful up to this point) that someone must be able to take on this new responsibility. We're not saying that you don't have very competent HR and OD folks. What we are saying is that you must discuss all this with these individuals and determine whether they can succeed before you anoint them as your culture specialist(s).

Ask the questions:

- What experience has this individual had in implementing any type of change initiative?
- If it is a merger or acquisition, has this individual ever managed the integration process before?
- How successful has this person been in implementing change strategies?
- Is the individual open to being on the change team or leading the team?
- Is the person a strategic thinker?

- Does the individual have good business acumen and are their methodologies grounded in hard-core business strategies?
- Is the individual and/or their function respected in the organization?

The type of individual that you must select is one who sees herself or himself as a change agent. Remember "The Change Game" exercise? We suggest that you have your prospective change agent complete that exercise. That exercise shouldn't be the sole tool in making your decision, but it will be a great basis for dialogue. Too often, we have seen really good people become incredibly frustrated (to the point of questioning their own competence) when they find themselves in a position for which they're not prepared or find they don't have the right tools to be successful. Remember the boogieman? It is very scary to be left alone in the dark.

The change agent must have a track record that demonstrates the ability to develop and implement effective business strategies to achieve higher market share, improve profitability, and create a sustainable competitive advantage. This individual must see the big picture and help others do the same. If you find that this person has some major gaps in these skills, then you must set the individual or individuals up for success. Function as advisor and coach. Know when to bring in external support. You can accomplish this by partnering with an external cultural specialist. This will increase your odds for success and your ability to capture huge gains.

One organization that we worked with was going through the biggest transition in its 100-year history. The management team failed to recognize that the individual (internal) who was chosen to lead this change strategy was not the right fit. She was very bright, but did not possess the core skills needed to pull this off. She was a taskmaster and tactician. She became bogged down in the details because she failed to trust in her people's ability and willingness to get the job done. She became extremely dysfunctional—a tyrant, really—yelling and screaming at her people. Needless to say, there was chaos, dissension, anxiety, and frustration. Ultimately, this did her in.

After a year of struggling, the organization finally realized that she needed support; however, by that point 50% of her staff had resigned, 25% of the organization was ready to jump ship, and the project schedule was set back by 14 months. This cost the organization millions of dollars.

If you decide to partner with an external cultural expert, view this person as the designated driver. Hiring a designated driver does not mean that the external person is leading the change initiative. Instead, the external expert is serving as a guide to assist you in getting through the CDD™ process. This person will help you get to your first destination safely. The magnitude to which CDD™ will change your organization will affect many aspects of your business and will require ongoing support and involvement from senior managers, middle managers, supervisors, and frontline employees. No consultant can rally that level of support; it must emerge from the process.

If you've decided to bring in external support, be very clear about the level of responsibility, lines of authority, objectives, and accountabilities. Paying attention to these details in advance is all about relationship building.

Bring someone from the outside to a) help build the internal strength and b) help the staff implement the CDD™ process, so that they are then equipped to conduct CDD™ independently. This is the essence of *real-time learning*.

We know that many of you are cringing at the thought of bringing in "another consultant." Be wise and conduct due diligence before selecting a partner. Don't just empty your pockets. Look for a partner who is interested in working with your organization to help the employees become self-sufficient.

Pick a Partner and Promenade

So how do you pick the right partners? Have they lived in the trenches? Look for a partner who has had real-life experiences, someone who has a track record for creating healthy, congruent cultures. You don't need someone who has just bounced from one organization to another as an external consultant, but someone who has "felt the pain." Then and only then, can they truly understand the challenges that you face as a business leader. This type of individual has the ability to go beyond the assessment phase of the Cultural Due Diligence™ process and can assist you in putting a solid action plan together and assist in powerful implementation strategies. Start by getting referrals from other professionals whom you know and respect. This will ensure a higher level of success. Ask for references. Learn what they have achieved. Are they results-oriented? Do not be fooled by an impressive client list. Find out what they did for the clients and how successful they were at meeting the agreed-upon goals and objectives. Did they add value? Did they make a positive difference? How? Don't be afraid to ask very specific questions about their past performance. Get examples of specific projects they have been responsible for from start to finish.

Good Listeners

Look for a partner who is a good listener—and one who asks the right questions. How can you determine that? After your first meeting, the effective consultant will be able to provide you with a detailed report of what was discussed in writing. What you should ask for is what we've come to call the "the situational summary" or "historical perspective." This summary/perspective must be very detailed, so much so that your reaction in reading it should be, "Gee! Did they have a tape recorder going during our discussion?" Or "Are you sure you haven't worked here before?"

Knowledgeable

Does she really know the subject or field she claims to be an expert in? Can she answer the majority of your questions without constantly referring to her notes? (The key word is "constantly." No consultant, particularly when working in a highly technical area, carries all the relevant knowledge in her head.)

Communication

How well does she communicate? Does she use jargon or does she communicate in simple, understandable terms? When asked to explain the jargon, can she clearly articulate what she means and not spew some incomprehensible variation of what she just said? A consultant who doesn't understand the terminology will not be able to apply the underlying concepts in your organization.

Choices

A good partner will offer alternatives. As the client, you should be given choices. The consultant can assist in determining what the best solution may be at any given time, but you are the customer, and you deserve to have choices. Do they present choices in modular form so you can pick and choose? The prospective consultant should also be prepared to explain the pros and cons of choosing one alternative over another. Ultimately, it is your choice, but you want to make a well-informed decision and the only way to do that is to consider all the facts.

Partner

External consulting should be about collaboration and partnership. The reason so many change initiatives have failed in organizations of all sizes and in all industries is that we get consultants to come in, identify the problem, tell us how to fix it, and then they go on to the next project. A true partnership is about seeing a project through to fruition. It's about ongoing support. It's about putting their plan into action. If consultants don't guarantee their work—BEWARE! If the clock is constantly running, be leery.

Implementation

Can the consultant move from concepts, models, and theory to implementation? Remember the article from *Fortune,* "Why CEOs Fail"? Lack of execution is one of the key culprits in CEO failure. Well, the same holds true for external consultants. To determine how effective your potential partner is, ask for specific examples of their success. For instance, have the consultant describe a recent situation in which he established a successful client relationship. What did the consultant do to make that relationship happen? What indication did the consultant get that the client valued his skills? Or you may have the consultant describe a recent change initiative in which he implemented a solution. What did the client have when the consultant started? When the consultant finished? What barriers were encountered in between? How did the consultant deal with those barriers? Ideally, you should find a consultant who has functioned as an internal consultant or line manager because the odds are better that he will deliver. Internal consultants and line managers absolutely have to have the ability to move from the conceptual stage to practical application of the concepts and implementation.

Personality/Chemistry

How does the individual fit within your current culture? Don't be fooled by all the wonderful credentials. Take the time to determine his style/approach. Does he see himself as a trainer, educator, or coach? Is he able to work well with individuals at all levels in your organization?

Jack/Jackie Of All Trades

Beware of the consultant who boasts he can do whatever it is you need. This is highly unlikely. Look for a consultant who has formed alliances with other professionals in order to provide the right/best service to you, the client. The bottom line is that the consultant should be in the business of coaching and helping individuals, groups and, ultimately, organizations to be healthier and more effective. Beware of the consultant who wants to fish for you—look for the consultant who wants to teach you and your organization how to fish.

Honesty And Integrity

When you bring an external consultant into your organization you are placing a high level of trust in her; therefore, it is absolutely critical that the individual be honest, have a high level of integrity, be willing to share information, and be comfortable with a high level of disclosure. You will be able to determine some of this through your interactions. However, the other alternative that we strongly suggest is to speak with previous clients.

Whatever your choice may be, make it one that will ensure a higher level of success for everyone involved—including the driver.

Beware of the Wolf in Sheep's Clothing

Once you've made the decision on who will lead the CDD™ charge, you must then develop a CDD™ team. Some critical questions that you must consider are:

- Do you have a supportive top team?

- How has that team supported you in the past? (Take the time to think of each individual on your team and conduct individual assessments. Think of particular situations when their leadership was required in support of any type of change initiative, and assess their performance.)

- Do the members of the top team show open opposition and hostility?

- Do they spend most of their time talking about "why this won't work," or are they more passive in their resistance?

- Do they withhold information?

- Do they drag their feet? Are they non-confrontational yet unproductive?

- Do they not attack the solution, yet not support it?

- Do they still have the "we've always done it this way" mentality?

- Do they tend to overcomplicate new ideas/changes?

Be prepared to deal with their resistance and confront it head on. Spend time sharing with them your vision of the CDD™ process. Explain why it is important and what you expect from them. If you begin to see resistance, address it immediately. Remember the statistics from "Why CEOs Fail"—not dealing with people issues is one of the biggest downfalls for a CEO.

Also remember to involve your employees, they are the ones who will really make things happen. View them as partners in your business, because you'll need their help whenever SHIFT HAPPENS.

The Responsibility Shifts to You

The foundation for the house has been poured. The blueprint is laid out on the drawing table. The materials have been identified, the tools defined, and hopefully you are now keenly aware of the crew you will need to build the house.

Conducting a cultural assessment will begin to send a strong message to your work force that the people side of your business is just as important as the infamous bottom line. What you do with the information once it is collected will also send a strong message to your employees. If you do nothing with the information, then it will be very clear that you have only given lip service to the human component. On the other hand, if you take the next steps and involve your employees in the process, you are well on your way to creating a congruent culture. If you follow this path, you will find your organization moving from a group of "MEs" to an energized collection of "WEs." It is in this transformation that you begin to create a sustainable, profitable work environment.

Keep It Alive

We are very interested in staying connected to our readers and making this an ongoing process in which we all continue to learn and grow from each other's experiences. Therefore, as you gain more insight, knowledge, and experience in the areas of organizational culture and change, we would like you to share those experiences with us so that we might pass them along to our readership.

Please contact us at http://www.change4u.com and share your stories: the good, the bad, and the ugly.

We hope you have enjoyed taking this journey toward a better understanding of your organization and yourself. During our own personal journey through the writing of this book, we met Barry Berns, M.D., physician, lecturer, and author. Barry touched our lives with his philosophy on the role of spirit and leadership and the role of core values.

We wish to share his thoughts with you in the Afterword of our book.

In closing, we are reminded again of an old Chinese saying "a book is like a garden you carry in your pocket." We hope the many seeds of wisdom from this book will allow your personal and professional gardens to flourish.

Afterword: Spirit and Leadership

by Barry R. Berns, M.D.

Introduction

What profits a man if he gains the world but loses his soul?

If you had one year to live, would wealth or happiness be your bottom line?

If your business had one year to live, would you extract all its profits and abandon it, or would you find a way to realign it so that its purpose, employees, and customers would find continuation, satisfaction, and completion?

How does the meaning and purpose of our personal lives fit with our work lives? How does the individual connect with work in a way to promote the welfare of both? How do personal core values fit in the paradigm of business success? Can we even speak of spirit in connection with the business world?

There is a powerful connection between spirit and work. We are never separated from our spirit. Spirit is the essence of our being, our life force. Spirit drives our values, purpose, desires and motivations. In the work world, we can more easily speak of spirit in its manifestation as core values. Core values connect us in positive relationship to others. They create integrity, vitality, extend positive energy, liberate our creativity and connect us to our hearts to what we love. Core values are our connection to spirit.

The Promise

The way we operate personally carries over into whatever we do. What do we do most? Work. There must be no incongruities between our personal, professional, and work values. If there is, disharmony and dysfunction arise between our inner and outer worlds. Following our **positive** core values directs our lives towards happiness and contentment.

When we realize that there is a very thin line between customer and employee we begin to promote the satisfaction of both. At a deeper level, we realize that we are all customers and employers of each other. As a physician, my ethical and competent work with my patients brings health and wellness not only to them but to me as well. Their peace of mind is also mine.

I too am a patient needing medical care, a customer of managed care, of home-care products, of food services, and of every facet of the life that connects us all. When I see all the interconnections, I realize that I am not alone and that what I believe and do affects others and the world.

Each of us is a mirror to the other. Stakeholder, shareholder, employee, manager or CEO, we have common, shared inner and outer experiences. Aligning the core inner spirit with outer actions promises integration of our highest interest with our common interests—it allows us to be congruent.

What could be a higher goal than to share prosperity with each other? Anything else is destined not only to failure, but also to conflict and suffering.

As a senior medical student in the clinic at our university hospital, I encountered a woman with high blood pressure. I spent an hour with her learning not only her medical history, but also her personal story. At the end of our visit, I prescribed an anti-hypertensive medication to help lower her high blood pressure.

In my heart, I knew that this medical intervention was only the tip of the iceberg. Her social, environmental, and family struggles were untouchable by the Western medical model. Her eyes told me of her surrender to an inescapable fate. And I had no idea of how to make a difference for that woman.

Have you ever had that feeling? At work, at home, or in some other area of your everyday experience?

How do we really help others? How do we join efforts and change things for the better? Who takes leadership to create such change? In our organizations, we sometimes think that significant change must come from the top down, until we find the story of the "little person" who changed someone's life or the conditions around them. In this way, those we serve feel the influence of our inner core values.

What difference does it make, you might ask, if in business we act with trust or betrayal? With truth or dishonesty? With care or contempt?

Would you accept betrayal, dishonesty, and contempt as your family's means of connection with each other? Would you sign on to serve a company with such virtues?

The promise that we make to each other in a relationship, whether a work relationship or a personal relationship, counts. This promise is an outer expression of our inner core values. A business that deceives at any level of operation, deceives itself and its customers.

The promise of a business to uphold its integrity and do what is best for its customers is the promise of the people in that business. There is no separation between the people and the business.

The Obstacles

What keeps us (personally and in business) from fulfilling this promise of integrity? The answer lies in our core values that are undefined, insufficient, or disregarded. It is that simple and profound.

Every day brings challenges of every sort. This is the world we live in. Our core values are what help us to meet those challenges. When we know them and act on them, we proceed into the unknown with confidence.

When our core values are poorly defined or disregarded, we betray ourselves and others in ways that cause harm.

Most of the obstacles to understanding and acting upon our core values come from old beliefs, knee-jerk emotional reactions, unhealthy loyalties, unhealthy commitment to historical precedents, and fearful expectations.

These obstacles are swimming in the personal or business unconsciousness, operating without proper scrutiny or open discussion. They are "under the table" precepts that underlie and put us into the reactive mode of the "fight or flight" survival response.

How we respond to crises without discussion, involving others or asking for help will open us to old patterns—beliefs and emotional reactions of the past. We can remain tied to obstacles from our past (old beliefs, knee-jerk emotional reactions, unhealthy loyalties, unhealthy commitment to historical precedents, and fearful expectations) or we can test them against our core values. When we examine our values through open discussion, we can determine which elements of the past are obstacles to be cleared away so that we can arrive at new concepts, new emotional reactions, and new loyalties, etc., that reflect our values and offer us new possibilities for desired solutions.

Turning Points

Crises are the messengers of change. They are paradoxical blessings that demand our attention and response. In the personal arena, crises come in the form of health problems, life-threatening illness, relationship and family crises, divorces, separations, job changes, financial losses, legal difficulties, and more.

These are mirrored in the business arena with similar scenarios, such as high employee turnover, absenteeism, employee theft, or distrust of management.

Common to all these scenarios is the need for response. And the basis for our response is grounded in our core values.

Acting and reacting from confused, unclear, or muddled values leads to a loss of energy, unfocused actions, emotional drain, mental exhaustion, and sometimes even physical illness. This often is referred to as "burnout."

Yet, it is in that moment of "hitting bottom" that a demand for deeper inner awareness and clarity is realized.

This is the call to investigate values, beliefs, emotional reactions, health conditions, family and relationship connections, business and work connections, loyalties and expectations before you encounter significant problems or difficulties.

Why wait for a major crisis? Why not act when the problems are minor?

There is an ancient wisdom that says, "Die before you die." This means that you deal with the deepest of all issues before you actually encounter them. In doing so, you live day to day, moment to moment, with peace of mind because you have already confronted the most significant of all problems.

Let me share a story.

Ten years ago, I was diagnosed with cancer. This crisis of health carried me into one of the deepest parts of my inner journey.

In the swirl of surgical biopsy and diagnostic testing, I lost whatever grounding I once had. I experienced tremendous pain and sorrow at the possibility of losing all I had come to know and love. All the positive aspects of my life seemed, in that moment, lost to me.

In particular, I had been opening a new door to closer relationships with my son and daughter. I felt such a deep love for both my children that the anticipation of losing connection to them was overwhelmingly painful, so much so I was unwilling to accept a verdict of doom.

It is interesting to note the word "doom." This was indeed how I felt. The diagnosis of cancer carried a cloud of hopelessness with it. I had been trained in the science of medicine, in which doom and hopelessness are characteristics attached to cancer. To Western ways of thinking, I was about to enter the wasteland of statistics where my fate was tied to numbers accumulated in experimental trials of medical treatments. I would be offered state-of-the-art treatment in a field of medicine where death was the anticipated outcome.

Yet, something clicked inside me as I confronted this challenge. I already had expanded traditional healing methods to include emotional, psychodynamics and addiction methodologies in order to deal with my own workaholism and family problems, realizing I could not live a life untrue to myself.

Now, I had to begin an even more risk-laden journey, one that had mortality written on it. I had to trust my intuitive inner guidance, not my rational mind, to find the path I now required. In the past, I tried to be in control of everything; now I knew that I had to surrender my control (the control that I never really had to begin with) and open up to something larger than myself.

What was I looking for? How was I to find it? Who could help me?

The one clear, guiding commitment I found in my heart was this: I had to do whatever was needed in order to participate fully and completely in my healing. "Participation" seemed the key word. I had to give up the thought that I had to be the one in control. I needed to exercise my ability and my responsibility to do my part, whatever it was to be, and then, surrender the outcome. I had to surrender to my spirit.

"Healing" was another key word. This was not about longevity. It was about coming into a deeper truth of being, no matter how much time I had left to live.

I can tell you now that I found that deep place of healing that I was looking for. It required a journey deep into the past, the journey itself being full of its own wonderful synchronicities and blessings.

Western medicine would say that I am in remission. I would say that cancer brought me a gift of healing. To be free of hate and to realize the true essence of love is a blessing.

This essence exists in each and every one of us at our core, but it is easily lost in the course of our lives. It is, very simply and deeply, the place of connection to our highest truth. And in this place is the love and joy we all crave.

How we get to this place of healing, into spirit, is the only real question. In my journey, I found a path that opened me to healing at all levels of the mind, body, heart, and spirit. It opened me to the experience of love and joy in the present moment (the only time there is), the eternal now.

Fulfillment

Once we've examined our behaviors and beliefs and discarded that which is contradictory and dysfunctional, we begin to choose our paths freely, instead of being governed by dark, unseen forces within. In the moment of success when core values are aligned with outcomes, we encounter enjoyment. If this remains elusive, we must ask, "What are those factors that keep me from happiness and contentment? What are those things that keep our business from enjoying its success?"

The culmination of our lives does not lie in retirement as our culture often believes and directs us. It lies in the moment-to-moment living of our truth. This brings joy to our experience of life, to our interactions with others, and sets the stage for all else to follow.

The words *happiness, contentment, satisfaction, enjoyment,* and *loving* touch something inside our innermost being that yearns for attention and completion.

Art and literature are packed with stories of men who suffer through their lives in competition and accomplishment, but feel empty in their hearts. Citizen Kane told that story, as did all of Hemingway's work and all of Shakespeare's tragedies.

Love itself is a most potent elixir. How painful it must be for those who seek only power and money, and miss that sweet taste, when they discover they cannot buy it.

When you come to that last breath, what do you say? What do you take with you? What is in your spiritual bank? When you drop all the impermanent forms, what do you have left? Do you really think that when you're on your deathbed you're going to say I wish I'd spent more time in meetings.

When you live your life according to truth of your core values, you experience something unnamable, yet deeply knowable. You come to know something of a higher awareness of being that is shared with other human beings, something of spirit that is common and most easily recognized when two people acknowledge that they are in love, or that they love their children, love their friends, or just love life itself.

This connection of life and love—NOT ONLY PERSONAL LIFE, BUT IN BUSINESS AS WELL—brings joy and happiness. We feel satisfied and at peace when we live an integrated life in harmony and congruent with our core values.

Faced with life-threatening disease or events, one looks at one's deepest priorities. What you gain in this material world, you lose eventually. The deathbed life review reveals our truest wishes. Who of us would say that we want to pass on to others money and possessions, but not love? Who would say that they would like to be remembered as an unloving person who attained great status and position? Who would like to have people forget or reject them?

This end point of life calls forth deep thought. Who am I? What is life all about? What is my life purpose and meaning? What is the legacy I want to leave to those I care for and love?

Awareness of our deepest purpose and meaning shows itself in the ways we live with others and in the ways we do our work and business. Crises provide the wake-up call to ensure that we pay attention.

Awareness brings opportunity. We can decide and choose. Then, act in accordance with our truth.

Appendix A

Phase I—We formed a core group whose objective was: "To enlist/engage people who would get involved, communicate and carry the vision of the new leader." They included formal and informal leaders from all levels of the organization; who view themselves as change agents and see problems as opportunities and are: vocal, energetic, committed, optimistic and customer focused.

The resulting twenty-five member "Customer Service Team" represented a cross section of the organization, from entry level to top managers.

Phase II—The Customer Service Team organized and was empowered to develop "a back to basics approach to attain levels of 90%+ approval by patients." The most important factor here was that although senior management and the CEO gave the direction for improvements, all (and I mean, all) actions were developed by the Team, communicated to all staff members and monitored by the Team. This was empowerment at its best!

Phase III—The first group of activities included the following:

- ID Badge—The members of the committee, including myself, had our ID badges remade showing just our first name and Customer Service Representative as our position.

- Catcher Program—The team defined three levels of Customer Service: A, B and C. For the first three months, members of the team would reward staff for performing level C (very basic customer service). Awardees received free lottery tickets or ice cream sundaes. After three months, Level C was the expected behavior and we moved on to rewarding level B, repeated the cycle, and moved on to level A.

- Sloppy Sally Fashion Show—We were receiving comments about the appearance of our staff. Patients had a hard time trusting people who were about to take blood samples from them, when they— 1) had no ID, and 2) were sloppy in their appearance. The Customer Service Team developed the Sloppy Sally Fashion Show, which was held in the cafeteria during lunch hours. It went something like this: Various staff members would model sloppy dress and appropriate dress and "walk the runway" between tables. There was an emcee and rating cards on the tables similar to those you see at the Olympics. The employees would then hold up cards rating the various forms of dress. It turned out to be hilarious and successful in getting our point across to the staff. Most organizations, when faced with this problem would more than likely write a rigid "dress policy," and enforce it with penalties, etc. We had a very innocuous policy and literally never had to enforce it. Better yet, the staff became our sentinels of the policy. When someone dressed inappropriately, they let their colleagues know about it. This never came up as an issue again in our customer surveys!

- Image Consultant—The committee had an image consultant come into the hospital to review every area to determine its ambiance and how it appeared to patients. They then submitted a plan to senior management that was, with a few minor changes, accepted and implemented over a two to three year period. They even held garage sales and raffles to fund some of the improvements. They did this on their own time!

- Revamped all signage—This was a part of the image work. We made our signs friendlier, and they were written in several languages.

- Nursing Unit Aesthetic Team—There was a tendency on the part of operating rooms to close down after the day's schedule was done and ignore last-minute requests. This unit developed a plan to accommodate these last-minute requests by juggling schedules to minimize overtime while still providing quality service. This group's actions helped us increase our volume, not only because they accepted after-hours cases; but, because the surgeons were now booking more of their regular cases with us.

- Translator Program—The North Shore of Massachusetts had a very heavy influx of Spanish, Laotian, Cambodian, Vietnamese, and Russian immigrants. We implemented a Translator Program to better understand the needs of these patients. In addition, the team recommended that we implement diversity training. All employees, including management, went through two days of training.

- Telephone Skill Training was conducted.

- Videotapes were produced for patients to view in their home *before* they came in for surgery.

- Room Service—(Phase I): we offered newspaper delivery, haircuts, shopping for basics.

- Room Service (Phase II): We added the prime feature of hotel room service: food ordering. We discovered that patients wanted the hospital to look and feel more like a hotel. The Customer Service Team researched the process, made a presentation to senior management, and the program was implemented in six months and was very successful. What was so exciting? Well food is usually the lowest-ranked area in a customer survey (you know all the jokes about hospital food); however, in our latest customer survey, food was one of the highest-ranked areas! In addition, in the most recent employee survey, this department had the highest employee commitment to the organization!

- Retreats focusing on customer service were held department by department with these objectives:

  1. Recognize that our employees are our most valuable asset
  2. Create understanding of customer service (internal and external)
  3. Identify how the department contributes to customer service
  4. Define and identify the customer
  5. Identify the needs of the customer
  6. Identify the barriers that prevent the department from providing exceptional customer service
  7. Brainstorm the process/problems that cause these barriers
  8. Develop suggestions for potential solutions to barriers
  9. Remove the barriers—the manager and the employees of the department worked together to remove the barriers

All of this was possible because leadership was able to relinquish control and truly empowered the team by giving them the responsibility and the authority to carry out their plans.

Appendix B

The value process was conducted in two phases. In PHASE I, we established the team and charged them with reviewing current values (Surprise, surprise! There were none!) so we had to go about establishing them. The team was made up of seventeen individuals, and, as I mentioned before, they came from several disciplines and a number of line and staff positions. We met twice a week for three months. At the end of that time, we were able to articulate the newly developed values, which gave the organization the base from which to develop a culture. We determined that the keepers of the values would be the Human Resources Department and myself. As a result, we (along with the senior team) developed the program each year to drive the values into the genetic code (culture) of the organization. It was very important to give all of the team members the time, resources and authority to carry out their mission. As CEO I served as the chief spokesperson and champion for the group.

PHASE II was really the implementation phase that followed refinement of the values. In our situation, this involved the following steps:

- assignment of primary responsibilities to Human Resources;
- prominent display of the written values at building entrances, on bulletin boards, in conference rooms, and any workplace gathering area;
- integration of the values into annual performance appraisals, 360-degree feedback documents, public-relations brochures, security information, new services, and service-award ceremonies;
- incorporation of the values into an Employee Opinion Survey, in which employees were asked to rate how well the organization lived up to the stated values;
- hosting open orientation sessions with new employees to discuss the values;
- holding at least annual sessions to discuss how our strategic and operational/budget objectives supported our values.

We often had spirited discussions at our meetings. Each major objective had to meet the intent of at least two values. If it did not, we would re-think the objective, determine its value, and modify it to pass through the screen.

Shared values are critical, and when we talk about the Cultural Due Diligence™ process, you will see that at the heart of creating a congruent culture is the congruency between our values as CEOs and those of our employees at all levels. When a breakdown of these core values begins, we leave ourselves wide open for mass chaos. Employees start to question what is acceptable and unacceptable behavior. Confusion sets in, energy levels decline. That's when morale goes in the basement. Implementation of our key strategic goals is threatened. This is a very unhealthy condition for our organizations. This state directly affects our attitude toward our customers. Dissatisfied employees = dissatisfied customers = decrease in revenues = decrease in earnings (DE=DC=DIR = DIE). That's the real bottom line.

Programs—Tried and True

Here are some other ways that I tried to 'talk the talk' and 'walk the walk' of an empowering leader.

Town Meetings

In the early days, they were called the CEO Forum. The name is not as important as how we conduct ourselves, what information we share, and our willingness, as CEOs, to shut up and listen during the Q & A session. We must treat the attendees as our customers!

My two basic objectives at these meetings were:

1. to share whatever information was appropriate with regard to the organization; and

2. to help employees understand why the organization was making specific decisions.

Some subjects that were discussed at Town Meetings were:

- annual budgets and objectives;
- new or changed benefit programs;
- potential personnel changes (layoffs) before they happened;
- merger, acquisition, affiliation agreements with other organizations;
- impact of environmental issues on the organization;
- "grapevine" issues e.g. Who is saying what about whom and is it true?

(Within reasonable limits of confidentiality).

At these meetings, we had a Q & A period at the end where I refrained from comment until I fully understood the questions or comments that were presented. I tried to address WIFM—what's in it for me? I ended each session by asking the attendees to "crank this information into their own personal lives," to see how it affected them, and to make decisions accordingly. (I didn't want anyone to face what my wife and I had encountered when we went on our spending spree thanks to misinformation.)

"Andy Over Easy"

I regularly met with small groups of ten to twenty-five employees since first becoming a CEO in 1976. Doing so allowed discussion of issues and concerns on a more intimate basis. In my most recent experience as CEO, my predecessors had conducted similar sessions, which were dubbed "Bagels with Bob" and "Eggs with Ernie. Even though these sessions by my predecessors had not been previously well received, I decided to be consistent with the attempt at humor, and we decided to call these sessions "Andy Over Easy,"

This is how it worked. Each month, we sent a birthday card to the employees who had a birthday that month. They were invited, not mandated, to have breakfast with me. We limited the number to twenty-five and would expand to more than one session, if necessary.

We opened each meeting with a welcome and some brief remarks. I then sat back and asked for questions. Sometimes, the attendees were reluctant to ask the first question, so I would offer $5.00 to anyone who would. (I think the word got out on this one!) Once the first question was asked, things started flowing. The majority of the time, such a meeting can be a great exchange between the CEO and the employees. You learn so much about the organization, the employees, and the customers. And always, trust the process—it works!

It is important to note some simple principles for these meetings.

First of all, attendance has to be voluntary. Also, such meetings are not a "bitching session," but a chance to exchange information and get answers. My remarks were limited to ten to fifteen minutes at the most, so the rest of the time was spent talking about what they wanted to talk about. It was clearly understood that everyone was free to talk about everything that was discussed at the meeting once they left. And finally, if we (the management team) could not answer a question, we would get back to them with an answer within seventy-two working hours.

I would also mention that the Senior VP of Human Resources attended all of the meetings since many questions related to that area. The types of questions people asked sometimes amazed me. I found it hard to understand where the breakdown in communication took place, but it was helpful to know that it existed.

It is important to remember to treat the group's members as your customers: Listen carefully, don't get defensive, and only answer those questions that you can really answer. This is not the forum for the "ole smoke and mirrors" routine. They will see right through that one.

At the end of each breakfast, we gave everyone a birthday present. It was a T-shirt with a logo of a chicken popping out of an egg and the caption: "I survived Andy Over Easy!"

A little levity goes a long way.

However, going through the motions isn't enough. Yes, the intimacy of a small group is great and the T-shirts are fun, but these breakfast meetings were successful because we were honest in our information and responses, we followed up on recommendations, and we treated everyone with respect. The key being that, although I was the CEO, I did not act like nobility and was not defensive. All this made people feel important!

Customer/Patient Dinners

This practice was implemented in an acute-care hospital setting, but can be adapted for use in any organization. This is a perfect example of how the Chief Empowerment Officer can 'walk the walk' regarding an organization's customer service.

We would send dinner invitations to forty-five randomly selected individuals who had been patients in our hospital for three or more days. They were asked to bring a friend and join members of the hospital management team for dinner and discussion.

On average, we would meet with sixteen people. Our customer-service representative, a nurse, another caregiver, and one manager joined me.

We would ask the former patient some questions based on their hospital stay. We would also ask the patient's guests to offer input about their experience if they had accompanied the patient to the hospital. After hearing the responses, we would go around the room and ask everyone the following question:

"If you were CEO for a day, what is the one thing you'd change or improve?"

We received some incredible suggestions and many were implemented immediately. For example, the idea for the two phases of Room Service mentioned in Appendix A came out of these dinners.

The information collected at these dinners was always shared with the other staff members and was used to supplement our patient surveys. Our Customer Service Team was then given the responsibility to follow up on open items and submit a report of any action taken.

Tour Of Duty

Here's one that is really easy and fun. Schedule monthly tours of duty for yourself in different areas of your organization. Walk a mile in some of your employees' shoes. You can get your hair messed up and your hands dirty! During my tenure as CEO, I washed and waxed floors, scrubbed toilets, drove a laundry truck, worked in the laundry, spent a day with staff in a locked mental-health unit, shadowed nurses, worked a security shift, and worked with the maintenance crew. I learned that these folks knew a lot more than I did about our organization.

Chapter Notes

Call to Action
1. Interview with Milt Bayer, 1999.
2. Interview with Carol Mangold, 1999.
3. James C. Collins and Jerry I. Porras, *Built to Last: Successful Habits of Visionary Companies,* (New York: HarperBusiness,1997), p. 196.
4. Neale D. Walsch, *Conversations with God, an uncommon dialogue, book 1,* (New York: G. P. Putnam's Sons, 1995), p. 3. Reprinted with permission.

The Change Game
1. Interview with Jerry Hurwitz, 1999.
2. Interview with George Burkholder, M.D.,1999.
3. Audrey Y. Williams, "Be Prepared for layoff, experts warn," *The Arizona Republic,* May 9, 1999. Reprinted by permission from The Charlotte Observer. Copyright held by The Charlotte Observer.
4. Stephen Bertman, "Hyperculture: The Human Cost of Speed," *THE FUTURIST,* 12/98, p. 20. Used with permission from the World Future Society, 7910 Woodmont Avenue, Suite 450, Bethesda, Maryland 20814. Telephone: 301/656-8274; Fax: 301/951-0394; **http://www.wfs.org.**
5. James A. Belasco, *Teaching the Elephant to Dance: The Manager's Guide to Empowering Change,* (New York: Crown Publishers, Inc., 1990), p. 244. Reprinted with permission.
6. Brock Yates, *Outlaw Machine: Harley-Davidson and the Search for the American Soul,* (New York: Little, Brown and Company, 1999), p. 166–7,172.

7. James A. Belasco, *Teaching the Elephant to Dance: The Manager's Guide to Empowering Change,* (New York: Crown Publishers, Inc., 1990), p. 17. Reprinted with permission.

8. Interview with Milt Bayer, 1999.

9. Angela Gonzales, "Keys to Emerging Businesses—Changes lead to firm's growth," *The Business Journal,* 11/14/97, p. 49. Reprinted with permission.

10. ProSci Study, Management Review, 12/98, p.8.

11. Interview with Steve Ruggles, 1999.

12. Interview with Patti Saathoff, 1999.

13. ProSci Study, Management Review, 12/98, p.8.

14. Ibid., p. 7.

15. Paul Levesque, Breakaway Planning: 8 Big Questions to Guide Organizational Change, (New York:AMACOM, 1998), p. 73.

16. Roger E. Herman and Joyce L. Gioia, "Making Work Meaningful: Secrets of the Future-Focused Corporation," THE FUTURIST, 12/98, p. 25. Used with permission From the World Future Society, 7910 Woodmont Avenue, Suite 450, Bethesda, MD., 20814. Telephone: 301/656-8274; Fax: 301/951-0394; **http://www.wfs.org.**

17. Ibid., p. 24.

18. Ron Ashkenas, Dave Ulrich, Todd Jick and Steve Kerr, The Boundaryless Organization: Breaking the Chains of Organizational Structure, (San Francisco: Jossey-Bass Inc., Publishers, 1995), p.4. Reprinted by permission of Jossey-Bass,Inc., a subsidiary of John Wiley & Sons, Inc.

19. ProSci Study, Management Review, 12/98, p.8.

20. Ram Charan and Geoffrey Colvin, "Why CEO's Fail," Fortune, 6/21/99, p.70. Reprinted with permission.

21. Herb Kelleher, "A Culture of Commitment," Leader to Leader, Spring, 1997, p. 21. Reprinted by permission of John Wiley & Sons, Inc.

22. Barbara Ettorre, "Change Management," Management Review, 5/99, p. 8.

Can We Talk—CEO to CEO

1. Richard Edler, *If I Knew Then What I Know Now,* (New York: G. P. Putnam's Sons, 1995), p. 230.

2. Ram Charan and Geoffrey Colvin, "Why CEO's Fail," *Fortune,* 6/21/99, pp. 69–70. Reprinted with permission.

3. Thomas J. Peters and Robert H. Waterman, Jr., *In Search of Excellence,* (New York: Warner Books, Inc., 1983), p. 306.

4. Christian Amoroso, M.D., "The Trust Ladder," 1993.

5. Max DePree, *Leadership Is An Art,* (New York: Doubleday, a division of Random House, Inc., 1989), p. xvi. Reprinted with permission.

6. Jenny McCune, "The Change Makers," *Management Review,* 5/99, pp. 19–20.

7. Ibid.

8. Ibid.

9. Mergerstat.com, 1998.

The Culture Vulture

1. Rob Goffee and Gareth Jones, The Character of a Corporation: How Your Company's Culture Can Make or Break Your Business, (New York: HarperBusiness, 1998), p. xv.

2. Ibid., p. 15.

3. Interview with Sal Caputo, 1999.

4. James C. Collins and Jerry I. Porras, *Built to Last: Successful Habits of Visionary Companies,* (New York: HarperBusiness, 1997), p. 123.

5. Ibid., pp. 121-4

6. Paul Roberts, "Total Teamwork: The Mayo Clinic," *Fast Company,* 4/99, p. 160.

7. "Make Yourself a Leader—Leadership Kit," *Fast Company*, 6/99.

8. Bennett Daviss, "Profits from Principle," *THE FUTURIST*, 3/99, p. 28. Used with permission from the World Future Society, 7910 Woodmont Avenue, Suite 450, Bethesda, Maryland 20814. Telephone: 301/656/8274; Fax: 301/951-0394; **http://www.wfs.org**.

9. Ibid.

10. Ibid., p. 28.

11. Ibid., p. 31.

12. "Fast Facts," *PR News*, 5/17/99, p.3.

13. Annie Brooking, *Intellectual Capital*, (London: International Thomson Business Press, 1996), p. 9.

14. Ibid., p. 8.

15. Sue Cartwright and Cary L. Cooper, *Managing Mergers, Acquisitions and Strategic Alliances: Integrating People and Cultures*, (Oxford: Butterworth-Heinemann, 1992), pp. 61–2. Reprinted by permission of Butterworth Heinemann Publishers, a division of Reed Educational & Professional Publishing, Ltd.

16. Rodney D. Fralicx and C. J. Bolster, "Preventing Culture Shock," *Modern Healthcare*, 8/11/97, p. 50.

17. Edgar H. Schein, *Organizational Culture and Leadership*, (San Francisco: Jossey-Bass Inc., Publishers, 1985), p. 384. Reprinted by permission of Jossey-Bass, Inc., a subsidiary of John Wiley & Sons, Inc.

18. Ibid.

19. Editorial Staff, "The Decline of Conversation," *THE FUTURIST*, 2/99, p. 18. Used with permission from the World Future Society, 7910 Woodmont Avenue, Suite 450, Bethesda, Maryland 20814. Telephone: 301/656-8274; Fax: 301/951-0394; **http://www.wfs.org**.

20. Ram Charan and Geoffrey Colvin, "Why CEO's Fail," *Fortune*, 6/21/99, p.70. Reprinted with permission.

21. Ibid.

22. Stewart B. Clifford, Jr., *The Excellence Files,* (Cambridge, MA: Enterprise Media, 1997), p. 31. Reprinted with permission.

23. Price Pritchett, *Culture Shift—The Employee Handbook for Changing Corporate Culture,* (Dallas, TX: Pritchett Publishing Company, 1993), p. 3. Reprinted with permission.

24. Ibid.

25. Editorial Staff, "The Computerized Kitchen," *THE FUTURIST,* 6-7/99, p. 16. Used with permission from the World Future Society, 7910 Woodmont Avenue, Suite 450, Bethesda, MD 20814. Telephone: 301/656-8274; FAX: 301/951-0394; **http://www.wfs.org**.

26. Ibid.

27. Stewart B.Clifford, Jr., *The Excellence Files,* (Cambridge, MA: Enterprise Media, 1997), pp. 20–2.

28. Ed Mickens, *100 Best Companies for Gay Men and Lesbians,* (New York: Pocket Books, 1994), p.2. Reprinted by permission from Simon and Schuster, Inc., Copyright 1994 by Ed Mickens.

29. Oren Harari, "The Trust Factor," *Management Review,* 1/99, pp. 28–9.

30. Interview with Jim Petrillo, 1999.

31. Robert Fulghum, *All I Really Needed to Know I Learned in Kindergarten,* Copyright ©1986, 1988 by Robert L. Fulghum. Reprinted by permission of Villard Books, a division of Random House, Inc.

Culture and Leadership

1. Edgar H. Schein, Organizational Culture and Leadership, (San Francisco: Jossey-Bass, Inc., Publishers, 1992), p. 374. Copyright© 1992 by Jossey-Bass Inc., Publishers. Reprinted by permission of Jossey-Bass,Inc., a subsidiary of John Wiley & Sons, Inc.

2. Pamela Kruger, "A Leader's Journey, Fast Company, 6/99, p. 118

3. "Make Yourself a Leader—Leadership Kit," Fast Company, 6/99, p.3.

4. Ibid.

5. Jeff Papows, "From Merger to Marriage," Management Review, 5/99, p. 13.

6. Ibid.

Due Diligence

1. Gordon Bing, Due Diligence Techniques and Analysis: Critical Questions for Business Decisions, (Westport, CT: Quorum Books, 1996), p.2.

2. Ibid., pp. 213–55.

3. Executive Summary of Watson Wyatt Worldwide's 1998/99 Mergers and Acquisitions Survey, **www.watsonwyatt.com**, 1999.

4. Ibid.

5. J. Robert Carleton, Cultural Due Diligence, (Conifer, CO: The Vector Group, 1997), p.2. Reprinted with permission.

6. Ibid.

7. Pamela Harper, "How to Take Charge of Clashing Culture Issues Before They Take Charge of Your Merger," Channel Magazine, Vol. 11: number 6, 8/98, pp. 8–9. Republished with permission from Semiconductor Equipment and Materials International, copyright August, 1998, Channel Magazine.

8. Gordon Bing, Due Diligence Techniques and Analysis: Critical Questions for Business Decisions, (Westport, CT: Quorum Books, 1996), p. 137.

9. Interview with Ben Gill, 1999.

10. Interview with Joe Dionisio, 1999.

11. Mitchell Lee Marks and Philip H. Mirvis, Joining Forces—Making One Plus One Equal Three in Mergers, Acquisitions, and Alliances, (San Francisco, CA: Jossey-Bass Inc., 1998), p. 65. Reprinted by permission of Jossey-Bass, Inc., a Subsidiary of John Wiley & Sons, Inc.

12. Chuck Salter, "Fast Change: Tivoli Systems Inc.," Fast Company, 4/99, p. 131.

13. Ibid.

14. Mergerstat.com, 1999.

15. Executive Summary of Watson Wyatt Worldwide Study, p.5.

16. Best Practices for Managing Change, Amherst Consulting Group's 1994 Survey of Business Initiatives, (Boston, MA: Amherst Consulting Group, 1994), p.6. Reprinted with Permission from Keane, Inc.

17. Ibid.

18. Ibid.

19. Interview with Jerry Hurwitz, 1999.

The Cultural Assessment Process

1. Edgar H. Schein, *Organizational Culture and Leadership,* (San Francisco, CA: Jossey-Bass, Inc., 1992), p. 5. Reprinted with permission from Jossey-Bass, Inc., a subsidiary of John Wiley & Sons, Inc.

2. Ibid.

Notes

Notes

Notes

Other Fine Titles From Five Star Publications, Incorporated

All titles are available through www.amazon.com

Letters of Love: Stories from the Heart
Edited by Salvatore Caputo
In this warm collection of love letters and stories, a group of everyday people shares hopes, dreams and experiences of love. Love won, love lost, and love found again. Most of all, they share their belief that love is a blessing that makes life's challenges worthwhile.   ISBN 1-877749-35-4

Linda Radke's Promote Like a Pro: Small Budget, Big Show
By Linda F. Radke and Contributors
In Linda F. Radke's *Promote Like a Pro: Small Budget, Big Show*, a successful publisher and a group of insiders offer self-publishers a step-by-step guide on how to use the print and broadcast media, public relations, the Internet, public speaking and other tools to market books—without breaking the bank!   ISBN 1-877749-36-2

The Economical Guide to Self-Publishing
By Linda F. Radke
This book is a must-have for anyone who is or wants to be a self-publisher. It is a valuable step-by-step guide for producing and promoting your book effectively, even on a limited budget. The book is filled with tips on avoiding common, costly mistakes and provides resources that can save you lots of money—not to mention headaches. A *Writer's Digest Book Club* selection.   ISBN 1-877749-16-8

Shoah: Journey From the Ashes
By Cantor Leo Fettman and Paul M. Howey
Cantor Leo Fettman survived the horrors of Auschwitz while millions of others, including almost his entire family, did not. He worked in the crematorium, was experimented on by Dr. Josef Mengele, and lived through an attempted hanging by the SS. His remarkable tale of survival and subsequent joy is an inspiration for all. *Shoah* includes a historical prologue that chronicles the 2,000 years of anti-Semitism that led to the Holocaust. Cantor Fettman's message is one of love and hope, yet it contains an important warning to new generations to remember—in order to avoid repeating—the evils of the past.   ISBN 1-877749-33-8

For the Record: A Personal Facts and Document Organizer
By Ricki Sue Pagano

Many people have trouble keeping track of the important documents and details of their lives. Ricki Sue Pagano designed *For the Record* so they could regain control—and peace of mind. This organizing tool helps people keep track and makes it easy to find important documents in a pinch.   ISBN 0-9670226-0-6

Joe Boyd's Build It Twice... If You Want a Successful Building Project
By Joe Boyd

In *Joe Boyd's Build It Twice... If You Want a Successful Building Project*, construction expert Joe Boyd shares his 40 years of experience with construction disputes and explains why they arise. He also outlines a strategy that will allow project owners to avoid most construction woes: Build the project on paper first!   ISBN 0-9663620-0-4

Profits of Death: An Insider Exposes the Death Care Industries
By Darryl J. Roberts

This book still has the funeral and cemetery industries reeling from aftershocks. Industry insider Darryl J. Roberts uncovers how the death care industry manipulates consumers into overspending at the most vulnerable time in their lives. He also tells readers everything they need to know about making final arrangements—including how to save up to 50% in costs. THIS IS ONE BOOK THEY CAN'T BURY!
ISBN 1-877749-21-4

Tying the Knot: The Sharp Dresser's Guide to Ties and Handkerchiefs
By Andrew G. Cochran

This handy little guide contains everything you want (or need) to know about neckties, bow ties, pocket squares, and handkerchiefs—from coordinating ties and shirts to tying a variety of knots.   ISBN 0-9630152-6-5

Phil Rea's How to Become a Millionaire Selling Remodeling
By Phil Rea

All successful remodelers know how to use tools. Too few, however, know how to use the tools of selling. Phil Rea mastered the art of selling remodeling and made more than $1,000,000 at his craft. He has shared his "secrets" through coast-to-coast seminars. Now, for the first time, you can read how to make the most of the financial opportunities remodeling has to offer.   ISBN 1-877749-29-x

The Proper Pig's Guide to Mealtime Manners
By L.A. Kowal and Sally Starbuck Stamp

Of course, no one in your family would ever be a pig at mealtime, but perhaps you know another family with that problem. This whimsical guide, complete with its own ceramic pig, gives valuable advice for children and adults alike on how to make mealtimes more fun and mannerly.   ISBN 1-877749-20-6

Shakespeare: To Teach or Not to Teach
By Cass Foster and Lynn G. Johnson

The answer is a resounding "To Teach!" There's nothing dull about this guide for anyone teaching Shakespeare in the classroom, with activities such as crossword puzzles, a scavenger hunt, warm-up games, and costume and scenery suggestions.   ISBN 1-877749-03-6

The Sixty-Minute Shakespeare Series
By Cass Foster

Not enough time to tackle the unabridged versions of the world's most widely read playwright? Pick up a copy of *Romeo and Juliet, A Midsummer Night's Dream, Hamlet, Macbeth, Much Ado About Nothing* and *Twelfth Night*, and discover how much more accessible Shakespeare can be to you and your students.

Household Careers: Nannies, Butlers, Maids & More:
The Complete Guide for Finding Household Employment
By Linda F. Radke

There is a wealth of professional positions available in the child-care and home-help fields. This award-winning book provides all the information you need to find and secure a household job.   ISBN 1-877749-05-2

Nannies, Maids & More: The Complete Guide for Hiring
Household Help
By Linda F. Radke

Anyone who has had to hire household help knows what a nightmare it can be. This book provides a step-by-step guide to hiring—and keeping—household help, complete with sample ads, interview questions, and employment forms.   ISBN 0-9619853-2-1

Kosher Kettle: International Adventures in Jewish Cooking
By Sybil Ruth Kaplan, Foreword by Joan Nathan
With more than 350 recipes from 27 countries, this is one Kosher cookbook you don't want to be without. It includes everything from wheat halva from India to borrekas from Greece. Five Star Publications is donating a portion of all sales of *Kosher Kettle* to MAZON: A Jewish Response to Hunger. A *Jewish Book Club* selection.   ISBN 1-877749-19-2

That Hungarian's in My Kitchen
By Linda F. Radke
You won't want that Hungarian to leave after you've tried some of the 125 Hungarian/American kosher recipes that fill this delightful cookbook. Written for both the novice cook and the sophisticated chef, it comes complete with "Aunt Ethel's Helpful Hints."   ISBN 1-877749-28-1